Applied Methods
of Regional Analysis

Westview Special Studies

The concept of Westview Special Studies is a response to the continuing crisis in academic and informational publishing. Library budgets for books have been severely curtailed. Ever larger portions of general library budgets are being diverted from the purchase of books and used for data banks, computers, micromedia, and other methods of information retrieval. Interlibrary loan structures further reduce the edition sizes required to satisfy the needs of the scholarly community. Economic pressures on the university presses and the few private scholarly publishing companies have severely limited the capacity of the industry to properly serve the academic and research communities. As a result, many manuscripts dealing with important subjects, often representing the highest level of scholarship, are no longer economically viable publishing projects--or, if accepted for publication, are typically subject to lead times ranging from one to three years.

Westview Special Studies are our practical solution to the problem. We accept a manuscript in camera-ready form, typed according to our specifications, and move it immediately into the production process. As always, the selection criteria include the importance of the subject, the work's contribution to scholarship, and its insight, originality of thought, and excellence of exposition. The responsibility for editing and proofreading lies with the author or sponsoring institution. We prepare chapter headings and display pages, file for copyright, and obtain Library of Congress Cataloging in Publication Data. A detailed manual contains simple instructions for preparing the final typescript, and our editorial staff is always available to answer questions.

The end result is a book printed on acid-free paper and bound in sturdy library-quality soft covers. We manufacture these books ourselves using equipment that does not require a lengthy make-ready process and that allows us to publish first editions of 300 to 1000 copies and to reprint even smaller quantities as needed. Thus, we can produce Special Studies quickly and can keep even very specialized books in print as long as there is a demand for them.

About the Book and Author

Promoting widespread economic growth while allowing a majority of those living in economically lagging regions to participate more effectively in productive activities and to obtain greater benefits from the development process is a fundamental development problem. Dr. Rondinelli offers an approach to regional spatial analysis that can help planners and policymakers build the productive and service capacity of settlements in rural regions. He describes methods of regional resource, settlement system, and spatial linkage analysis that identify and locate investments in productive activities, social services, and physical infrastructure that will more effectively promote widespread regional development. Application of these methods is illustrated by examples from several developing countries.

Dr. Dennis A. Rondinelli is professor of social science and development planning at the Maxwell School of Citizenship and Public Affairs, Syracuse University. He is the author of *Secondary Cities in Developing Countries: Policies for Diffusing Urbanization* (1983) and *Development Projects as Policy Experiments: An Adaptive Approach to Development Administration* (1983).

Applied Methods
of Regional Analysis
The Spatial Dimensions
of Development Policy

Dennis A. Rondinelli

Westview Press / Boulder and London

A Westview Special Study

Published in 1985 in the United States of America by Westview Press, Inc.,
5500 Central Avenue, Boulder, Colorado 80301; Frederick A. Praeger,
Publisher

Library of Congress Cataloging in Publication Data
Rondinelli, Dennis A.
   Applied methods of regional analysis.
   (A Westview special study)
   Bibliography: p.
   1. Regional planning--Developing countries. 2. Rural
development--Development countries. I. Title.
HT395.D44R66 1985   307'.12   84-20825
ISBN 0-8133-7022-1

Printed and bound in the United States of America

10 9 8 7 6 5 4 3 2 1

Contents

Tables and Figures

FIGURES

Foreword

The Urban Functions in Rural Development (UFRD)
Project began in 1976 as an attempt by the Office of
Urban Development of the U.S. Agency for International
Development to introduce spatial analysis into regional
development planning in Third World countries. This
subject has a long history in the academic literature,
particularly in geography, regional science, regional
economics and rural sociology and in the initial
formulation of UFRD leading authorities in those fields
actively participated in discussions and workshops. It
is interesting to note, however, that while a rich
academic literature with theory, concepts and empirical investigations was readily available, little
effort had been made by international assistance organizations to apply them to practical planning problems.
It was only through considerable personal effort by Dr.
Eric Chetwynd, Jr., and Dr. William R. Miner that this
seminal spatial project was initiated within USAID.
    Dennis Rondinelli became the field leader of the
UFRD efforts, beginning in 1976, and he remains today
its leading proponent. He formulated what is now
called the "UFRD Approach" from the perspectives of the
theorist E.A.J. Johnson, and like Johnson's his view is
principally that of a development planner who recognizes that Third World policy-makers face pressing day-
to-day problems that must be met with actionable programs and viable projects. But, as a result of its
characteristics as a rapid, low cost and simple way to
begin the long and difficult task of spatial analysis
and regional planning, UFRD has often had to be
defended from the criticisms of some academics, who saw
it as an overly simplified interpretation of a complex
reality, of some Third World planners, who wanted more
definitive prescriptions for solving pressing problems,
and of official donor agencies, for whom regional planning plays a minor role in international development
assistance. Rondinelli has responded repeatedly that

UFRD is only the first step to a better comprehension
of the critical roles that towns and cities play in the
regional development process.

Since 1976, and after numerous demonstrations of
UFRD in the Philippines, Bolivia, Upper Volta, the
Cameroons and Guatemala, this book closes the first
chapter on attempting to achieve that comprehension.
While Rondinelli maintains that UFRD is an invaluable
tool in development planning, he recognizes from the
experiences of the demonstration projects that other
key issues also influence the results of regional
development activities. Since the UFRD approach was
first conceived, Rondinelli has helped to formulate
studies for USAID which concentrate on food marketing
chains in rural areas as they are reflected in the
dynamics of periodic markets and small market towns,
and he has been one of the principal architects of yet
another USAID thrust which focuses upon the middle-size
or secondary cities in developing countries as centers
of employment generation and service provision for
rural areas. I and my colleagues at Clark University
and a network of development planners are privileged
to work with Dennis Rondinelli, and we are all indebted
to USAID for its foresight in recognizing the critical
importance of a regional perspective in development
planning. This book serves, in an invaluable way, to
express the merits of that perspective to a larger
audience.

Gerald J. Karaska
Clark University

Acknowledgments

This book reflects a large number of intellectual debts that I owe to friends and colleagues. The concepts and methods described here were developed and tested in field projects funded by the United States Agency for International Development. Eric Chetwynd, Jr., played a central role in the Urban Functions in Rural Development (UFRD) projects on which the book is based. Without his advocacy, interest and support for nearly a decade, the projects could not have been undertaken.

I have drawn heavily on the field work of collaborators in the Philippines and Bolivia, without whose help this process of regional planning and analysis would not have been applied. Emmanuel I. Astillero and Junio M. Ragragio made an important contribution in the Bicol River Basin of the Philippines. Field studies in Bolivia were carried out under the supervision of Hugh Evans, from whose reports I have borrowed freely for illustrations and examples. Evans, over a two-year period as resident advisor, and I on frequent visits to Bolivia worked closely with a dedicated staff of the Development Corporation of the Department of Potosi (CORDEPO), including Alfredo Bellott, Braulio Ore, Hugo Solis and their colleagues.

This book was completed with strong support from the Cooperative Agreement on Human Settlements and Natural Resources Systems Analysis at Clark University. Gerald J. Karaska and Eric Belsky sharpened my thinking, focused my attention on the strengths and weaknesses of the UFRD approach and provided the necessary logistical support.

All of these people and organizations, however, should be absolved of responsibility for the interpretations and conclusions that follow. The UFRD approach to regional analysis and planning remains controversial. It attempts to combine time-tested, perhaps some would call them conventional, methods with new techniques and field applications to provide a process that is flexible and adaptable under a wide variety of economic, political and cultural conditions, that is easy to use

with limited data and skilled personnel, that can be
understood by policy-makers who have little or no experience in regional science or planning, and that can be
completed quickly to influence on-going investment
decision-making. Some readers will undoubtedly question
whether or not such an approach is appropriate; others
if, in fact, it meets all of these objectives.

In ten years of testing and revising the methods
described here, I have come to appreciate Disraeli's
aphorism that "it is easier to be critical than to be
correct." More testing and revising and searching for
alternatives need to be done. But if these concepts
and methods, at this stage in their evolution, help planners, community organizations, public officials and
private investors to understand better the regions that
they are trying to develop, then they will have served
their purpose. My hope is that those who use these
concepts and methods will join the effort to improve
them.

Dennis A. Rondinelli

1
Spatial Planning and Regional Development

This book addresses a basic development problem: how to promote widespread economic growth in ways that will allow a large majority of people living in rural areas and in economically lagging regions to participate more effectively in productive activities and to obtain greater benefits from the development process. It offers an approach to spatial analysis and regional planning that focuses on building the productive and service capacity of settlements of different sizes and functional characteristics--rural service centers, market towns, intermediate-sized cities and regional centers--to provide the services, facilities and economic activities that can promote rural and regional development. It seeks to describe the locational dimension of regional and rural development planning and to offer guidelines for improving the capacity of settlements to offer an appropriate range of services, facilities, infrastructure and economic activities for their own residents and those of surrounding rural areas.

This approach to regional development planning is based on a fundamental assumption: that if governments in developing countries want to achieve geographically widespread development, they must invest in a geographically dispersed pattern. The concentration of investments in one or a few large cities will not result automatically in the spread of development through trickle-down processes. In most countries the spread effects of investments are highly constrained. At the same time, many of the services, facilities and productive activities that are needed for regional development cannot be provided economically or efficiently to widely dispersed populations living at very low densities. Few developing countries have sufficient financial resources to offer a wide range of basic services everywhere at the same time. Essential services and facilities must be located in places that

1

have a sufficiently large concentration of population or a broad enough market area to support them economically. Thus, if economic development is to be achieved with greater social and geographical equity, investments must be made in a pattern of "decentralized concentration." That is, they must be strategically located in settlements that can serve a large population living in and around them, and to which people living at relatively low densities in rural areas have easy access.

This pattern of "decentralized concentration" can be achieved most efficiently and effectively through an articulated and integrated system of settlements. A hierarchical or diffuse settlement system can provide not only the critical mass of services and facilities needed in rural areas to increase agricultural productivity and income but also provide the trade, transportation, administrative and social linkages that integrate a region into a self-sustaining economy.

This book describes an approach to spatial analysis that can help policy-makers at national, regional and local levels to allocate investments in services, facilities and infrastructure in ways that build up the capacity of settlements to serve residents more effectively and to stimulate development throughout a region. The approach has been tested in more than a dozen developing countries under a variety of labels: block-level planning in India, settlement systems analysis in Indonesia, market center analysis in Kenya, Peru and Ecuador, growth center analysis in Ghana, Malawi and Thailand, "urban functions in rural development" planning in the Philippines, Bolivia and Upper Volta, and central place analysis in other countries.[1] Whatever it is called, the general approach to settlement system analysis described here seeks to provide a spatial and locational dimension to regional planning by (1) identifying settlements that can most effectively act as service, production and trade centers for their own populations and those of surrounding areas; (2) determining the strength of linkages among these settlements and between them and their rural hinterlands; and (3) delineating those areas in which people have little or no access to town-based services and facilities. It attempts to provide the information needed by planners and policy-makers to allocate investments in services, facilities and productive activities to the smallest efficient units of settlement and to maximize the access of rural residents to those communities. Thus, it provides a spatial or locational framework for incrementally increasing the capacity of a larger number of communities to serve their residents more effectively.[2]

The process of planning and analysis described here was most recently tested in a series of pilot projects sponsored by the U.S. Agency for International Development in the Philippines, Bolivia and Upper Volta. They were known as Urban Functions in Rural Development (UFRD) projects and the process has widely been referred to as "the UFRD approach." This book draws heavily on the Philippines and Bolivia experiences in describing this process of regional planning.

UFRD focuses not only on the spatial or locational dimensions of regional planning, but also on strategies for integrating urban and rural communities into a system of settlements through which a wide range of mutually beneficial economic, social and physical interactions can occur. It is meant to supplement sectoral, technical and problem-oriented planning and not to supplant them. It seeks to add a locational and spatial dimension to other forms of regional and national planning rather than to produce a comprehensive regional development plan. Thus, UFRD concentrates on locational factors and spatial concerns; it is assumed that many other factors of equal or more importance in regional development are being considered through other forms of planning and analysis. An underlying assumption of the UFRD approach is that planning and decision-making are continuous processes to which spatial analysis can make an important contribution. UFRD is a place-oriented approach to regional analysis that can be used to supplement sectoral and technical planning, as well as "people-oriented" approaches to social services planning.

CONCEPTS OF SPATIAL DEVELOPMENT

Three major concepts of spatial development have emerged in recent years. They have been described as the growth pole, functional integration, and decentralized territorial approaches.[3]

Growth Pole Concept

The growth pole concept of spatial development suggests that by investing heavily in capital-intensive industries in the largest urban centers, governments in developing countries can stimulate economic growth that will spread outward to generate regional development. The economies of scale found in the largest cities would provide high rates of return on investment, support the commercial, administrative and infrastructural services needed by industries to operate efficiently, and bring about the diversification of the growth pole's economy. It is assumed that the goods produced in the growth pole would be exported to the country's metropolitan center and abroad, that other manufactured goods would come from the metropolitan center to the

growth pole, and that the free operation of market
forces would create "ripple" or "trickle down" effects
that would stimulate economic growth throughout the
region. Investment in industry at the growth pole
would be the "engine of development" for agricultural
and commercial activities.[4]

But where growth pole policies were tried in
developing countries--mostly in Latin America and
Africa--they generally failed either to promote the
economic growth of the cities selected as poles or of
the regions in which the growth poles were promoted.[5]
Experience suggests that ripple and trickle down
effects were not strong enough to generate regional
development, and that if they worked at all, growth
poles often became "enclaves" of modern activities that
drained raw materials, capital, labor, and entrepreneurial talent from surrounding rural areas. Hansen
argues that "the trickling down of modernization has
not reached the poor, especially in rural areas, or
else has yielded to them no more than marginal benefits." He concludes that "the optimistic view that
economic growth would result in a convergence of
regional per capita income has not been supported by
evidence."[6]

In many countries with highly polarized settlement
systems, failure of development to spread is attributed
at least in part to inadequately articulated and integrated systems of settlements through which innovation
and economic stimuli could be diffused. Without an
articulated and integrated system of growth centers--as
opposed to one or a few growth poles--the impulses of
concentrated investment could not spread and the economic incentives for widespread productivity could not
be created. Under such conditions, as Berry has
observed, "growth and stagnation polarize; the economic
system remains unarticulated."[7]

Functional-Spatial Integration

An alternative approach is based on the concept
that a well-articulated and integrated system of growth
centers of different sizes and functional characteristics can play an important role in facilitating more
widespread regional development. It assumes that in
most developing countries the primary stimulus to
regional development must be through agricultural
rather than industrial development. The goals of this
strategy are to achieve higher levels of food production, expand employment and achieve higher levels of
income for larger numbers of people, especially those
living at or below subsistence levels. The primary
beneficiaries of investments must be small-scale farmers, landless laborers, and those engaged in small-
scale commercial enterprises--that is, people usually
living on the margin of the organized economy. If

greater productivity and higher income are to be
achieved, some critical mass of services must be available in rural areas, including appropriate agricultural
technology, research and extension services, high-
yielding seed varieties, adequate credit and other
inputs. Organizing accessible financial institutions
that increase the flow of capital to and promote
savings among rural people is crucial, as is the creation of a stable marketing system through which farmers
can sell their products.

Building the institutional framework for rural
development is essential to promote regional growth and
to transform subsistence farming into commercial agriculture. Rural residents must have access to self-
sustaining organizations capable of identifying and
solving rural development problems and of delivering
needed services. Greater opportunities for nonagricultural employment in rural areas must accompany
increased agricultural production. Jobs must be found
for those freed from agricultural employment as productivity increases. Agricultural processing and distribution activities must be established, and industries
must be created to provide low-cost inputs and equipment for farmers. Finally, if rural development is to
go beyond simply increasing farm output, attention must
be given to providing for basic human needs--health and
education services, vocational training, safe drinking
water, sanitary facilities, and adequate shelter.[8]

A crucial element in providing the basic preconditions for the commercialization of agriculture is a
well-articulated and integrated system of settlements
in which services and facilities can be efficiently
located and to which rural people have easy access.
The absence of such a system of central places, some
theorists argue, obstructs the emergence of a sectorally and geographically balanced pattern of economic
growth. E.A.J. Johnson argues that the "varied hierarchy of central places has not only made possible an
almost complete commercialization of agriculture but
facilitated a wider spatial diffusion of light manufacturing, processing and service industries... [and pro-
vided] employment of a differentiated variety," in most
countries with more advanced economies.[9] Without
access to an integrated system of market centers
farmers cannot easily sell their surpluses, obtain
inputs, modernize their technology and adapt products
to consumer demand. Nor can they easily obtain the
services needed to make living in rural areas acceptable.

Theorists such as Brian Berry have long insisted that
in market or mixed economies a diffuse and integrated
system of central places usually emerges with economic
growth and is a necessary but not sufficient condition

for achieving widespread development.[10] A network of central places—settlements that serve populations from a surrounding hinterland—is necessary to distribute goods produced in specialized locations to consumers in other places. Central places make available to people living in rural areas those services requiring fixed locations or large numbers of customers. Goods produced in various locations must be assembled in local collection points and distributed to consumers through markets, thus making specialized goods and services of particular communities available to consumers in other places.

Fisher and Rushton point out from their experience with area development planning in India and Indonesia, that creating an integrated system of service, trade and production centers has benefits both for governments attempting to promote regional development and for people living in the region. They note that an integrated hierarchy of service centers:

1. Is convenient and efficient for the consumer because it allows for the satisfaction of several different needs on the same trip out of the village.
2. It reduces the amount of transportation required to connect villages to facilities because, from among the many possible transport links between places, those few links connecting villages to their local service center and to more important places will be recognized by all to be the priority links where public transportation facilities should be provided.
3. It reduces the length of roads that require improvement before every village is connected to places having facilities to which they need access.
4. It economizes on the cost of providing services to the facilities themselves, because these costs can be shared among several facilities located in the same place.
5. It enables a more economical and effective monitoring of the regulated activities in market and service centers.
6. It facilitates the exchange of information and qualified personnel between related activities.
7. It focuses the development efforts for a region on a few places with superior locations and resources and this increases the likelihood that some of the places will spontaneously generate additional activities catering to the needs of their hinterland region.[11]

Others have also noted the benefits of an integrated system of settlements for regional development.
Bromley contends that "such central places are indis-
pensible elements in the functioning of rural and
regional economies, articulating the diverse specialized forms of production and consumption, and facilitating numerous forms of interaction and exchange."[12]
Roy and Patil note in their analysis of central places
in India that "there is a symbiotic relationship
between the development of service centers and the
development of service areas around them."[13] In a
region with a well articulated and integrated system of
central places, people living in or near towns of different sizes and functional characteristics have easy
access to basic necessities, convenience goods and
services in local markets as well as to more diversified and higher order functions that must be located in
cities of larger size. "All of these concepts" Roy and
Patil point out, "convey the idea of locating at different levels primary and secondary goods and services
that are functionally interlinked, mutually complementary and supplementary, well-integrated vertically and
inter-sectorally, to maximize the benefits to users and
minimize the costs." A well-integrated system of
settlements provides potential access for people living
throughout a region to markets of different sizes and
to a wide variety of urban amenities and inputs needed
for agricultural development. The objective of locational strategies based on the functional integration
approach is "to identify the lowest level service
center and villages within its gambit, which together
form a viable unit which can support a minimum package
of services."[14]

Decentralized concentration of investment through
settlements of different sizes and functional characteristics, Rondinelli and Ruddle point out, can:

1. Create economies of scale, spillover and spread
    effects that are beneficial to both residents of
    those centers and people living in surrounding
    rural areas;
2. Help organize the economies of rural hinterlands
    through supply, market, administrative and
    service delivery systems that provide increased
    and diversified employment opportunities;
3. Aid in attracting creative and innovative person-
    alities and entrepreneurs with values, attitudes
    and behavior patterns that can create an environ-
    ment conducive to further innovation;
4. Provide returns from previous investment that can
    be used for future development and for creating
    comparative locational advantages and more and
    better opportunities for future growth through
    inducement effects;

5. Create pressure and demand for extending new
   services, facilities and infrastructure, thus
   creating a continuing cycle of growth and expansion;
6. Create physical and economic linkages among
   settlements and between them and their rural
   hinterlands that increase the accessibility of
   central places;
7. Attract related economic and social activities
   that create--through economies of proximity--new
   markets for raw materials, semi-finished goods
   and new commodities.[15]

Perhaps most importantly, decentralized investment
in strategically located settlements can create the
minimal conditions that enable rural people to develop
their own communities through "bottom-up" and autonomous processes. For higher levels of government, Roy
and Patil claim, "the major utility of the service
center strategy is the combination of social, economic
and spatial planning."[16]

Decentralized Territorial Approach

A third concept of spatial development is sometimes called a decentralized territorial, agropolitan,
or selective regional closure approach. It is usually
based on the argument that urban growth centers--even
market towns and intermediate-sized cities--are parasitic; that they allow town-based elites, large corpor-
ations and central government agencies to exploit the
rural population and to drain rural areas of their
resources. The implication is that investments should
not be located in these places, but dispersed in rural
areas where people have direct access to them. If
small towns and cities are encouraged to grow they will
simply become the instruments through which the privileged classes will exploit rural people more effectively. Schatzburg, for example, insists that the
"structures and organizations of these small towns
usually benefit the already wealthy elements of local
society who have the means and skill to co-opt most
developmental resources and initiatives that originate
with the national governments." Thus, he maintains,
even small towns are "structured to enhance the well-
being (social, economic and political) of those who are
relatively advantaged." Their development, he implies,
would be detrimental to the rural poor because small
towns and cities "are both centers of extraction that
siphon off financial and human resources from the
countryside and blockage points that inhibit the downward flow of resources as well."[17]
Others argue that rural people have limited access
to farming innovations and that this lack of access

makes small towns and cities ineffective in disseminating modern ideas and practices. Moreover, although farm people participate actively in town-based market trade, urban traders dominate the markets and merely seek to maximize their profits. They are not interested in diversifying the agricultural economies of the areas in which goods are produced or in increasing the incomes of the producers. It is argued that capital and credit are controlled by townspeople who are reluctant to lend to farmers. Strengthening the linkages between small towns and cities and the metropolitan centers would make many rural workers redundant, undermine the network of local trading and petty production activities and weaken the economic structure of small towns, making them dependent on the metropolitan economy.

The policy implications of such concepts are not always clearly stated. At one extreme it is suggested that nothing done at the local level within developing countries will be effective until the world economic order, which allows exploitation of the rural poor, is changed.[18] Others argue that development strategies should seek to create self-reliant rural economies with minimal linkages to the metropolitan economy. Friedmann and Douglass suggest an "agropolitan" approach of concentrating development activities in rural districts with from about 50,000 to 150,000 people. Planning and decision-making authority would be decentralized so that people living in the districts would be primarily responsible for their own development.[19] Stohr and Todtling have suggested a strategy of "selective spatial closure" as a way of protecting small towns and rural populations from potentially adverse effects of interaction between rural areas and larger cities.[20]

A counter argument is that small towns and cities per se are not necessarily parasitic; many perform beneficial functions that are essential to rural development. Nor is interaction with larger, more modern and economically diversified urban centers necessarily exploitive. Much depends on how the economies of small towns and cities are developed and the ways in which the linkages between them and larger communities are organized.

Once urbanization begins, even at very low levels, it is impossible to expect spatial closure. Leeds argues that no nucleated settlement can be closed because its very existence is based on some degree of specialization. Specialization requires exchange, and thus "no town is an island of itself." The concentration of people in towns is based on exchange and interaction and thus, "theoretically, never should one expect to find autonomy, closure or boundedness. On

theoretical grounds one should <u>always</u> expect flows of
goods, services, personnel, property, knowledge, information or possibly other values going in and out of any
locality."[21] Moreover, a good deal of empirical evidence suggests that small towns and cities can and do
perform beneficial functions for rural people. Not all
of the interactions between urban and rural people are
detrimental to the latter. New linkages with larger
communities can create new opportunities for the poor
in the hinterlands of smaller towns and intermediate
cities.

Preston found in his study of highland towns in
Bolivia, for example, that their negative impact on the
rural poor was usually minor, and that many offered new
economic opportunities to rural residents. He found
that the most important influence on agricultural innovation in highland Bolivia had been personal contacts
among farmers and that those contacts most often took
place in market towns. Farmers, he points out, are
"much more likely to be impressed by seeing large
healthy new varieties of potatoes in the market rather
than being told about them or even to some extent than
actually seeing them growing."[22] The degree to which
market towns made available new products was crucial in
disseminating agricultural innovations. Moreover, he
found little systematic or serious exploitation of
rural people by market operators or merchants, nor did
individuals or institutions in the towns seem to be
obstacles to capital accumulation by farmers. Preston
concluded that "there is little feeling of injustice at
the distribution of income" and that most rural families could get access to some capital. Likewise, the
negative effects of administration in the towns were,
with the exception of a few individual cases, not a
serious problem for farmers and, indeed, municipal
officials had a good deal of popular support.[23]

Other studies of market towns indicate that rural
people can compete fairly with townspeople and that the
linkages between the towns and rural areas are the primary channels through which rural people derive income.
Studies of marketplace interaction in the Guatemalan
town of Antigua, for instance, document the ability of
rural people "to establish themselves as permanent
market participants in competition with urban vendors,
to obtain permanent rights in market space, to cope
with hostile administrative structures and to form
trading partnerships with urban customers."[24] Indeed,
the very existence of the urban market in Antigua
depends on linkages between the city and its rural
hinterland, linkages in this case that seem to benefit
rural residents as much as townspeople. Swetnam points
out that

> While the Antigua Guatemala market-place is an
> institution organized and maintained by the city
> government, the bulk of its trade lies in the
> hands of rural middlemen. Vendors from outside
> Antigua outnumber city dwellers not only among the
> ranks of producer-sellers but also among the
> middlemen who constitute two-thirds of the selling
> population. ...The market is not a spot where
> urban merchants fleece rural producers, but rather
> an institution in which urban and rural dwellers
> mix freely playing the role of both buyer and pro-
> fessional market trader.[25]

Only about one-fifth of the market participants live in
the city; more than half come from the surrounding
rural hamlets or from other municipalities. Rural
vendors come to the thrice-weekly market from as far as
100 kilometers away. Linkages between small towns and
cities and larger metropolitan centers do not necessarily work to the disadvantage of the towns.
    Dannhaeuser's studies of Dagupan City--a medium-
sized town in Pangasinan Province of the Philippines
that has had strong trade relationships with the pri-
mate city, Manila, as well as with other towns and
cities in its region--conclude that trade and commercial linkages have not been detrimental to Dagupan's
economic development nor to those people living in the
town's surrounding areas. Sales penetration and
contractual-ownership penetration by large Manila-based
firms changed but did not destroy local trade relationships. Instead, they stimulated local innovations in
distribution and opened new employment opportunities.
Over a twenty-five year period of high inflation,
household income in and around Dagupan remained stable.
"Moreover, the expansion of infrastructure in Dagupan
and Pangasinan, the rise in revenue base, continued
brisk trade and vigorous demand in the province and in
the city do not convey a picture of large segments of
the population sinking into poverty" Dannhaeuser concludes.[26] He argues that trade with Manila was one of
the major factors that has kept capital within the
Dagupan region instead of being transferred elsewhere.
The expansion of active marketing by Manila-based firms
in Dagupan seems to have mobilized local capital and
labor resources that had previously been idle. The
economic ties did not impose a political dependency on
the city. Local officials have levied high license
fees on companies and taxes on salesmen doing business
in the city, often to the dismay of the large companies.
    Richardson comes closer to the truth in pointing
out that "neither the 'diffusion pole' nor the 'parasitic' views of the role of small cities are correct as

a general rule. Much depends on how the functions of
these cities have evolved with respect to their hinterlands, on the institutional and cultural features of
the country in question and on how policies for strengthening the small cities are formulated and implemented."[27]

A CONCEPTUAL FRAMEWORK FOR SETTLEMENT SYSTEMS

The Urban Functions in Rural Development (UFRD)
approach to regional planning is based primarily in the
functional integration concept of spatial development.
It is based on the assumption that settlements of
various sizes and functional characteristics--and especially smaller rural service and market centers--can
and do play important roles in regional and rural
development, but that in most developing countries the
settlement system may not be well enough articulated
and integrated to allow these centers to perform their
potential functions effectively.

Roles of Settlements in Regional Development

Although the literature on small towns and
intermediate-sized cities in developing countries has
grown so large in recent years that it is impossible to
summarize it all here, samples can be cited to indicate
the range and types of functions that these settlements
can perform. Studies of towns in West Bengal, India,
for example, reveal that even those with as few as
5,000 residents can act as "minimal urban centers" for
their rural regions. West Bengal towns:

> (1) serve as economic, political and cultural
> centers for the population of the villages in the
> surrounding rural micro-region, (2) provide the
> market where products not locally produced and
> specialized goods and services are available, and
> where local products may be sold; (3) provide the
> wide range of occupational specialists not usually
> found in rural villages, but necessary for the
> continuing existence of a primary agricultural
> rural population; (4) serve as centers in which
> administrative and educational specialists repre-
> senting wider society and its urban centers meet
> and interact with the local rural populations;
> (5) are characterized by extreme diversity in
> occupation and heterogeneity in population com-
> pared to their relative size as urban centers (as
> rural towns, such settlements exist to serve a
> nonresident population dispersed in agricultural
> villages) and (6) characteristically draw a large
> segment of the elite population from far outside

the immediate locality, recruiting on the basis of
education and experience in specialized administrative, professional and educational posi-
tions.[28]

Johnson found in his studies of small central
places in India that they are particularly conducive to
the types of commercial and industrial activity that
cater to local, short-radii market demand and that have
a small potential number of customers who are within
easy reach by foot, bicycle or other forms of transport.[29] Thus small towns in India frequently contain a
wide array of retail stores, personal and commercial
services, and cottage processing, fabricating or simple
manufacturing operations. Those activities that cater
to a small portion of a larger region can also be
located successfully in small towns and cities if adequate transport and ancillary services are present.
The most frequently found economic activities in Indian
towns are weight-losing and bulk-reducing processing
activities, such as sugar mills, saw mills, livestock
slaughtering houses, canneries and oil crushing mills.
These localized activities in turn create demand for
transport and supply services, brokerage, credit and
insurance services.
World Bank analysts assert that nonfarm enterprises and activities--especially small scale construction, commerce, service, transport, processing and
manufacturing--are an important source of employment
and income for more than a quarter of the rural labor
force in developing countries. They are also a significant source of secondary or supplementary income for
farm households and they provide on-the-job training
and apprenticeships in commercial and processing activities for rural youth.[30]
Studies of rural industries in South Korea and
Taiwan indicate that small towns and cities, in addition to supporting resource processing activities, are
also good locations for small market-oriented activities such as animal feed shops, ice manufacturing
plants, clay building products, earthenware and hand
tool producers and makers of small concrete products.
Medium-sized towns support a wider variety of services
including commercial printing, motor vehicle repair and
small machine, galvanizing and metal processing shops.
Simple assembly, mixing or finishing activities and
separable manufacturing operations can also be efficiently located in small towns and cities if they have
good transport linkages with larger urban centers.[31]
In Southern Thailand towns from 14,000 to 57,000
in population provide health clinics, small hospitals,
postal and district government services, elementary and

secondary schools, small libraries, banks, bus service, telephone exchanges, and some types of vocational and higher education. Although few systematic studies have been done of the "influence" areas of small towns and cities in developing countries, estimates made in South Thailand indicate that the larger and more diversified centers--with median populations of about 33,000--have influence areas averaging almost 10,000 km^2 and serve hinterland populations averaging 630,000. Such centers are linked to up to 22 smaller and less diversified towns within their influence areas.[32]

Studies of the people who migrated from rural villages to small towns and cities in northeastern Thailand found a high level of satisfaction. Most migrants were able to increase their incomes and find better educational and health facilities than in their villages of origin. Although housing conditions in the towns seemed to be of lower quality, the studies revealed that migrants on the whole were "rather pleased with their new life in town," and that among those who migrated voluntarily to small towns and cities "there is widespread satisfaction with the quality of life found at the destination."[33]

Indications that small towns and cities in Latin America can perform important economic and social functions come from Mexico, Bolivia, Honduras and Guatemala. Small cities in Mexico--such as Oaxaca--are important market centers for their regions.[34] The market in Oaxaca, for example, provides outlets for agricultural goods, livestock, nonagricultural products such as fibers and firewood, and a wide variety of artisanal products--pottery, baskets, mats and household and agricultural implements. An impressive array of people find employment directly or indirectly through market activities--carpenters, stonecutters, healers and curers, butchers, blacksmiths, small-parts sellers, and marriage arrangers, mechanics and seed and equipment vendors. The market offers opportunities for farmers to sell their own goods and for a large number of intermediaries to engage in trade. Oaxaca supports traders who buy and resell goods within the market, traders who travel to small rural markets to collect goods for resale in the urban market, and traders who buy goods in the market and resell them door-to-door in town. The market offers opportunities for rural people to shop in stores located on the market's periphery and to visit doctors, dentists, clinics, lawyers and lenders. Wholesalers collect small quantities of local products in the Oaxaca markets and sell them in bulk to retailers in larger cities; they also buy manufactured goods in the city to sell in small lots back in Oaxaca. The city's market and other commercial activities provide employment for field buyers, agents, truckers and small-load haulers.[35]

Even very small towns in Mexico—those with 2,000 to 5,000 residents—can support minimum basic services that are not available in rural villages—primary schools, medical doctors' offices, health clinics, pharmacies, gasoline stations, secondary schools, cinemas, restaurants, small banks and hotels and in some places dentists, lawyers, veterinarians and technical schools.[36]

The degree to which intermediate-sized towns and cities absorb rural-to-urban migrants in Mexcio depends very much on the settlement structure within states. The degree of primacy has been found to be an independent factor in migration. In those states with the highest degree of primacy more migrants are attracted to the largest city than in states with a more diffuse pattern of urbanization. Studies have found that

> The mere existence of a greater number of medium and large cities in a nonprimate state provides options for maximization of choice which are denied to migrants in a primate state. Migrants pushed from rural areas in primate states do not have the same spectrum of options for settlement and job opportunity.[37]

Field studies of small towns in Honduras and Bolivia indicate that even in the poorest countries of Latin America, towns with average populations of 10,000 to 12,000 can provide basic health, agricultural supply, educational, and commerical services. They are most important as transport and distribution centers and as markets for agricultural products grown in surrounding rural areas.[38] The degree to which markets in small towns facilitate and promote interaction between urban and rural residents is seen in anthropological studies of towns such as Antigua in Guatemala, where the bulk of trade is controlled by rural middlemen and where rural vendors travel long distances to participate in the periodic market.[39]

Similar roles are played by small towns and cities in many African countries. In Tanzania small towns provide the only real opportunities for employment in the nonagricultural sectors. On average about one-quarter of the economically active labor force in Tanzanian towns is employed in agriculture. The other three quarters are in nonagriculture jobs—about 10 percent are employed in manufacturing, about 15 percent in construction, utilities and communications, another 15 percent in commerce, and about 32 percent in services.[40] Small towns in Ghana—like Techiman with less than 20,000 population—are periodic market centers for their rural areas. Wunsch notes in his study of Techiman that trucks come on market day from as far away as

Kumasi, Tamale, and Accra, as well as from rural areas
in Upper Volta, Mali and the Ivory Coast. The town
supports retail stores, schools, hospitals and a wide
range of skilled and semi-skilled craftsmen, including
tailors, carpenters, masons and mechanics, physicians,
nurses, ministers and civil servants. Larger towns
like Obuasi, with a little more than 30,000 residents
have a wider range of agro-processing, marketing, service, commercial and informal sector activities. Moreover, it encompasses population that is socially, reli-
giously and ethnically heterogeneous. In the 1970s, it
had more than 90 voluntary associations including religious, ethnic, occupational, trade, religious, and
recreational associations, unions and trade associations, lodges and secret societies.[41]

The Underdevelopment of Small Towns and Cities in Rural Regions

Growing evidence that small towns and cities can
perform the wide variety of functions just described
has been accompanied by strong indications that relatively few of them that could promote growth, transformation and integration in rural areas actually do.
There is usually a wide gap between potential and actual performance in poorer rural regions.

The settlement systems of rural regions and of
many of the poorest developing countries are inadequately articulated and integrated for three basic
reasons:

1. Lack of Sufficient Numbers of Lower Order Central
Places. As noted earlier, in many countries a large
majority of the rural population is scattered in settlements that are simply too small and too isolated to
support even basic services and facilities and to perform the variety of functions that larger and more
accessible places can and do perform.

Studies of rural settlements in Northern Nigeria,
for example, conclude that the vast majority of villages are "too small to provide the minimum population
threshold for the successful provision of such amenities as water, electricity, health, postal facilities
and educational centers." They also emphasize the fact
that villages are "too far apart to be conveniently
grouped into one central service system."[42]

In the poorest Latin American countries only a
small percentage of rural settlements perform important
functions. Studies of Honduras indicate that less than
one percent of the country's settlements have a sufficient range of functions to be considered central
places for their rural hinterlands. Less than 800 of
the nearly 20,000 villages and towns that are non-

central places have more than a few services or facilities that serve their own populations. Moreover, in a
sample of 925 towns and cities ranging in population
from less than 1,000 to more than 160,000 surveyed in
1980, it was found that 88 percent were non-central
places, having from none to less than 12 basic services
and facilities. All had populations of less than
5,000. Only 23 towns were market centers and 75
offered services for their own residents.[43]

Similar results were found in surveys of settlements in Bolivia. That country's recent five year plan
noted that the majority of urban centers "do not completely fulfill a dynamic role for their respective
areas of influence because they do not function ade-
quately as marketing centers and as centers for the
diffusion of cultural and technological innovation."[44]
A survey of 112 settlements in the Department of Potosi
found that about 63 percent did not have a sufficient
range of functions to be considered central places.
Another 26 settlements were so small in size and lacking in services, facilities and infrastructure that
they could only serve their own residents. Only 16
towns had a wide enough range of functions to act as
sub-regional or rural service centers and these were
not widely distributed throughout the region.[45]

Studies of Melanesia--Papua New Guinea, Vanuatu
and the Solomon Islands--found only a small number of
towns performing central functions.[46] Studies of the
Bicol River Basin in the Philippines yielded similar
findings. Of the 1,419 discrete settlements in Camarines Sur and Albay Provinces, only 2 had a sufficient
range of functions to act as provincial service centers
and only 11 others served significant numbers of people
outside of their boundaries. About 43 small towns--
mostly with periodic markets--served some residents of
their immediately surrounding areas, but over 1,300--
about 96 percent--were non-central places. They had
average population sizes of less than 1,000 and provided either no services or facilities at all or less
than 9, most of which were small-scale residentiary
functions.[47]

The underdevelopment of small towns in Thailand
creates significant opportunity costs. Douglass points
out in his studies of the Central Plain region that the
government could use existing administrative districts
(amphoe) to organize the 100,000 to 200,000 population
usually living in them, and the more than 800 lower
order centers ranging in population from 2,000 to
40,000, to create integrated settlement networks linking rural villages to urban centers.[43] He argues that
with proper services, facilities and linkages to
smaller and larger settlements many towns could "by
generating non-farm employment opportunities, increase
incentives for local investment and production which

might retain those rural surpluses now being transferred to the metropolis and abroad."[49]

    2. <u>Inadequate Distribution of Services and Facil-
ities Among Small Towns and Cities in Rural Regions</u>.
Part of the reason that small towns and cities in rural
regions are underdeveloped is that they lack essential
services, facilities and infrastructure. A survey of
the distribution of services, facilities and organizations in settlements in Honduras indicate that less
than 7 percent had even the most ubiquitous function,
an elementary school, less than 4 percent had a minimal
water supply facility and that less than 3 percent had
a third-level post office. Less than 3 percent of the
925 settlements surveyed in 1980 had grain marketing
facilities, public health clinics, small hospitals, a
permanent market or a postal facility. Only about 4
percent had a government store, second class market or
complete secondary school, all of which could be efficiently located in small central places.[50] In the
Potosi region of Bolivia, only 5 of the 112 settlements
surveyed had more than half of the 56 functions found
in the largest town. In the Bicol River Basin of the
Philippines, less than 1 percent of the settlements had
half of the basic services, facilities and infrastructure found in the largest town. Nearly 90 percent of
all of the types of services, facilities, organizations
and infrastructure in the Basin appeared in less than
20 percent of the settlements. Moreover, nearly 60
percent of these functions could be found in less than
20 percent of the towns that were capitals of their
municipalities.[51] These highly skewed distributions of
services and facilities are not unusual, they are
reported in both small island countries in the South
Pacific and poor regions of large countries such as
India and the Sudan.

    3. <u>Lack of or Weak Linkages Among Settlements in
Rural Regions</u>. The relatively small number of settlements performing central functions and the highly
skewed distribution of services and facilities would
not in themselves necessarily be serious problems if
those settlements that do perform central functions
were accessible to their rural populations and were
linked to each other and to larger cities and towns.
In an integrated settlement system, not all settlements
provide all services and facilities: people can easily
travel to the most convenient next larger center to
obtain goods and services that are not located in
smaller and less diversified centers closer to where
they live. Indeed, the value of an articulated and
integrated settlement system is that it is locationally
efficient--it allows clusters of services, facilities
and infrastructure that cannot be economically located

in small villages and hamlets to serve a widely distributed population from an accessible central place.

But large opportunity costs are incurred in
developing countries because of the inadequate number
and distribution of small central places. They are
exacerbated by weak linkages among those settlements
that do perform central functions. Johnson was led in
his studies of the settlement system in India to conclude that although that country was not lacking in
central places, "what is amiss is that they rarely con-
stitute a functional hierarchy and for this reason they
fail to provide an intermeshed system of exchange that
will provide the requisite incentives for increased
application of labor, capital and human skills."[52] A
similar situation exists in Papua New Guinea, where in
the 1970s, there was not a single road network linking
towns and villages to each other. The Wards found that
"no roads join the northern and southern side of the
mainland and the principal towns of the 13 mainland
provinces have no road links with any other major
town."[53] In some provinces more than 40 percent of the
population lives more than a 2-hour overland journey
from any town.

In the Bicol River Basin of the Philippines no
level of the settlement hierarchy is well integrated
with the others. Most of the rural population lives in
settlements that are not easily reached by roads. The
cost of transporting farm products in interior rural
areas is up to six times the amount in areas connected
by access roads. Rural settlements are poorly connected to periodic markets and, as a result, they
rarely attract people from more than 15 kilometers
away. As will be seen later, studies show that as a
result of the weak or incomplete linkages among settlements, the health, educational and other facilities
located in some towns tend to serve only people living
in them or those from nearby barangays (villages).
Social interaction among communities is limited, inter-
municipal travel is low and trade and communications
between the two largest towns in the Basin are weak.[54]
The access of rural people to town-based services and
facilities was also found to be weak in the Potosi
region of Bolivia. Surveys indicate that because of
the paucity of central places, the highly skewed distribution of central functions, and weak physical linkages among them, "overall accessibility throughout the
Potosi region is extremely low."[55]

Thus, increasing evidence shows that small towns
and cities in developing countries can perform a wide
range of social and economic functions that contribute
to economic growth and social transformation in rural
areas and that integrate these rural areas with urban
centers. But in many countries the full potential for
development is lost because of the paucity of small

central places, the highly skewed distribution of functions among them, and the weak linkages between them
and larger and smaller settlements.

SPATIAL POLICY AND REGIONAL DEVELOPMENT

The foregoing analysis suggests that small towns
and cities in developing countries can and do perform a
wide variety of social, economic, and service functions
that are important to regional and national development, although not all towns perform all of these functions and many do not perform them well. Moreover,
under proper conditions, small towns and cities can be
positive forces for developing their hinterlands, for
transforming subsistence rural societies into commercial agricultural areas and for integrating urban and
rural economies within developing nations. Creation of
industrial "growth poles" in the ways attempted by many
developing countries during the 1960s, however, seems
to be neither appropriate nor sufficient to generate
widespread development. Service, distribution, commercial, marketing, agro-processing and other functions
may offer a far better base for stimulating the growth
of towns and cities in rural regions than large scale
manufacturing.[56]
And even if industrialization is one of the means
of promoting the growth and diversification of small
towns and cities, it is clear that the economic activities encouraged within them must create and serve
regional demand as well as external markets. Although
cities can have a strong and pervasive influence on the
development of their regions, their areas of influence
are clearly limited and the impact of urban centers on
villages and rural populations declines with distance.
Stohr's studies of diffusion influences in Latin
America suggest that the spread effects from intermediate cities tend to deteriorate rapidly;[57] Gilbert's
studies of the development impacts of the second
largest city in Colombia found that they were highest
within a 25 kilometer band around the city and dropped
sharply for towns and populations located more than 50
kilometers away.[58]
Thus, the creation of selected industrial "growth
poles" in rural regions is not sufficient to stimulate
widespread economic growth in rural areas, nor to
spread the benefits of development throughout a region.
Because the spread effects tend to weaken rapidly with
distance, a system of towns and cities--in which larger
settlements are linked to rural villages and farm
settlements--seems necessary to ensure wider diffusion
of innovation, the stimulation of economic activities in
rural areas and greater access for rural people to town-
based services and facilities. Stohr argues that the
only urban centers in Latin America that have been able

to act effectively as regional growth centers are those
that have developed a combination of externally-oriented
and regionally-based economic activities. These towns
and cities, "while producing for extra-regional
(national or international) demand, usually possess
sufficient integration between regional supply factors
(capital, technology, labor, societal innovation) and
regional demand (effective purchasing power) to provide
for self-sustained growth."[59]

Regional development policies must be focused on
increasing agricultural production and the marketing
of agricultural goods, supporting small-scale agro-
processing industries and diversifying the economic base
of market centers. Activities must be organized to link
town-based enterprises with rural supply areas and to
make services, facilities and inputs essential for agricultural production and marketing easily accessible to
rural populations living at low densities or scattered
widely over the landscape. Investment in farm-to-market
roads and all-weather access roads are essential to
linking rural areas and central places. Attention must
be given to providing water, basic housing, health and
social services in towns to increase the productivity of
the labor force. Attention must also be given to providing off-farm job opportunities and urban amenities
that will keep people in rural areas.[60]

Not all small towns and cities can or should be
developed as central places, nor should they all have a
full range of services, facilities and infrastructure.
As noted earlier, one of the benefits of an articulated
and integrated settlement system is that it provides
access to a wide range of functions without each settlement having to provide them all. Thus, regional
development requires careful planning to ensure that
essential services and facilities are provided in strategically located settlements and that these places are
linked to their rural hinterlands. The Urban Functions
in Rural Development approach to spatial analysis can
help planners to make better locational decisions.

The rest of this book describes the UFRD approach
to regional planning. Chapter Two examines in more
detail the conceptual framework, procedures of planning
and characteristics of the UFRD methodology. Chapter
Three outlines methods and techniques of macro-regional
analysis; Chapter Four surveys the methods of analyzing
the settlement system and the distribution of functions
among settlements; and Chapter Five describes approaches
to identifying and assessing the strength of linkages
among settlements and between them and their rural hinterlands. In Chapters Six and Seven the applications
and implications for implementation in a regional set-
ting are examined.

NOTES

1. For details see S.M. Shah, "Growth Centers as
a Strategy for Rural Development: India Experience,"
Economic Development and Cultural Change, Vol. 22, No.
2 (January 1974), pp. 215-228; R.P. Misra and K.V.
Sundaram, "Growth Foci as Instruments of Modernization
in India," in A. Kuklinski (ed.), Regional Policies
in Nigeria, India and Brazil (The Hague: Mouton,
1978), pp. 98-188; H. Benjamin Fisher, "Methods of
Identification of Agro-Urban Centers at the Kabupaten
and Provincial Levels," Jakarta: Ford Foundation,
1975; R.A. Obudho, Urbanization in Kenya: A Bottom-Up
Approach to Development Planning, Lanham, Md.: University Press of America, 1983; R. Bromley, Periodic
and Daily Markets in Highland Ecuador, Ann Arbor,
Michigan: University Microfilms Ltd., 1975; D. Grove
and L. Huszar, The Towns of Ghana, Accra: University
of Ghana Press, 1964; Republic of Malawi, Development
of District Centers Feasibility Study: Final Report,
Vol. I, Dusseldorf, Germany: GEITEC Consult GMBH,
1980; D.A. Rondinelli, "Spatial Analysis for Regional
Development: A Case Study in the Bicol River Basin of
the Philippines," Resource Systems Theory and Methodology Series, No. 2 (Tokyo: United Nations University,
1980); H. Evans, Urban Functions in Rural Development:
The Case of the Potosi Region in Bolivia, Parts I and
II, Washington: U.S. Agency for International Development, 1982; and S. Fass, "Urban Functions in Upper
Volta: Final Report," Washington, USAID, 1981.
2. For a description of the concepts underlying
UFRD see Dennis A. Rondinelli and Kenneth Ruddle, Urbanization and Rural Development: A Spatial Policy
for Equitable Growth, New York: Praeger, 1978.
3. Avrom Bendavid-Val, Regional and Local Economic Analysis for Practitioners, New York: Praeger,
1983.
4. See John B. Parr, "Growth Poles, Regional
Development and Central Place Theory," Papers of the
Regional Science Association, Vol. 31 (1973), pp. 173-
212; D.F. Darwent, "Growth Poles and Growth Centers in
Regional Planning--A Review," Environment and Planning,
Vol. 1 (1969), pp. 5-32; M.D. Thomas, "Growth Pole
Theory: An Examination of Some of its Basic Concepts,"
in N. Hansen (ed.), Growth Centers in Regional Economic
Development (New York: Free Press, 1972), pp. 50-81.
5. Michael E. Conroy, "Rejection of Growth Center
Strategy in Latin American Regional Development Plan-
ning," Land Economics, Vol. XLIX, No. 4 (1973), pp.
371-380; Harry W. Richardson and Margaret Richardson,
"The Relevance of Growth Center Strategies to Latin
America," Economic Geography, Vol. 51, No. 2 (April

1975), pp. 163-178; Milton Santos, "Underdevelopment, Growth Poles and Social Justice," Civilizations, Vol. 25, Nos. 1 and 2 (1975), pp. 18-30.

6. Niles Hansen, "The Role of Small and Intermediate Sized Cities in National Development Processes and Strategies," paper delivered at Expert Group Meeting on the Role of Small and Intermediate Cities in National Development (Nagoya, Japan: United Nations Center for Regional Development, 1982), p. 1.

7. Brian J.L. Berry, "Policy Implications of an Urban Location Model for the Kanpur Region," in P.B. Desai et al. (eds.), Regional Perspective of Industrial and Urban Growth: The Case of Kanpur (Bombay: MacMillan, 1969), pp. 203-219; quoted at p. 207.

8. See Rondinelli and Ruddle op. cit., Chapter 4.

9. E.A.J. Johnson, The Organization of Space in Developing Countries (Cambridge, Mass.: Harvard University Press, 1970), p.171.

10. Brian J.L. Berry, Geography of Market Centers and Retail Distribution, Englewood Cliffs, N.J.: Prentice-Hall, 1967.

11. H.B. Fisher and G. Rushton, "Rural Growth Centers: Experiences in the Pilot Research Project 1969-1974," paper presented at the Annual Meeting of the Association for Asian Studies, San Francisco, 1975, p. 6.

12. Ray Bromley, "Market Center Analysis in the Urban Functions in Rural Development Approach," paper presented at International Symposium on Small Towns in National Development (Bangkok: Asian Institute of Technology, 1982), p. 1.

13. Prodipto Roy and B.R. Patil, Manual for Block Level Planning (Delhi: The MacMillan Company of India, 1977), p. 25.

14. Ibid., pp. 25-26.

15. Rondinelli and Ruddle, op. cit., Chapter One.

16. Roy and Patil, op. cit., p. 7.

17. Michael Schatzberg, "Islands of Privilege: Small Cities in Africa and the Dynamics of Class Formation," Urban Anthropology, Vol. 8, No. 2 (1979), pp. 173-190; quote at p. 174.

18. See, for example, Aidan Southall, "What Causes Overconcentration or Decentralization in the Urbanization Process?," Urbanism Past and Present, Vol. 7, No. 13 (Winter-Spring 1982), pp. 38-41.

19. John Friedmann and Mike Douglass, "Agropolitan Development: Towards a New Strategy for Regional Planning in Asia," paper presented at the Seminar on Industrialization Strategies and the Growth Pole Approach to Regional Planning and Development (Nagoya, Japan: United Nations Centre for Regional Development, 1975).

20. Walter Stohr and Franz Todtling, "Spatial Equity--Some Anti-Theses to Current Regional Development Doctrine," Papers of the Regional Science Association, Vol. 38 (1977), pp. 33-53.

21. Anthony Leeds, "Towns and Villages in Society: Hierarchies of Order and Cause," in T.W. Collins (ed.), Cities in a Larger Context (Athens, Georgia: University of Georgia Press, 1980), pp. 6-33.

22. David A. Preston, Farmers and Towns: Rural-Urban Relations in Highland Bolivia (Norwich: University of East Anglia-Geo Abstracts, 1978), p. 69.

23. Ibid., pp. 176-177.

24. John J. Swetnam, "Interaction Between Urban and Rural Residents in a Guatemalan Market Place," Urban Anthropology, Vol. 7, No. 2 (1978), pp. 137-153; quote at p. 137.

25. Ibid., p. 141.

26. Norbert Dannhaeuser, "Commercial Relations Between Center and Periphery in Northern Luzon: Detrimental Dependence or Generative Interdependence?," Philippine Studies, Vol. 29 (1981), pp. 144-169; quote at p. 165.

27. Harry W. Richardson, "Policies for Strengthening Small Cities in Developing Countries," paper prepared for Expert Group Meeting of the Role of Small and Intermediate Cities in National Development (Nagoya, Japan: United Nations Centre for Regional Development, 1982), p. 14.

28. Lauren Anita Corwin, "The Rural Town: Minimal Urban Center," Urban Anthropology, Vol. 6, No. 1 (1977), pp. 23-24; quote at p. 39.

29. E.A.J. Johnson, "Scale Economies in Small Agro-Urban Communities," in F. Helleiner and W. Stohr (eds.), Proceedings of the Commission on Regional Aspects of Development of the International Geographical Union, Vol. II (Toronto: International Geographical Union, 1974), pp. 583-612.

30. World Bank, Rural Enterprises and Nonfarm Employment, (Washington: World Bank, 1978), pp. 7-8.

31. Sam P.S. Ho, Small-Scale Enterprizes in Korea and Taiwan, World Bank Staff Working Paper No. 384, Washington: World Bank, 1980.

32. Government of the Kingdom of Thailand, National Economic and Social Development Board, South Thailand Regional Planning Study, Vol. 2 (Bangkok: Hunting Technical Services, Ltd., n.d. 1979?), pp. 27-34.

33. Theodore D. Fuller, "Migrant Evaluations of the Quality of Urban Life in Northeast Thailand," Journal of Developing Areas, Vol. 16, No. 1 (October 1981), pp. 87-104; quotes at pp. 92 and 101.

34. Ralph L. Beals, The Peasant Marketing System in Oaxaca, Mexico (Berkeley: University of California Press, 1975), pp. 120-121.

35. <u>Ibid.</u>, Appendix 1 provides a detailed description of these activities.

36. See P.A. Doherty and J.M. Ball, "Central Functions Small Mexican Towns," <u>Southeastern Geographer</u>, Vol. XI, No. 1 (1971), pp. 20-28.

37. Diane E. David, "Migration, Rank-Size Distribution and Economic Development: The Case of Mexico," <u>Studies in Comparative International Development</u>, Vol. XVI (1981), pp. 84-107; quote at p. 102.

38. See Joseph F. Lombardo, Jr. "Introduction to the Human Settlement System in Honduras," Unpublished Report, Tegucigalpa, Honduras: U.S. Agency for International Development, 1982; and Hugh Evans, <u>Urban Functions in Rural Development: The Case of the Potosi Region in Bolivia</u>, Part I, Washington: U.S. Agency for International Development, 1982.

39. Swetnam, <u>op. cit</u>.

40. M.A. Hirst, "A Functional Analysis of Towns in Tanzania," <u>Tijdschrift voor Econ. en Soc. Geografie</u>, Vol. 64, No. 1 (1973), pp. 39-59.

41. James S. Wunsch, "Political Development and Planning in Ghana: A Comparative Study of Two Medium Cities," in R.A. Obudho and S. El-Shakhs (eds.), <u>Development of Urban Systems in Africa</u> (New York: Praeger, 1979), pp. 137-156.

42. J.O.C. Onyemelukwe, "Settlement Structure as Sociocultural Constraint on Nigerian Rural Development," <u>Ekistics</u>, Vol. 7, No. 284 (1980), pp. 353-355; quote at p. 355.

43. Lombardo, <u>op. cit</u>.

44. Quoted in Michael McNulty and Michael E. Conroy, "An Evaluation Report on Potential Sites in Bolivia and Paraguay for the Urban Functions in Rural Development Project" (Washington: U.S. Agency for International Development, 1977), mimeographed, p. 10.

45. Evans, <u>op. cit</u>., and Dennis A. Rondinelli and Hugh Evans, "Integrated Regional Development Planning: Linking Urban Centers and Rural Areas in Bolivia," <u>World Development</u>, Vol. 11 (1983), in press.

46. See R.G. Ward and M.W. Ward, "The Rural-Urban Connection--A Missing Link in Melanesia," <u>Malaysian Journal of Tropical Geography</u>, Vol. 1 (September 1980), pp. 57-63.

47. Dennis A. Rondinelli, "Spatial Analysis for Regional Development: A Case Study in the Bicol River Basin of the Philippines," <u>Resource Systems Theory and Methodology Series</u>, No. 2 (Tokyo: United Nations University, 1980) and Dennis A. Rondinelli, "Applied Policy Analysis for Integrated Regional Development Planning in the Philippines," <u>Third World Planning Review</u>, Vol. 1, No. 2 (1979), pp. 150-178.

48. Mike Douglass, "Thailand: Territorial Dissolution and Alternative Regional Development for the

Central Plains," in W.B. Stohr and D.R. Fraser Taylor (eds.), Development from Above or Below? (London: Wiley and Sons, 1981), pp. 183-208.

49. Ibid., p. 199.

50. Lombardo, op. cit., pp. 3-4.

51. Rondinelli, "Spatial Analysis for Regional Development," op. cit., pp. 22-27.

52. Johnson, The Organization of Space in Developing Countries, op. cit., pp. 70-71.

53. Ward and Ward, op. cit., p. 59.

54. Rondinelli, "Spatial Analysis for Regional Development," op. cit., pp. 28-38.

55. Evans, op. cit., p. 74.

56. See Dennis A. Rondinelli, Secondary Cities in Developing Countries: Policies for Diffusing Urbanization, Beverly Hills: Sage Publications, 1983.

57. Walter B. Stohr, "Some Hypotheses on the Role of Secondary Growth Centers as Agents for the Spatial Transmission of Development in Newly Developing Countries--The Case of Latin America," in Helleiner and Stohr, op. cit., pp. 75-111.

58. See Alan Gilbert, "A Note on the Incidence of Development in the Vicinity of a Growth Center," Regional Studies, Vol. 9 (1975), pp. 325-333.

59. Stohr, op. cit., pp. 98-99.

60. See Dennis A. Rondinelli and Kenneth Ruddle, "Integrating Spatial Development," Ekistics, Vol. 43, No. 257 (April 1977), pp. 185-194.

2
The UFRD Approach
to Regional Planning

Urban Functions in Rural Development (UFRD)
emerged from a series of pilot projects sponsored by
the U.S. Agency for International Development (USAID)
during the late 1970s and early 1980s. The projects
that were initiated in the Philippines, Bolivia and
Upper Volta drew heavily on experience with similar
approaches to planning in other developing countries.
They were motivated by the recognition that despite the
economic and social progress made in much of the developing world during the previous two decades, a substantial portion of the population in the Third World still
lives in dire poverty. In many countries, the gaps
between the richest and poorest groups continue to
widen. The World Bank estimated that the number of
people living in absolute poverty--"a condition of life
so characterized by malnutrition, illiteracy and dis-
ease as to be beneath any reasonable definition of
human decency" and in which people survive on a per
capita income of less than $75 a year--at 780 million
in 1980. This represents an increase over a decade of
30 million people living at or below subsistence
levels. Millions more people live in relative poverty,
with incomes substantially below the average of their
countries.[1] According to studies undertaken by the
International Labor Office (ILO) the incomes of many of
the poorest families in Asia fell during the 1970s and
the percentage of rural population with incomes below
the poverty line increased. Inequities in the distribution of income and wealth in some developing countries were more pronounced by the mid-1970s than they
had been 15 years earlier.[2] The UFRD projects were
aimed at both helping to alleviate rural poverty and to
increase productivity and income in rural regions.

27

THE DIMENSIONS OF UNDERDEVELOPMENT IN RURAL REGIONS

About 85 percent of the people living in absolute
poverty in developing countries can be found in rural
areas. The distribution and severity of poverty in
developing countries are closely related to levels of
agricultural productivity and regional resource development. In most poor regions people have limited
access to the natural and man-made resources needed to
satisfy basic needs, increase productivity, diversify
economic activities and raise incomes. Growing disparities can be seen in levels and rates of economic
growth between those countries and regions that have
been able to mobilize and use their resources effectively to stimulate agricultural and industrial development, and those less able to do so. Serious disparities in levels of living also appear between urban and
rural areas and among subnational regions with different levels of resource endowments and productive
assets.[3]

Ironically, the majority of the poor live in areas
with relatively favorable climates and with potentially
productive resources. They remain poor because they
lack access to the means of procuring, transforming or
distributing those resources more effectively.[4] They
inhabit areas where competition for existing resources,
especially agricultural land, is intense; where the
physical, social and administrative infrastructure
needed to transform and use resources is scarce; or
where deliberate patterns of government investment have
placed them at a disadvantage in competing with other
regions in national or international markets.

In much of the developing world the intense competition for arable land is a primary cause of poverty.
"Within the rural sector," the World Bank has found,
"at the very core of the poverty problem are families
who either own and cultivate very small holdings or own
no land at all."[5] Severe pressures on land resources
from high rates of rural population growth are expected
to continue in areas with the highest levels of poverty
for the rest of this century.

But problems also arise from inefficient use of
existing resources: from the inability to identify
productive uses for indigenous renewable resources or
from inefficient resource transformation and delivery.
Inefficient use of labor--its low productivity and
sporadic employment--is perhaps the most apparent
example of underused resources in rural regions. The
ILO has found, however, that "labor is not the only
resource that is poorly utilized; in many countries
land and other resources are not efficiently exploi-
ted."[6] The intense competition for available resources
is often exacerbated by lack of credit facilities and

marketing outlets for small farmers and entrepreneurs, the inadequacy of cooperative organizations or other arrangements for selling goods or obtaining inputs, poor communications, insufficient physical infrastructure and poorly organized agricultural research and extension services. Most subsistence activities, moreover, depend on manual labor or animal power; the technology needed to transform resources and increase productivity are not available to the rural poor. In addition, the administrative and institutional arrangements needed to provide and maintain services, facilities and infrastructure are often missing or inadequate.[7]

As noted earlier, the rural poor generally lack access to town-based services and facilities that would allow them to increase their productivity and to market their goods. Their limited access to market towns and small cities, in which the services and facilities they need to promote rural development are located, places rural people at a serious disadvantage.[8]

By the mid-1970s many governments in developing countries and most international assistance organizations recognized that if they are to ameliorate rural poverty, integrate poor regions into the national economy and increase agricultural productivity, they must promote development in a way that supports the internal growth of rural economies.[9] Redistribution alone does little to overcome rural poverty of the magnitude found in most developing countries. The emphasis on equitable growth that emerged during the 1970s requires the development of new resources in rural regions and the steady inclusion of marginal and subsistence populations in productive economic activities.[10] This in turn requires extensive investment in physical infrastructure, services and productive activities in rural regions, located strategically in intermediate-sized cities, smaller towns and rural market centers. The growth of "rural service centers" that link towns to rural hinterlands must also be encouraged in order to increase the access of rural people to basic services and facilities.[11]

The investments, moreover, have to be located in such a way as to create an articulated and integrated regional settlement system capable of (1) strengthening markets for agricultural goods and other rural resources; (2) distributing more widely services such as health, education, family planning and vocational training, the technical inputs needed for increased agricultural production such as new seed varieties, appropriate technology, farm-to-market roads, and rural electrification, as well as communications and transportation; (3) creating new rural employment opportunities, especially in agro-processing, agribusiness,

small-scale manufacturing and cottage industries that
use local resources as the primary inputs for production, and (4) slowing the rate and altering the pattern
of rural to urban migration.[12]

Those within the U.S. Agency for International
Development who promoted the UFRD pilot projects recognized that spatial and locational factors were crucial
to the success of rural and regional development and
that urban centers played an important role in rural
transformation. "In addition to being loci of opportunities for off-farm employment," they noted, "urban
centers provide marketing, storage, processing, supply,
credit, health, educational and other services to the
rural areas." They concluded that rural populations
"without access to fully functional and efficient centers are denied their full development potential."[13]
Strengthening the linkages between rural areas and
urban centers can extend services and facilities into
rural areas and expand markets for agricultural products. Major economic linkages for rural areas are
established almost entirely through urban activities
and institutions, making cities essential components of
any strategy for developing rural regions. "The system
of cities and towns in any country is a totality,"
USAID's Working Group on the Rural Pool pointed out.
"There are a number of linkages and interdependencies
between the essentially rural based centers at the
lower end of the urban hierarchy and the larger cities
in the urban system which ought to flow in both directions, up and down the hierarchy."[14] But the critical
problem in most developing nations is that almost all
linkages needed to promote and sustain agricultural
growth are downward, because the lower levels of the
national spatial system are neither well-developed nor
properly organized. USAID strategists argued that in
most developing nations villages are too small to support the services needed for growth, that vertical
linkages between farms, small towns and cities which
could provide rural areas with needed services and
facilities and link them to the national economy have
been neglected in previous development strategies, and
that linkages must be created between rural settlements
and urban centers if development policy is to
succeed.[15]

The importance of the spatial dimension of equitable growth policy was strongly confirmed in research
conducted for USAID in the mid-1970s. The study found
that settlement systems in many developing countries
were not conducive to widespread regional development.
Although metropolitan centers and smaller cities could
play important roles in facilitating economic growth,
in most less developed countries they were not widely
dispersed and were often weakly linked to rural hinterlands. Thus, the rural poor generally lacked access to

the services, facilities and productive activities concentrated in them. As a result these towns and cities
did not provide the stimuli needed to develop new
resources, increase agricultural production or generate
new employment.[16]

The report also emphasized that locational factors, which were often overlooked or neglected in rural
development planning, were crucial in implementing
regional development programs effectively. It noted
that proper location of public services and facilities
and private investment stimulates development in a
number of ways. Even within relatively small and homo-
geneous countries, regions differ in their suitability
for, and attractiveness as, locations for investment.
The creation of locational advantages in the future
depends in part on past decisions--on the quantity and
quality of facilities available for production, and on
the existence of infrastructure and services that
attract and support investment. Although suitable
natural resources--land, water and mineral endowments--
must be available, man-made facilities are also crucial. The existence of a transport network, of rail,
air, water and highway linkages, for instance, determines the cost of moving raw materials from supply
sources to points of production and finished goods to
distributors and final markets. Public investment in
water supply, waste disposal and energy helps determine
the productivity of the labor force and of economic
enterprises. Social services can contribute to the
quality of human resources and to general standards of
living in the community.[17]

The report pointed out that in developing nations
the proper location of services and facilities is particularly important, for with scarce resources, limited
administrative capability, increasingly urgent needs to
expand food production and manufacturing, projects must
be assessed not only by their efficiency and feasibility, but also by their "multiplier effects."

Distribution of services and facilities is crucial
not only for promoting economic growth, but also for
achieving social equity and improving the quality of
life. Disparities in economic and social well-being
are often measured by the number and diversity of productive and social functions located within a community
or region. The growing gap between the richest and
poorest groups in developing nations is largely attri-
butable to differences in access to productive activities and social services. In a policy paper on rural
development, World Bank officials argue that any strategy for dealing with poverty in the Third World, to be
effective, must recognize that "the need for special
intervention to raise rural production and income
applies also to the provision of social and other

services, such as health and education. . . . Compared
with urban areas, rural areas have a smaller share of
economic infrastructure services such as domestic
water, electricity and waste disposal." And even in
areas where services do exist, Bank analysts observe,
"the poor often do not have access to them because
organization is inadequate and the cost is high. A
special effort is needed to provide appropriate social
and economic infrastructure for the rural poor, and it
is important to integrate these components into rural
development projects."[18]

The USAID report proposed a general framework for
analyzing regions and determining the degree of articulation and integration of the settlement system and the
linkages between urban and rural areas. Functional
analysis of settlement systems in developing countries
could help determine the services and facilities needed
at each level of the spatial hierarchy and the means of
providing better access for the rural population to
those functions. The study pointed out, however, that
any analytical framework would have to be modified in
application, adapted to local conditions, and tested in
a number of developing countries because of the scarcity of data and general unreliability of statistics in
developing nations, and the need for analytical techniques that could be easily applied by planners and
readily understood by policymakers in rural regions.

The report suggested that the pilot projects focus
on three areas of analysis:

1. Analysis of Regional Resources and Characteristics: including such factors as physical characteristics of the region, land and resource uses, cropping
patterns, volume and diversity of agricultural production, population distribution and rural settlement
patterns, services and facilities distribution, non-
agricultural and commercial activities, and subsistence
system characteristics;

2. Analysis of Settlements: including the location of market towns, small cities, intermediate or
regional centers; the size, composition and density of
towns, the location, concentration and dispersion of
central functions, changes in the size and concentration of social and economic activities over time, and
the labor force and income distribution characteristics
of settlements; and,

3. Analysis of Spatial Linkages: including
physical, economic, population movement, technological,
social service delivery, political and institutional
interaction patterns among settlements within the
region, and linkages with urban centers in other
regions.

A number of specific analytical techniques, and
the types of information needed to apply them, were

also described. The report emphasized, however, that
the pilot projects should be tailored to the needs and
constraints found in the regions under study. A pre-
designed package of methods could not be imposed;
methodology should be designed in collaboration with
local planners and researchers only after initial data
inventories and surveys of available information were
conducted.[19]

CONCEPTS USED IN THE UFRD APPROACH

The Urban Functions in Rural Development approach
used in the Philippines, Bolivia and Upper Volta drew
on central place and service center concepts described
in Chapter One. Among the most important assumptions
underlying these concepts are the following derived by
Roy and Patil from their studies of spatial development
in India:

1. People are distributed in various size
   settlements in space;
2. They have bio-physical as well as socio-
   economic needs;
3. They utilize physical and human resources,
   i.e., goods and services to satisfy their
   needs;
4. They form settlements in space in the
   form of homesteads, hamlets, villages,
   towns or cities and continue to stay
   together as long as resources are
   adequate to meet their needs;
5. They utilize resources for basic needs
   which are limited or wants which are
   unlimited; and,
6. They go to other places in search of
   goods and services that are not (or
   cannot be) available in their own
   settlements.[20]

Other important assumptions were, as noted earlier,
that central places--market towns, small cities,
regional centers and metropolitan areas--all play
important roles in regional economic and social development. Their number, geographical distribution and
functional characteristics are crucial factors in the
way regional development occurs and in its pace and
pattern. Moreover, the linkages among settlements must
be strong if access to services and facilities located
in central places is to be extended and if social,
political, economic and physical interaction among
centers of different sizes and specializations is to be
enhanced. Three types of linkage are especially
important:

1. Those between a central place and its
   surrounding rural areas (hinterland);

    2.   Those among central places within a
        region (internal); and

    3.   Those between central places within a
        region and places outside the region
        (external).

The UFRD approach employs a number of concepts of
regional economics and geography which are defined in
the following way.[21]

    Urban functions are those services, facilities,
infrastructure, institutions or economic activities
that must be located in settlements of some minimum
population size in order to be offered economically and
efficiently. Some functions serve only the residents
of the place in which they located and are called local
or residentiary functions; others serve a larger market
or the residents of other settlements and are called
basic or central functions.

    Settlements with a significant number of basic
functions are called central places. The number of
people required to support a function, or a combination
of functions, is called a threshold population level.
Each function has a different population threshold.
Some provide daily goods and services and require only
a relatively small number of people to make their operations profitable and efficient. Large numbers of
these functions are found in a region and some are
located in nearly every settlement. Others offer goods
and services that are rarely needed or that are expensive to produce or deliver. These require large market
areas and populations to support them and are located
only in larger urban centers. The degree to which a
settlement acts as a central place depends, therefore,
on (1) its number, concentration and diversity of basic
functions; (2) its population size and density and the
size of the population in its market or service area;
(3) the volume of interaction among activities located
within it and with similar complementary functions in
other locations, and (4) the degree of convenience it
offers as a point of interaction among people living in
the geographical area in which it is located.

    Generally, the larger the number of basic func-
tions located in a settlement, the greater their diversity and the higher their population threshold, the
higher is the settlement's centrality. A central place
consists of a core area in which basic functions are
physically located, and service area or hinterland from
which people come to avail themselves of services and
facilities located in the central place. The market,
service or hinterland area--sometimes called a complementary region--is determined largely by distance, cost
of travel, and the ranges of services and facilities
provided in a center. "The range of a good is the
farthest distance a dispersed population is willing to

go in order to buy a good offered at a place," Berry and Garrison point out.[22] Other things being equal, the range will be lower if there are competitive goods being offered by nearby centers. Usually goods and services will have a larger range in larger places and a smaller range in smaller places. "Range is actually a ring with an upper limit beyond which a good can no longer be obtained from a center, and a lower limit which is determined by the minimum amount of consumption which is necessary before production or offering the central good will pay."[23] Settlements within a region can be ranked in a hierarchy, based on their levels of centrality. The service areas of central places can be determined and the degree of interaction or trade among them can be estimated.[24]

Regions that have a well developed hierarchy of central places--settlements of different sizes with different combinations of central functions--are considered to have more articulated spatial systems. For various reasons such as a unique location, an important natural resource base, or large numbers of people with particular kinds of skills, some settlements achieve a larger concentration of one or two functions than others, and are considered to be functionally specialized communities. They may be industrial, commercial, administrative, mining or agricultural marketing centers in which a large percentage of local residents are employed in producing goods or providing services of a particular type. Strong trade linkages usually develop among such highly specialized centers.

Those regions in which all, or nearly all, of the population have easy access to at least one central place, in which the service areas of the larger centers "overlap" with each other and encompass the service areas of small centers, and in which the central places of different sizes are physically linked with each other in such a way as to allow their populations to interact, can be considered integrated.[25] In an integrated and articulated region, "there is a system of central places comprising several size-types, determined in general by the spatial effects of the upper and lower limits to the range of central goods," Berry and Garrison observe. "Lower order centers and their complementary regions 'nest' within those of larger centers."[26]

The degree of integration in a spatial system depends, therefore, on the degree of articulation in the settlement hierarchy, the distances among centers, the effective access that people have to other centers, and the diversity and magnitude of functions within centers. Thus, integration is primarily determined by the amount of interaction that takes place among settlements within a region. In turn, integration is

an indicator of the degree to which a region has a
viable internal economy and participates in mutually
beneficial interaction with external regional or
national economies.

There is also a minimum population size and
service area below which settlements are not able to
supply central goods and services. These settlements
usually only offer ubiquitous functions for their own
residents, or may offer nothing more than the benefits
of mutual security from having houses and families
clustered together in spatial proximity. Service
center theory suggests that the lowest order central
place is one that provides basic inputs for agricultural producers. In its guidelines for rural
service center planning, the UN Economic and Social
Commission for Asia and the Pacific suggests that they
perform the following functions: (1) facilities or
arrangements for the marketing and collection of agricultural surplus production; (2) services and facilities for the distribution of essential farm inputs such
as fertilizers, tools, implements, and credit; (3) services and facilities for basic agricultural processing
both for subsistence and commercial purposes; and
(4) services and facilities that fulfill basic human
needs.[27] Those settlements that do not offer these
basic services and goods are considered to be non-
central places.

There are few, if any, absolute standards for
measuring these characteristics of a regional system.
All are relative concepts and must be defined within
the social, economic, physical and cultural context of
the societies in which they are examined. Spatial and
economic factors are closely related in the development
of regions in nearly all societies, however, and effect
each other over time. The degree of articulation and
integration in a settlement system depends on past
rates and patterns of economic development, which in
turn have been influenced by the interaction of people,
the performance of activities and the flow of resources
in geographic space. Thus, over time, the pattern of
economic development in a region strongly influences
the pattern of spatial development, which shapes the
future rate and direction of economic growth and the
distribution of its benefits among people and places
within the region.

THE PROCESS OF SPATIAL ANALYSIS

Urban Functions in Rural Development is a process
of analysis and planning that involves the following
stages or phases:[28]
    1. An overall regional resource analysis and
socioeconomic and demographic profile that serves as a

data inventory for planning purposes and as a "baseline" study for monitoring and evaluation;

2. An analysis of the existing system of settlements, describing its elements, the functional complexity and centrality of settlements, the hierarchy of
central places, and the distribution of and patterns of
association among functions within the region;

3. Description and analysis of the major socio-
economic, organizational and physical linkages among
settlements within the region and between them and
centers located in other regions of the country;

4. Mapping of information obtained from the functional complexity, settlement hierarchy and spatial
linkages analyses to determine "areas of influence" or
service areas of various settlement categories within
the region;

5. Delineation of areas where linkages are weak
or nonexistent, and of marginal areas that are unserved
by central places or in which rural populations have
poor access to town-based services and facilities that
are crucial for regional development;

6. Comparison of information from the regional
resources survey, settlement system, functional distribution and linkage analyses to regional development
plans and objectives to (a) determine the adequacy of
the spatial system to meet development needs and
facilitate equitable growth and (b) identify major
"gaps" in the spatial system, in service areas for crucial functions, and in linkages among subareas of the
region;

7. Translation of the spatial analyses into
investment proposals that identify the projects and
programs that will be needed to ameliorate major development problems, to strengthen and articulate the
regional spatial structure, and to integrate various
levels of settlement within it;

8. Integration of projects identified through
spatial and economic analyses into spatially and functionally coordinated "investment packages" for different locations within the region, and combination of the
investment packages into a priority-ranked and
appropriately-sequenced investment budget for the
development of the region over a given period of time;

9. Creation of an evaluation system for monitoring the implementation of projects and programs, and
for determining the substantive results of development
activities on areas and population groups within the
region; and

10. Institutionalization of the planning procedures in local and regional public agencies charged
with investment decision-making and with revising the
spatial analysis and development plans at appropriate
intervals.

These phases of the process evolved from experiments with spatial analysis in the Philippines and Bolivia. However, they should be seen only as guidelines for regional development planning rather than as a "tool-kit" of methods or an invariable series of steps that must be followed slavishly in every situation. Each region has different problems and characteristics, and planning agencies in every region have different capabilities and requirements for information. Thus, the UFRD approach can only provide a point of departure for analysis rather than a comprehensive model. In some areas, such as the Eastern Region in Upper Volta, only some of the stages and methodologies were used. In Bolivia, new methods and techniques and different approaches to analysis were added to those applied in the Philippines. In some countries the analyses suggested here can be expanded and followed by more detailed and comprehensive studies. In other situations, a "quicker and dirtier" version of the approach can be applied to gather essential information rapidly. More systematic approaches can be used later when more time and resources are available.

Thus, although the chapters that follow describe the UFRD approach in the sequence described above, it should be remembered that in any given region the process should be tested anew and adapted or tailored to local needs. Other appropriate methods and techniques can be added to or substitute for those that are described here. The ultimate objective is to develop a process of spatial analysis that can be used effectively in local planning and decision-making and that can be adapted and up-dated as time goes on.

CHARACTERISTICS AND PRINCIPLES OF UFRD

The UFRD approach is based on six principles or characteristics, some of which are inherent in its conceptual framework, some of which have emerged from early field testing, and some of which arose from experience with applying similar methods of analysis in other countries. Among the principles underlying UFRD are the following:

1. UFRD should focus on the spatial and locational dimensions of regional development and be primarily a "place-oriented" form of planning and analysis.

Unlike most forms of regional planning used in developing countries, UFRD focuses primarily on the spatial and locational dimensions of regional development. It seeks to add a spatial dimension to the sectoral and technical planning that is more frequently

done in developing countries. UFRD is used to analyze
a regional settlement system in order to determine the
degree to which settlements of different sizes and
functional characteristics are accessible to people
living in different areas of the region and the degree
to which those settlements are linked to each other and
to their rural hinterlands. The information gathered
through spatial analysis can give sectoral and technical planners a framework for locating services,
facilities, infrastructure, and productive activities
more effectively to serve a larger number of people and
to strengthen the settlement system's capacity to
facilitate spontaneous or induced development activities.

The UFRD approach is a process of regional spatial
analysis that gathers information about four basic
questions:

    a.   How are functions (services, facilities,
        infrastructure, socioeconomic activi-
        ties) distributed geographically among
        settlements or communities?

    b.   How much physical access do residents of
        settlements and of rural areas surround-
        ing them have to the functions located
        in central places?

    c.   How widely do services and facilities
        located in settlements throughout the
        region serve their rural hinderlands?
        and,

    d.   How can the distribution of functions
        and of settlements be improved and how
        can physical access of rural residents
        be increased?

The UFRD approach is primarily descriptive; it is
a means of gathering information about the spatial
system that will contribute to normative or prescrip-
tive plans. As Fass noted in his review of the UFRD
approach in Upper Volta, "where the UFRD concept and
method differs from more conventional sectoral
approaches is that it does not presuppose which of the
'functions' would have the most significant effects,
does not presuppose which of the effects are most
appropriately called 'significant' and does not presuppose that the same set of functions can be, or ought
necessarily to be, universally applied in all
places."[29] UFRD attempts to find out "what is located
where" as a means of analyzing better how to achieve
what planners and policy-makers conclude "ought to be."
Moreover, the UFRD methodology is based on the assumption, as Fass notes, that "in any region there is
heterogeneity and that social, economic, or environmental circumstances can vary considerably. Thus, the
kinds of functions which would be appropriate to and or

strengthen one place might not necessarily be the same
in another. In other words, the UFRD concept is 'place
specific' rather than sector specific and represents a
kind of integrated or multisectoral approach to rural
development."[30] In asking "what kinds of functions are
located where?" the analyst is implying that some of
the missing functions provide opportunities for new
investments. But it should be remembered that more
intensive studies than those encompassed in the UFRD
approach must be carried out to determine whether or
not the lack of services and facilities in some places
is a problem. Much depends on what sectoral, technical
and regional planners and local residents want to
accomplish through regional development activities.

    2. <u>The UFRD approach should seek to create an on-
going planning process rather than to produce a comprehensive regional development plan</u>.

    Because the objective of the UFRD methodology is
to add a spatial and locational dimension to regional
analysis and planning, it should not be seen as a process that will produce a comprehensive regional development plan or supplant sectoral, program or technical
plans. Spatial analysis can complement and strengthen
other forms of planning and provide locational guidelines for the formulation, design and allocation of investment projects. Although the spatial analysis must
be presented clearly, sometimes in the form of a spatial plan, UFRD is most effectively used as a method of
assessing the spatial distribution of services, facilities, infrastructure and productive activities among
settlements in a region on a continuing basis. To do a
spatial analysis once and present it as a long range
plan for regional development both ignores the real-
ities of the decision-making process in most developing
countries and makes the analysis static rather than
dynamic. In a sense, UFRD presents a picture of the
spatial structure of the region at the time the study
is completed. But the spatial system within regions
changes continuously as economic, social, political and
physical changes occur. Thus, spatial analysis must
also be continuous in order to provide a better understanding of those changes. Although the emphasis of
the following chapters of this book is on the methods
and techniques of spatial analysis and planning, it
should be kept in mind that they are less important
than the <u>process</u> for which they serve merely as instruments.

    3. <u>UFRD should be a process of spatial analysis
that is policy- and problem-oriented and indicative and
adjunctive in nature</u>.

The planning activities and spatial analyses embodied in the UFRD approach should be attuned to the decision-making processes and requirements of regional planning agencies, regional offices of national government ministries and agencies, provincial and local governments, private investors and community groups that are involved in making investments and location decisions in a region. The analyses can be used to add a place-oriented dimension to sectoral and technical planning as well as provide a framework for making better regional development decisions.[31] As such, UFRD is strategic rather than comprehensive planning, it is an adjunct to other forms of analysis and planning in which private organizations and government agencies are already engaged.

Rather than leading to a long range comprehensive plan, adjunctive planning seeks to facilitate inter-action among a wide variety of organizations and interests within a region, focus attention on solving remediable aspects of known problems, identify courses of action that move marginally and incrementally--through successive approximation--away from unsatis-factory social and economic conditions, especially when "optimal" or ideal goals cannot be agreed upon. It is used to explore alternatives upon which diverse interests can act jointly.[32] Strategic planning seeks to disaggregate problems into decisions that can be made incrementally and that can be dealt with through discrete but related investments over a long period of time.

To be most effective, the UFRD approach should be used in a way that elicits widespread participation--not only of national, regional, provincial and local governments, but of private sector organizations and community groups as well. Technical analysis alone will not provide "answers" to locational questions about investment and development activities. It will merely provide information that can be used by various groups within a region to make more informed deci-sions.

In this sense, UFRD should be seen as a process of learning about the settlement system and the distribu-tion of functions among communities within a region. UFRD is a process of indicative planning. It should lead planners and policy-makers to ask better and more informed questions about why the spatial system and geographical distribution of functions exist as they do; how changes might be brought about by reinforcing the growth of existing settlements or stimulating the development of new ones; what types of investments might be needed in different places; when it is pos-sible for communities to support new functions or com-binations of activities; and which organizations and

agencies might play an important role in helping them
to do so.

Ultimately, rather than providing answers to these
questions or solutions to regional development problems, the UFRD approach allows planners and policy-
makers to gather important information quickly, and to
ask more refined and detailed questions that will help
them make better judgments from a spatial or locational
perspective. Being adjunctive, indicative and focused
on the spatial dimensions of regional development, UFRD
must be used in combination with other forms of economic and social analysis in order to be useful for
policy-making and problem-solving.

4. The UFRD approach should use research methods
and techniques that are easily applied by regional
planners and easily understood by policy-makers.

UFRD's analytical techniques are intended to be
used in applied policy analysis and to be appropriate
for the relatively low levels of planning capacity
found in most developing countries. Those tested in
the USAID pilot projects in the Philippines, Bolivia
and Upper Volta were designed to avoid many of the
limitations of the sectoral systems analysis and
regional planning models used by USAID during the 1960s
and 1970s. Those models were found to be of limited
value for project and program planning. Sectoral
systems analysis and comprehensive planning models came
under increasing criticism during the 1970s because
they were usually inappropriate for the conditions in
and needs of developing countries. Evaluations indicate that there were severe difficulties in obtaining
adequate and reliable data by which to make the models
operational. Most of the sectoral systems studies had
to be designed and applied by contractors or Western
experts because of the shortages of professionals in
developing countries trained in systems analysis and
regional economics. Moreover, the models could not be
easily calibrated, not only because of the lack of
adequate data but because the models were often too
complex or comprehensive in scope. Analysts had to use
inaccurate, unrealistic or greatly simplified assumptions about sectoral activities or regional economies
that made the results of limited value to government
officials. Few policy-makers below the central government level, or within international assistance agencies, fully understood the models, the results of their
application, or their policy implications. As one
USAID evaluation concluded, "computerized sector models
are rarely understood by more than a half score of
people in many LDCs and these are unlikely to be
decision-makers. And what people do not understand

they may well be skeptical of and the approach itself may be self-defeating."[33] Thus, few governments used the results of sectoral or regional systems analysis in decision-making and project design.

The UFRD approach was designed to reflect the fact that decisions are made continuously; they rarely await comprehensive and systematic analysis. Information must be gathered and analyzed quickly if it is to influence regional investment decisions. UFRD is based on the assumption that studies done to influence decision-making cannot rely on time-consuming, sophisticated and costly techniques. Nor can they use methods that impose overly complex, costly or time-consuming requirements on planners and policy-makers. They must, instead, adopt methods and techniques that are relatively easy to apply and that do not require sophisticated equipment or high levels of technical skill and training. If the results are to be useful in regional planning and decision-making the analytical methods must be applied quickly, make use of calculations that can be done manually or with easily acquired and operated equipment such as desk calculators or simple micro-computers. They should be relatively easy to learn by planners and their results should be comprehensible to technical planners who lack special training in spatial or regional analysis and especially to government officials and local leaders who may not have high levels of formal educational attainment. In most developing countries, the methods most likely to meet these requirements involve descriptive statistics that can be presented easily in maps, charts, graphs and tables.

5. The UFRD approach should use as much existing data for analysis as possible and limit new data collection to areas where significant information gaps appear.

Regional and sectoral planning are often criticized for being merely extensive data gathering exercises. They often take years to complete and are not well structured at the outset, so that only the most important information for decision-making will be collected. As a result, data gathering and statistical analyses often become ends in themselves. Many of the data collected are never analyzed and much of what is analyzed is never used. Moreover, a careful search of government offices and organizations in a region often uncovers similar data already collected for other purposes or information that could have been used for regional planning that was collected for special studies, feasibility analyses or previous investment decisions.

The UFRD approach attempts at the outset to inventory existing data and to make as much use of them as possible in spatial analysis and regional planning. New studies are designed and carried out only when crucial "information gaps" appear. As will be seen in Chapter Three, the emphasis at the beginning of the planning process is on inventorying and ordering existing data, on identifying information needs and on tailoring new data collection activities that are focused on specific spatial and locational issues. In the UFRD approach data collection is seen as an instrument for better decision-making and not as an end in itself.

6. The UFRD approach should use a combination of analytical methods and rely heavily on "ordinary knowledge" about the area under study.

In situations where analysis must be done under severe time constraints and with limited resources, it is not possible to engage in comprehensive, systematic and long term research. Policy proposals must be produced quickly if they are to influence investment decisions. Usually, formal statistical analyses must be replaced or supplemented with "softer" methods of qualitative analysis, participant observation, interviewing of key informants, short case studies, and descriptive analyses. Planners must be encouraged to be creative in developing methods of information gathering that are suited to the conditions and needs of the area in which they are working. They must employ a wide variety of techniques for collecting data, and cultivate and use their own knowledge of the region in arriving at judgments and conclusions. They must elicit information from a variety of sources. Under such conditions planners must depend heavily on what Lindblom and Cohen call "ordinary knowledge", that is "common sense, casual empiricism or thoughtful speculation or analysis."[34] They point out that although such knowledge is not derived from systematic, scientific research it is information that is commonly held by people who have lived in an area and which is used "as a basis for some commitment to action."[35] More formal scientific inquiry usually only modifies and never fully replaces ordinary knowledge in decision-making; therefore, effective methods of spatial analysis and regional planning must draw on both.

The UFRD approach makes heavy use of techniques and methods of analysis--especially in describing the settlement system and distribution of functions among settlements--that can substitute easily gathered qualitative and ordinal information for quantitative data needed in more sophisticated techniques. Such methods

as scalogram analysis, which is described in Chapter
Four, require only information about the presence or
absence of functions in settlements. Unlike factor
analysis, which is used in many studies of settlements
systems in scholarly or academic research, scalogram
analysis does not require quantitative data. Yet,
Voelkner and others have found that simple scalogram
studies can often produce results that are highly cor-
related with those of more complex factor analyses.
Voelkner notes that "factor scores per community have a
very high correlation with scale scores and that if
mapped produced nearly exactly the same development
contours." Where quantitative data do not exist or
cannot easily be collected, or where studies must be
done quickly and cannot await the collection of quanti-
tive data, less complex methods such as scalogram analysis can produce comparable results.[36] Collecting
information on the presence or absence of functions or
activities does not require highly sophisticated surveys; information can be gathered from key informants
or from local residents. Voelkner points out that
drawing an ordinary knowledge is essential in many
rural regions and commonly yields more reliable information than formal surveys:

> Professionals working in the field with rural
> development have often experienced that tra-
> ditional populations do have an acute aware-
> ness of many relevant data on their social
> and physical environment. This awareness is
> in terms of the presence or absence of
> clearly recognizable phenomena especially
> material manifestations of structure or
> behavior. Rural people recognize when wells
> or rivers dry up more often than before, when
> rivers become too dirty for drinking, washing
> or bathing, when fields become infertile or
> erode. They also know where they are able to
> obtain agricultural production inputs and
> whether they can afford them or not. Simi-
> larly, they know where to obtain essential
> items for living, whether for housing, or
> clothing or sickness. They know whether in
> their own community or how far away are such
> services as a dispensary, a school, or a
> variety store. Quite often, they also know
> who in the community has a radio, or whether
> anybody uses synthetic fertilizers. In the
> close proximity in which people live in tra-
> ditional society, there is little that
> remains secret to community knowledge, even
> whether and which contraceptives are used for
> family planning.[37]

Although the UFRD approach makes use of formal
statistical techniques and surveys whenever possible,
it does not rely on them exclusively. A wide variety
of methods, both "hard" and "soft", must be used to
gather the kinds of information that will be useful for
regional planning and development decision-making.
UFRD is less concerned with achieving scholarly standards of research than with gathering, classifying and
assessing information about spatial and locational
dimensions of regional development in as effective a
manner as possible and presenting it in forms that are
understandable to the people who participate in
regional planning and decision-making.

In Chapters Three, Four and Five, the methods and
techniques that were tested in the Philippines, Bolivia
and a few other countries are described and their uses
are examined. In each chapter the methods and techniques used in the UFRD approach are identified and
described and illustrations of their application and
results are drawn from two pilot projects--the Bicol
River Basin in the Philippines and the Department of
Potosi in Bolivia.

NOTES

1. World Bank, World Development Report, 1980,
Washington: World Bank, 1980.
2. International Labour Office, Poverty and Land-
lessness in Rural Asia, Geneva: ILO, 1977.
3. World Bank, Rural Development Sector Policy
Paper, Washington: World Bank, 1975.
4. The argument is made in more detail in Kenneth
Ruddle and Dennis A. Rondinelli, Transforming Natural
Resources for Human Development: A Resource Systems
Approach to Development Policy, Tokyo: United Nations
University Press, 1983.
5. World Bank, World Development Report, 1978,
(Washington: World Bank, 1978), p. 38.
6. International Labor Office, op cit., p. 14.
7. See Dennis A. Rondinelli and Kenneth Ruddle,
"Local Organization for Integrated Rural Development:
Implementing Equity Policy in Developing Countries,"
International Review of Administrative Sciences, Vol.
XLIII, No. 1 (January 1977), pp. 20-30.
8. See Dennis A. Rondinelli and Kenneth Ruddle,
"Coping with Poverty in International Development
Policy," World Development, Vol. 6, No. 4 (1978), pp.
479-498.
9. Dennis A. Rondinelli and Kenneth Ruddle,
"Appropriate Institutions for Rural Development:
Organizing Services and Technology in Developing Coun-
tries," Philippine Journal of Public Administration,
Vo. XXI, No. 1 (1977), pp. 35-52.
10. Dennis A. Rondinelli and Kenneth Ruddle,
"Political Commitment and Administrative Support: Pre-
conditions for Growth with Equity Policy," Journal of
Administration Overseas, Vol. XVII, No. 1 (1978), pp.
43-60.
11. E.A.J. Johnson, The Organization of Space in
Developing Countries, Cambridge, Mass.: Harvard
University Press, 1970.
12. Dennis A. Rondinelli, "Regional Disparities
and Investment Allocation Policies in the Philippines:
Spatial Dimensions of Poverty in a Developing Country,"
Canadian Journal of Development Studies, Vol. 1, No. 2
(Fall 1980), pp. 262-287.
13. U.S. Agency for International Development,
Office of Urban Development, "Urban Functions in Rural
Development Project Paper," mimeographed, (Washington:
USAID, 1976), p. 4.
14. Ibid., p. 4.
15. Ibid., pp. 6-7.
16. See Dennis A. Rondinelli and Kenneth Ruddle,
Urbanization and Rural Development: A Spatial Policy
for Equitable Growth, New York: Praeger, 1978.
17. Ibid., Chapter 1.

48

18.   World Bank, <u>Rural Development Sector Policy</u>
<u>Paper</u>, <u>op</u>. <u>cit</u>. p. 5.
19.   Rondinelli and Ruddle, <u>Urbanization and Rural</u>
<u>Development: A Spatial Policy for Equitable Growth</u>,
op. cit., Chapter 7.
20.   Prodipto Roy and B.R. Patil, <u>Manual for Block</u>
<u>Level Planning</u>, New Delhi: The Macmillan Company of
India, 1977), p. 25.
21.   See Dennis A. Rondinelli and Hugh Evans,
"Integrated Regional Development Planning: Linking
Urban Centers and Rural Areas in Bolivia," <u>World Devel-</u>
<u>opment</u>, Vol. 11, No. 1 (January 1983), pp. 31-54.
22.   Brian J.L. Berry and William Garrison,
"Recent Developments in Central Place Theory," <u>Papers</u>
<u>and Proceedings of the Regional Science Association</u>,
Vol. IV (1958), pp. 107-120.
23.   Brian J.L. Berry and Frank E. Horton, <u>Geo-</u>
<u>graphic Perspectives on Urban Systems</u>, (Englewood
Cliffs, N. J.: Prentice-Hall, 1970), p. 172.
24.   <u>Ibid</u>
25.   <u>Ibid</u>., pp. 172-173.
26.   Berry and Garrison, <u>op</u>. <u>cit</u>.
27.   United Nations Economic Commission for Asia
and the Pacific, <u>Guidelines for Rural Centre Planning</u>,
(New York: United Nations, 1979), pp. 64-65.
28.   See Dennis A. Rondinelli, "Spatial Analysis
for Regional Development: A Case Study in the Bicol
River Basin of the Philippines," <u>Resource Systems</u>
<u>Theory and Methodology Series</u>, No. 2, Tokyo: United
Nations University Press, 1980.
29.   Simon Fass, <u>Urban Functions in Rural Develop-</u>
<u>ment in Upper Volta</u>, (Washington: U.S. Agency for
International Development, 1981), p. 3.
30.   Idem.
31.   See Evans, <u>op</u>. <u>cit</u>.
32.   Dennis A. Rondinelli, "Adjunctive Planning
and Urban Development Policy," <u>Urban Affairs Quarterly</u>,
Vol. 7, No. 1 (1971), pp. 13-39; and Dennis A. Rondinelli, <u>Urban and Regional Development Planning: Policy</u>
<u>and Administration</u> , Ithaca: Cornell University Press,
1975.
33.   E.B. Rice and E. Glasser, "Agriculture Sector
Studies: An Evaluation of AID's Recent Experience,"
<u>AID Evaluation Paper No. 5</u>, (Washington: U.S. Agency
for International Development, 1972), pp. 44-45.
34. Charles E. Lindblom and David K. Cohen, <u>Usable</u>
<u>Knowledge: Social Science and Social Problem Solving</u>
(New Haven: Yale University Press, 1979), p. 12.
35.   <u>Ibid</u>., pp. 12-13.
36.   H.E. Voelkner, <u>Shortcut Methods to Assess</u>
<u>Poverty and Basic Needs for Rural Regional Planning</u>,
Part II, Geneva: United Nations Research Institute for
Social Development, 1978).
37.   <u>Ibid</u>., p. 43.

3
Regional Resource Analysis

If one does not already exist, it is useful to
begin the study of a region by creating a profile of
socioeconomic and physical conditions. In the UFRD
approach, a "macro-analysis" of a region is based primarily on data that have already been collected. The
information is organized into categories that enable
planners and policy-makers to analyze the region's
level of development compared to other regions in the
country and the levels of development of various areas
within the region. This "regional profile" serves
three important purposes. First, it encourages planners to make a thorough inventory of existing data in
censuses, special studies, project analyses, feasibility studies and other reports about the region. The
information is used not only to create a profile of
conditions within the region but also to formulate programs and projects in later stages of spatial analysis
and regional planning. The exercise gives planners an
overview of the region and an appreciation of the kinds
of information that have already been gathered. Time
and money can be saved by not duplicating studies that
have been done or that yield information that can be
used for other purposes. Second, the data gathered
through this exercise can be compiled into a regional
statistical compendium that can provide planners, government officials, private investors and community
groups with information about the region that previously had been scattered in inaccessible or little-
known reports. Third, the profile provides a baseline
analysis of conditions within the region that can be
used later in assessing changes that result from
regional development programs and projects.
More specifically, the objectives of creating a
social, economic, demographic and physical profile of a
region are to:
    1. Describe the overall strengths and weak-
        nesses of the regional economy by assess-

ing the types, characteristics and distribution of human and physical
resources;

2. Compare the level of development of
human, economic and physical resources of
the region with those of other regions in
the country;

3. Determine the relative position of the
regional economy within the national
economy;

4. Identify subareas of the region with
particular strengths and weaknesses for
development, with lagging or underdeveloped economies, and with higher than
average levels of poverty;

5. Compare the distribution of human, economic and physical resources and their
levels of development among administrative jurisdictions or market areas within
the region; and

6. Identify historical trends and changes in
the development of the region that help
explain its position in the national
economy and the conditions of communities
within it.

Such an analysis can also help to classify regions
within the country, or areas within a region, by various socioeconomic and physical characteristics. This
can help planners and policy-makers to understand the
region's unique circumstances and its relative position
within the national space-economy.

ORGANIZING A REGIONAL PROFILE ANALYSIS

Data on the human, social and physical resources
of a region can be organized in a variety of ways. No
single approach is universally correct or always useful: much depends on the amount and quality of information available, the types of problems or issues that
are important to local and regional planners, and prevailing concepts of the region's potential for development. Since the purpose of creating a regional profile
is to collect and order information in ways that will
assist planners and policy-makers to understand better
the conditions of areas within the region and the dynamics of growth or underdevelopment, the choice of
methods for organizing it should be based on local
judgments about which approach is likely to achieve
those objectives most effectively.

Ultimately, however, prevailing concepts of the
region's potential for development inevitably influence
the ways in which planners and policy-makers think
about policy problems and determine how information is

organized and interpreted. Alternative perceptions of
regional development allow planners to determine what
information to collect, how to organize it and how to
interpret it. Some of the major concepts and their
implications for collecting and categorizing information include the following.

Regions as Agricultural Production Systems

One view of regions, especially in countries that
are predominantly rural, is that they are primarily
agricultural areas. Regional development policies and
programs focus on improving agricultural output and
farm efficiency. Information about the region would be
related to the factors that must be managed in order to
increase agricultural productivity. In its manual on
rural service center planning, the Economic and Social
Commission for Asia and the Pacific (ESCAP) considers
the farm and farm-household as the basic units of activity accounting for regional agricultural productivity.[1] Information therefore should be collected about
agricultural land, labor, capital and management conditions in the region and about the composition, subsistence needs, preferences and requirements of farm households (see Figure 3-1). Farms and farm-households in
turn are influenced by the condition of the physical
environment (climate, vegetation, soil, pests and dis-
ease), the region's demographic characteristics (population size, density, and composition), sociocultural
factors, the level of economic and social services,
prices and conditions of trade in the world market, as
well as national price and support policies. Policy
formulation and implementation would focus on coordinating those inputs needed to increase regional and agricultural production and income.

Regions as Core-Periphery Areas

Others view a region as a set of social and economic relationships between core urban centers and peripheral rural areas. Friedmann classifies regions and
areas within regions by various socioeconomic indicators that determine the relationships among them in a
larger space-economy.[2] He classifies core areas as
those with high potential for growth and for dispersing
innovation stimuli for development. They consist of
one or more clustered cities and their immediately surrounding rural hinterlands. Upward-transitional areas
have characteristics that relate favorably to core
areas and have the capacity for more extensive use of
their resources. Generally they respond to increasing
demand at the core and are areas of net immigration.
Resource frontiers are areas in which there is new

FIGURE 3-1

REGION AS AN AGRICULTURAL PRODUCTION SYSTEM

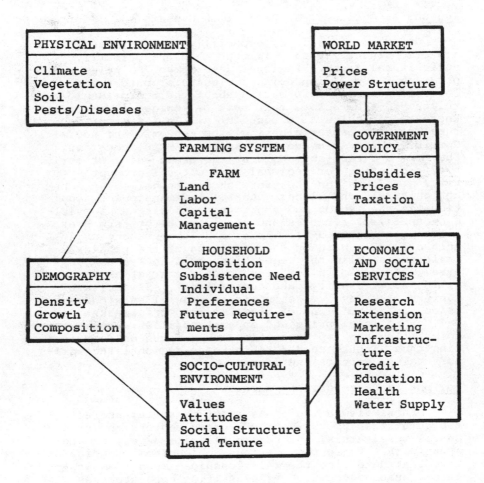

Source: After UNESCAP, <u>Guidelines for Rural Center Planning</u>, New York, United Nations, 1979

settlement by populations taking advantage of favorable agricultural or natural resources. Downward-
transitional areas are older, long settled areas of net
emigration in which rural economies are either stagnant
or declining. Special-problem areas are those, such as
river basins, with particular locational or resource
constraints that require specialized development strategies.

Friedmann suggests that information be collected
on the social and economic characteristics of a region
in order to characterize areas with it. Information on
spatial organization; locational characteristics of
major economic activities; land use types; social,
economic and infrastructural characteristics of urban
centers; demographic trends and behavior; human
resource characteristics; natural resource complexes
and characteristics; economic activities and trade
patterns; and indicators of regional economic performance would be included in the profile.[3]

In a manual on rural center planning, ESCAP officials note that regional planning rarely takes place in
entirely undeveloped areas.[4] Careful attention must be
paid therefore to existing patterns of settlement,
economic interaction and physical endowments. Information about a region that indicates how it has developed
in the past is important for distinguishing among areas
within Friedmann's core-periphery framework. Thus, a
regional profile should, at least, describe:

1. Already existing settlement patterns--
including the location, level, and functions of existing centers and their relationships to each other;

2. Location and characteristics of existing land-
scapes and land use and physical constraints, such as
mountains, rivers, marshes and deserts;

3. Administrative boundaries and political constraints;

4. Existing and proposed communications patterns
and their linkages;

5. Variations in regional development levels,
potentials and constraints;

6. Differences in main economic activities; for
example, the existence of mining, industrial, forestry,
cattle breeding, plantation, irrigated agriculture and
rainfed farming areas; and

7. Variations in social, cultural, ethnic and
religious characteristics in the way people live, their
needs and economic prospects.

Regions as Economic and Trade Areas

Others view regions as systems of economic production and interaction. Regional development is seen as

a process through which regional factors of production
are mobilized and invested in ways that increase the
region's productive and social capacity to attain
higher levels of production and income in the future.
Rondinelli and Jones contend that regional development
occurs primarily through the internal mobilization and
investment of regional resources in activities that
increase gross regional product (GRP) and social
decision-making and problem-solving capacity.[5]
Increases in productive and social capacity yield
higher levels of regional income, which allow higher
levels of savings, consumption and import of goods
needed for production. New capital resources can be
used to create a greater capacity for the region's
social system to sustain itself in the future by raising the level of entrepreneurial skills, providing new
social goods and services, satisfying the political and
social interests of a wide variety of groups, acquiring
new social resources and adapting existing legal and
social codes to changing economic and social conditions. Capital resources can also be used to adapt or
invent new technology, extend communications systems
and promote social progress (see Figure 3-2).

Higher levels of regional expenditure and greater
capacity to mobilize social resources increase expecta-
tions about the potential for development by creating a
favorable investment climate and greater social commitment to the region's economic growth and progress.

The perception that a region is likely to develop
in the future reduces the leakage of resources through
investment in other regions or countries, increases the
willingness of entrepreneurs to re-invest their
resources locally and expands the flow of external capital into the region. Moreover, a favorable regional
development climate reduces population out-migration,
increases people's incentives to seek higher education
and better training and stimulates entrepreneurial
effort. The resulting increases in capital and human
resources can be used to enhance the region's physical
resources, increase entrepreneurial skills, raise the
quality of the labor force and expand investment, leading to higher levels of development in the future.

One approach that has been used to organize information within this framework for regional development
is what Bendavid-Val calls the HINCO format.[6] Data are
organized into human, institutional, natural, capital
and other aspects:

1. Human aspects include data on population
    size and demographic characteristics,
    labor force characteristics, skills,
    income and wages, health, productivity,
    and educational characteristics of the

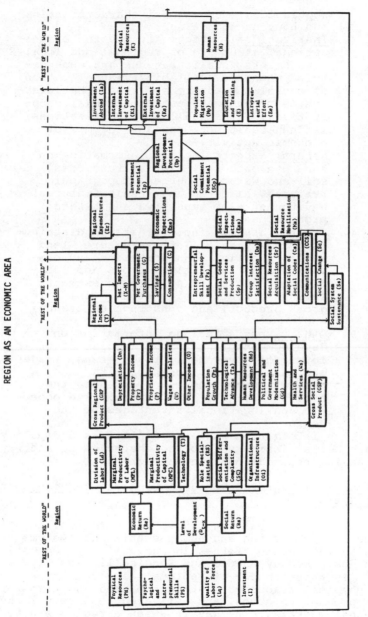

FIGURE 3-2

REGION AS AN ECONOMIC AREA

Source: D. Rondinelli and B. Jones, "Decision-Making, Managerial Capacity and Development: An Entrepreneurial Approach to Planning," African Administrative Studies, No. 13 (1975).

population, occupational characteristics
and housing conditions;
2. Institutional aspects include the organizational structure of regional and local
governments, public revenue and expenditure patterns, availability and location
of social and public services, characteristics of business establishments, cooperatives, trade and labor organizations,
landownership patterns and the mix of
economic activities;
3. Natural aspects include information on
land use patterns, mineral resources,
soil and water resources, topographic
features, historic and scenic features,
environmentally sensitive and hazard
prone zones;
4. Capital aspects include data on distribution and types of infrastructure, land
use potentials, transportation and communications facilities, types and location of public and private investment,
savings rates, housing stock, firm size,
gross product, and construction trends;
and
5. Other aspects include information on
development plans and strategies of other
levels of government, trade areas, trade
and exchange relationships with other
areas, energy resources, and data that
provide insights into the relative economic and locational advantages of the
region.
Such information would give planners and policy-
makers better insights into the obstacles to and ways of
increasing regional development potential.

Regions as Integrated Resource-Production-Human Settle-
ment Systems

A more encompassing concept of a region, in which
resource, production and human settlement systems are
seen as interacting forces in regional development, has
been described by Ruddle and Rondinelli (see Figure 3-
3).[7] In this concept of regional development natural
and physical resources must be procured and transformed
into productive goods, and delivered to internal and
external markets. The way in which a region's natural
resources are transformed depends not only on the application of technology and capital but also on behavioral,
perceptual and cultural factors, social characteristics
of the human population, regional economic factors, and
the pattern of settlement and interaction. National and

FIGURE 3-3

REGION AS INTEGRATED RESOURCE-HUMAN SETTLEMENT SYSTEM

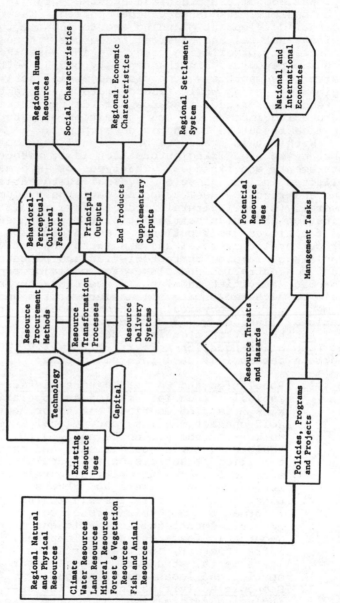

After Ruddle and Rondinelli, 1983

international economic conditions also affect how the
regional economy is organized and the potential uses to
which regional resources can be applied. The tasks of
regional development planning are to enhance the
region's natural and physical resources, increase the
productivity of existing uses, and increase the quality
of human resources and the capacity of the settlement
system to support new economic and social activities.
Regional planning would also promote new potential uses
of resources, reduce resource hazards and threats, and
in so doing improve the transformation of natural and
man-made resources for human development.

Within this framework of regional development, one
approach to organizing information is by resources,
settlements and linkages. The types of information
collected include those on physical characteristics,
land and resource use, cropping patterns, volume and
diversity of agricultural productivity, population distribution and human settlement patterns, and services
and facilities distribution. Also information on non-
agricultural commercial and manufacturing activities,
subsistence farming characteristics and patterns, location, concentration and dispersion of major social and
economic activities and labor force characteristics
would be gathered. Data on the interaction among settlements through physical, economic, social, and organizational linkages would be analyzed as well.

Another way of organizing data about the region is
the Population-Location-Activities format.[8] This
approach categorizes data into six groups:

1. Population and Social Characteristics--
   including such information as population
   size, age distribution, family or household characteristics, educational levels,
   work experiences, income and wealth,
   health and living conditions, and characteristics of subsets of the population
   such as farmers, minorities, rural population, urban dwellers and others.
2. Location Characteristics--including
   information on physical resources,
   natural, locational, climatic and other
   geographic features, social capital,
   infrastructure, and transportation
   investments, structure of government and
   spatial and locational linkages;
3. Economic Activities Characteristics--
   including information about firm size,
   concentration and distribution of economic activity, value added, gross regional
   product, productivity, farm characteristics, investment and capital accumulation, and industry mix characteristics;

4. <u>Population-Location Relationship Charac-
   teristics</u>--including data on population
   size, density, and distribution, travel
   patterns, migration and land-ownership
   patterns;
5. <u>Population-Activity Relationship Charac-
   teristics</u>--including information on
   employment by industry, income and wages
   by employment source, unemployment by
   industry, labor productivity and labor-
   capital ratios; and
6. <u>Location-Activity Relationship Character-
   istics</u>--including information on the
   location of commerce and industry, intra-
   and inter-regional trade flows and linkages, trade areas, labor-market characteristics, and economic relationships
   with other regions.

Other concepts of regional development may prevail
in a region and can also be used to classify data for a
regional profile. The point is that planners should
invest an adequate amount of time in thinking about how
to select and organize the data they need for spatial
analysis and regional planning <u>before</u> beginning data
collection. Collecting data is not an end in itself.
The information that is gathered about a region should
provide a statistical profile that is meaningful to
public officials, private investors, local interest
groups and others who participate in development activities. The profile should provide a broader framework
for interpreting the results of the analysis of settlements and spatial linkages from a regional perspective.

Four major methods or techniques are used in the
UFRD approach to analyze and present data collected in
the first phase of planning. They include: (1)
descriptive statistics for comparing the region with
other regions and for assessing economic conditions of
communities or areas within the region; (2) ranking and
scaling techniques to highlight differences among areas
within the region; (3) measures of distribution, specialization, concentration and association to show comparative strengths and weaknesses within the regional
economy; and (4) indexes of levels of development of
administrative units or economic areas within the
region. The methods are applied at two levels. Intra-
regional analysis attempts to compare the economy of
the region with that of others in the country. Intra-
regional analysis attempts to compare communities,
administrative sub-divisions, or economic sub-units
within the region.

INTER-REGIONAL PROFILES

Information about the region described earlier can
be used to obtain insights into its comparative
strengths and weaknesses within the national economy.
Descriptive statistical measures and mix-and-share
analysis are two easily applied techniques for interpreting the information.

Descriptive Statistical Measures

Most of the information that is already available
from censuses, surveys, special studies, feasibility
analysis and other sources can be reorganized and summarized using simple descriptive statistics--averages,
percentages, ranges, ratios, frequency distributions,
indexes, rates of change and time series. These measures can be calculated quickly and are easy for people
involved in regional development to understand and interpret. They can be presented effectively in tables,
charts, graphs, curves, pictographs and analytical
maps. They emphasize important relationships, trends
and classifications.[9]

These methods were used to summarize information
about the region in relationship to other regions in
both the Bicol River Basin in the Philippines and in
the Department of Potosi in Bolivia.

The profile of the Bicol region in the Philippines, for example, showed clearly its relative depri-
vation within the national economy and highlighted
reasons why Bicol continues to be at a disadvantage
within the national economy. One detailed profile (see
Table 3-1) compared number of families, average family
income, percentage of families with income below the
poverty level, percentage of families with incomes
below the minimum food needs level, enrollment rates in
elementary and secondary schools, population per hospital bed, physician and midwife, percentage of malnourished children, index of industrial production, and
index of agricultural productivity. All of the information for this inter-regional profile came from secondary sources--that is, from information collected and
published by government agencies.[10]

The profile indicated that the six-province
national planning region of which the Bicol River Basin
is a part was one of the poorest in the Philippines.
Average family income during the mid-1970s, when the
Bicol UFRD project began, was nearly 26 percent below
the national average and the second lowest in the country. More than 70 percent of the families in the Bicol
Region had incomes below the amount needed to obtain
adequate food; it had the third highest percentage of
families with incomes below the food threshold. More

TABLE 3-1

SOCIO-ECONOMIC CHARACTERISTICS OF BICOL AND OTHER REGIONS IN THE PHILIPPINES

Region	Number of Families (000s)	Average Family Income (Pesos)	Percent Difference in Average Family Income from National Average	Percent of Families Below Food Threshold	Percent of Families Below Poverty Level	Percent Malnourished Children
Ilocos	558	5,525	-5.3	72.6	85.2	31.0
Cagayan Valley	329	5,102	-12.6	75.8	84.8	29.3
Central Luzon	662	7,773	-1.1	36.5	68.5	32.2
Southern Tagalog	888	5,441	-6.8	30.6	54.5	29.2
Bicol	518	4,280	-26.7	70.9	87.3	30.6
Western Visayas	679	5,484	-6.1	65.3	84.5	39.0
Central Visayas	441	4,834	-17.2	70.7	85.4	27.0
Eastern Mindanao	595	5,172	-11.4	73.3	86.4	36.3
Western Mindanao	370	3,803	-34.9	NA	NA	28.9
Northern Mindanao	433	6,307	+7.9	65.1	86.1	28.2
Southern Mindanao	314	5,062	-3.0	58.3	79.8	24.9
Central Mindanao	301	5,025	-13.9	NA	NA	27.7
Metro Manila	770	10,469	+79.3	24.7	NA	30.4
Philippines	6,859	5,840	100.0	59.0	79.4	30.6

(continued)

TABLE 3-1 (continued)

Region	Enrollment Rates in Schools		Population Per			Percent Irrigable Land Irrigated	Index of Industrial Production	Agricultural Productivity
	Elementary	Secondary	Hospital Bed	Physician	Midwife			
Ilocos	114.7	84.2	769	2,000	2,707	56	53	60
Cagayan Valley	116.9	30.0	1,428	4,762	6,667	36	24	90
Central Luzon	113.0	37.4	1,428	4,167	5,882	79	89	118
Southern Tagalog	86.1	49.7	NA	NA	NA	30	102	100
Bicol	111.3	29.1	1,667	5,263	9,091	32	25	86
Western Visayas	139.2	64.3	2,000	3,703	5,263	46	91	137
Central Visayas	101.0	74.0	1,111	3,030	6,250	25	81	68
Eastern Mindanao	101.0	37.4	1,667	6,250	8,333	31	27	90
Western Mindanao	93.3	17.2	2,500	6,667	9,091	24	24	132
Northern Mindanao	98.1	35.9	1,428	4,762	5,556	11	41	110
Southern Mindanao	131.9	51.4	1,667	6,667	9,091	19	59	129
Central Mindanao	99.4	64.3	2,500	6,667	7,143	15	32	84
Metro Manila	85.5	47.3	334	1,724	5,556	NA	391	135
Philippines	105.1	48.0	833	3,125	5,882	38	100	100

Source: Republic of the Philippines, National Economic and Development Authority; World Bank and USAID.

than 87 percent of its families had incomes below the poverty level--the highest in the Philippines. Although enrollment rates in elementary schools were relatively high, those for secondary schools were the second lowest in the country. Population per hospital bed, physician and midwife were extremely high compared to the average in the Philippines, indicating relatively low levels of health care services in the Region. Nearly a third of the children in Bicol were found to be malnourished. Only a third of the irrigable land was irrigated. Bicol's agricultural productivity was only 86 percent of the national average. The Bicol's industrial production was about one-quarter that of the Philippines.

Socio-economic profiles were also constructed for the Bicol River Basin from statistics published for Camarines Sur and Albay, the two provinces that were included in the Basin's boundaries when the project began. Indicators for population density, average net population growth rates, percent population under 14 years old, average annual family income, percent of household population over 10 years old in gainful occupations, sectoral distribution of employed population, farm-land tenure status, percent of farm households with off-farm employment, birth and death rates, quality of housing and percent of municipal revenues derived from local sources formed this profile (see Table 3-2).

These data, along with others collected for the two provinces allowed planners to describe the Basin as an agricultural production area. They showed that this economically depressed region at the southern tip of the Luzon peninsula manifests almost classic characteristics of what in Friedmann's classification would be a perhiperhal, downward-transitional area.

The profile indicated clearly that the Basin's poverty was due in large part to its physical isolation and to a physical environment that was hostile to productive activity for much of the year. In relationship to other areas of the Philippines, Bicol lacks the physical infrastructure, social services and productive inputs to increase its agricultural and manufacturing output. The profile suggested that the predominantly subsistence agricultural economy of the basin created chronic underemployment and serious malnutrition among the population and encouraged relatively high rates of outmigration. About 28 percent of the labor force was either unemployed or seriously underemployed and non-agricultural job opportunities in the rural areas were limited. Income levels of the Basin's population were not only low, but income and wealth were inequitably distributed. Ten percent of the households in the Basin received 43 percent of total income. The poorer half of the population received only 13 percent of the income.

TABLE 3-2

COMPARATIVE SOCIO-ECONOMIC INDICATORS FOR BICOL RIVER BASIN,
THE BICOL REGION, AND THE PHILIPPINES

Indicator	Bicol River Basin	Bicol Region	Philippines
Population Density (No. of People Per Square Kilometer)	226	168	140
Annual Average Net Population Growth Rate	1.6	1.6	2.9
Percent Population Under 14 Years Old	48.1		45.7
Average Annual Rate of Natural Increase in Population	2.4	2.5	3.0
Average Annual Family Income (Pesos)	4,778	4,280	5,840
Percent of Household Population Over 10 Years Old in Gainful Occupations	41.0	40.4	42.6
Percent of Household Population Over 10 Years Old Gainfully Employed by Sector			
Agriculture, Fishing, Forestry and Related	59.2	66.2	54.3
Mining and Quarrying	0.1	0.3	0.5
Manufacturing	13.3	8.5	10.7
Gas, Electric, Sanitation, Water	0.2	0.2	0.3
Construction	2.9	2.4	3.4
Commerce	6.4	5.5	8.3
Transportation, Communication, and Storage	2.7	2.4	4.2
Services and Other Activities	15.2	14.6	18.4

TABLE 3-2 (continued)

Indicator	Bicol River Basin	Bicol Region	Philippines
Tenure Status of Farms			
Full Owner	51.9	59.0	58.0
Part Owner	10.5	9.0	11.4
Tenant	36.0	30.4	29.0
Manager	0.1	0.2	0.1
Other	1.4	1.4	1.6
Percent of Farm Households Reporting Off-Farm Employment	31.4	27.8	17.9
Birth Rate (Per 1,000)	34.8	28.0	26.0
Death Rate (Per 1,000)	8.4	8.0	7.0
Population Per Physician		5,263	3,125
Population Per Midwife		9,091	5,882
Type of Housing Construction			
Strong	18.0	15.5	38.4
Mixed	37.8	40.9	36.5
Light	44.6	43.6	25.1
Percent of Municipal Revenues from Local Sources	78.0	78.5	83.5

These people lived on about $45 per capita a year, only
enough to buy basic necessities.[11]
Other data collected by the UFRD project staff
indicated that standards of living in the Basin were far
below those of the Philippines. More than half of the
children suffered some form of malnutrition. A majority
of the population was inflicted with water-borne enteric
diseases and intestinal parasitism, resulting from con-
taminated water supplies and poor environmental sanitation. Nearly 73 of every one thousand infants born in
the Bicol River Basin died during their first year, primarily of pneumonia, gastro-enteritis and bronchitis.
There was only one physician for every 4,600 people and
most of the doctors were located in larger towns,
inaccessible to rural people. Surveys estimated that no
more than one-quarter of all women living in the Basin
had ever visited a health clinic, hospital or family
planning center; most rural families sought assistance
from healers or midwives during pregnancy.
Housing conditions outside of the larger towns
were also poor. In rural areas homes were built of
scrapwood and nipa, with grass roofs and bamboo or dirt
floors. Less than one-third of the Basin's households
had adequate water supplies or sanitary toilets.
Sounder structures, more typical of the towns, were
scattered in rural barangays, but the overwhelming
majority of houses throughout the Basin were constructed of weak building materials, highly susceptible to
fire, flooding or destruction during typhoons. Few
homes were served by piped water or electricity; in the
vast majority kerosene or wood was used for lighting
and cooking.
The population growth rate of 3.3 percent a year
resulted in a high dependency ratio--nearly half of the
population was under 14 years old--and more than one
percent of the population migrated out of the Basin
each year, resulting in an average annual net population growth rate of 1.6. Most migrants were younger,
more productive people seeking job opportunities in
larger towns outside the Basin, and usually in Metropolitan Manila. The Bicol Region, of which the basin
is a part, had the lowest net domestic product (NDP) in
the Philippines, which was declining in real terms at a
time when the national average was growing. The Bicol
Region had the lowest share of employment and production among all regions in the Philippines as well as
the lowest proportion of modern manufacturing establishments to population in the country. Nearly all
manufactured goods sold in Bicol were imported from
Manila.[12]
The profile also indicated that, ironically, most
Bicolanos lived in poverty in a land of abundant

natural resources. Properly irrigated and cultivated,
the Basin's rich alluvial soil could produce enough rice
to sustain an additional 8 million people. Production
of corn, abaca, sugar, coconuts and vegetables was only
a fraction of its potential under favorable conditions.
The Bicol had a wealth of untapped mineral resources--
about 30 percent of marble deposits, 75 percent of per-
lite and about 20 percent of the coal reserves of the
Philippines. The Tiwi Geothermal plant, located on the
Basin's northeastern border, generates substantial
amounts of energy.

But as a regional economy, the Bicol River basin
was poorly equipped for increased productivity and widespread development. Through much of the year the Basin
was battered by frequent typhoons, bringing high winds
and heavy rains. The perennial flooding destroyed crops
and homes, pushed saline water into interior rice fields
and caused widespread silting and erosion. The area was
physically isolated from the rest of the Philippines
during the worst of the typhoon season and poorly linked
to other regions or to Manila even during good weather.
A single paved highway that weaves tortuously through
the mountains of central Luzon connects Bicol to Manila.
During the typhoon season even this link became tenuous
as sections of the road were washed out and collapsed
down the side of steep mountain banks. Daily flights to
and from Manila, buses, and one railway provided limited
capacity for travel or interregional communications, and
small ports in coastal villages provided limited access
for inter-island trade. Regional transportation and
communications are not much better, limiting travel and
marketing, and leaving the Basin's settlement system a
scattering of relatively isolated and poorly integrated
clusters of villages.

Those people living in coastal areas depended on
traditional fishing methods that yielded small catches.
Much of the catch was consumed locally. The rest was
dried and sent to markets within the region or to Manila. In either case the prices fishermen received were
low and provided only subsistence incomes.

Nor were land tenure arrangements conducive to
increasing family incomes. Farm holdings were small and
fragmented. From a third to half of all rice and corn
farmers worked as tenants or landless laborers, and farm
productivity was nearly 10 percent lower than that of
the Philippines. Owners of large landed estates rein-
vested little of their profits in the Basin over the
years, and agricultural technology on both large and
small farms was primitive. Manpower and draft animals
provided the bulk of agricultural labor. Relatively few
milling or processing facilities had been established,
marketing networks in rural areas were poor and storage
capacity was limited. Because productivity and income

were so low, both tenants and small landowners were
continuously in debt. Whatever small surpluses they
accumulated were quickly spent on baptisms, weddings,
funerals, children's schooling and the annual fiesta,
and on repaying former loans. Only about half of the
basin's 100,000 hectares of potentially irrigable rice-
lands were irrigated; nearly 50,000 hectares of prime
agricultural land was flooded during the typhoon season
and that located adjacent to the Bicol river suffered
from saline intrusion.[13]

In the Department of Potosi in Bolivia, the inter-
regional profile compared principal socio-economic
characteristics of the department with those of the
other eight departments in the country. It compared
these administrative regions in terms of population
trends, migration flows, the composition of economic
activities as measured by labor and capital inputs, the
value of output, per capita income and location coef-
ficients. The profile illustrated a familiar paradox:
a region that had provided great wealth for the Spanish
empire for nearly two centuries and much of Bolivia's
foreign earnings more recently, had become the most
backward area of the country. The rich mineral deposits of silver, tin and other metals had created an
enclave economy in Potosi that provided wealth for
foreign investors but meagre benefits for the local
population.[14]

The profile of Potosi, moreover, showed that
although the mining sector still dominated the economy,
it had generated few forward linkages to related activities. The industrial sector was extremely weak.
Although mineral processing plants had been built in
the area, they used capital-intensive technology that
generated little local employment. The multiplier
effects of industrial activities within the local economy were highly constrained.

The profile indicated that Potosi was a region
with characteristics common to economically lagging or
downward transitional areas. Table 3-3 indicates that
more than 70 percent of the population lived in rural
areas, the population growth rate of the Department was
substantially lower than that of the other regions in
the country and that it had the highest average annual
rate of outmigration. The productivity of Potosi's
economic activities was the lowest in Bolivia. Heavy
outmigration and high mortality rates resulted in a net
population growth rate of less than one percent a year
during the quarter century between 1950 and the mid-
1970s. Per capita income in Potosi was 30 percent
lower than the average in Bolivia and less than 60 percent of the income of the adjoining Department of
Oruro.[15]

TABLE 3-3

SELECTED CHARACTERISTICS OF DEPARTMENTS IN BOLIVIA

Department	Population (000s)	Percent of Population in Rural Areas	Average Annual Population Growth	Percent Annual Average Migration	Regional Product Per Capita	Annual Growth Rate of Regional Product Per Capita	Per Capita Gross Regional Product (in Pesos)	Regional Product As Percent of National Product
Potosi	657.7	71.0	0.99	-0.64	458	2.3	2,884	10.3
Chuquisaca	358.5	87.4	1.23	-0.59	515	5.8	3,092	6.0
La Paz	1,465.0	52.4	2.07	-0.11	619	5.6	3,872	31.1
Cochabamba	721.0	62.3	1.79	-0.12	694	7.1	4,312	17.0
Santa Cruz	710.7	47.3	4.09	+1.49	767	8.0	4,683	18.6
Oruro	310.4	48.9	1.84	-0.51	802	6.0	5,049	8.6
Tarija	187.2	61.1	2.28	+0.74	681	11.7	4,099	4.2
Beni	168.4	51.8	3.28	-0.61	595	13.0	3,601	3.4
Pando	34.5	89.4	2.88	+0.96	698	12.8	4,421	0.8
Bolivia	4,613.5	58.3	2.05		637	6.3	3,951	100.0

Source: Hugh Evans, Urban Functions in Rural Development: The Case of the Potosi Region in Bolivia, Washington: USAID, 1982.

Although a large portion of the population of
Potosi derived its living from agriculture, the cultivation of crops was confined to a transitional area of
temperate valleys between the soaring mountains that
dominate the physical terrain of Potosi in the western
and eastern parts of the Department. The wheat, corn,
potatoes, other vegetables and some fruits grown in
Potosi were used primarily for subsistence. On the
altiplano and the mountains, sheep and llama raising
and cereal grain production were the main sources of
income. Farm output of Potosi generated less than 7
percent of agriculture's contribution to gross national
product in Bolivia and contributed only about 6 percent
to Potosi's gross regional product. Potosi's gross
regional product was nearly 30 percent below that of
the average for all departments in the country (see
Table 3-4).

In constructing the regional profile planners
found that Potosi, being relatively isolated from other
parts of Bolivia due to its mountainous terrain and
poor air, road and rail service, had little economic
interaction with other regions of the country. They
also confirmed that rural areas within the Department
were poorly linked to the few towns that had the infrastructure, services and facilities that might stimulate
rural development. Lack of access roads made travel to
the nearest towns for most rural people a long and
arduous journey.

As the Bicol and Potosi cases show, descriptive
statistics can provide planners with a general outline
of the major strengths and weaknesses of the regional
economy, but other methods and techniques must often be
used to analyze and interpret these data, especially in
assessing the region's position in the national economy.

Mix-and-Share Analysis

One technique of comparing changes in regional
economic activity--such as in employment or occupational composition--with changes taking place nationally, is mix-and-share analysis.[16] Underlying mix-
and-share analysis is an assumption that changes in
employment in a region are influenced by three sets of
factors:
1. Changes in total employment in the
   national economy,
2. The distribution of the labor force in
   particular industries or sectors in the
   region that may be growing slower or
   faster than those sectors or industries
   nationally, and

TABLE 3-4

PERCENT CONTRIBUTION BY SECTOR OF REGIONS TO GROSS DOMESTIC PRODUCT – BOLIVIA, 1977

Sector	La Paz	Cocha-bamba	Santa Cruz	Oruro	Potosi	Chuqui-saca	Tarija	Beni	Pando	Total	Sectoral Contribution to GDP
Agriculture	17.5	22.0	22.5	3.3	6.8	11.3	7.1	31.9	1.1	100.0	15.6
Minerals	32.0	3.0	--	25.0	40.0	--	--	--	--	100.0	8.4
Petroleum	--	--	81.3	--	--	12.2	6.5	--	--	100.0	1.6
Manufacturing	39.9	19.8	19.3	8.2	3.0	4.3	3.6	1.4	0.5	100.0	15.3
Construction	36.1	18.0	25.1	6.8	4.4	4.3	3.8	1.2	0.6	100.0	4.3
Energy	39.5	25.3	18.1	4.0	5.0	3.4	3.1	1.0	0.6	100.0	1.5
Transportation and Communications	25.0	20.0	20.0	9.0	9.8	6.0	4.5	4.2	1.5	100.0	8.8
Commerce and Finance	32.0	16.5	18.0	8.3	9.7	6.0	4.5	3.5	1.0	100.0	19.3
Government	44.0	15.0	15.0	6.0	9.0	5.0	3.0	2.0	1.0	100.0	9.0
Housing and Real Estate	35.0	17.0	16.3	7.5	9.0	6.5	4.5	3.2	1.0	100.0	7.7
Other Services	28.5	18.0	19.0	8.8	10.8	6.4	4.2	3.5	0.8	100.0	8.0
Percent Regional Contribution to GDP	31.1	17.0	18.6	8.6	10.3	6.0	4.2	3.4	0.8	100.8	

Source: Government of Bolivia, Ministry of Planning and Coordination; H. Evans, Urban Functions in Rural Development: The Case of Potosi Region in Bolivia, Washington: USAID, 1982.

3. Changes in the region's share of total
    national employment in each sector or
    industry.

Mix and share analysis helps explain changes in a
region's employment (R) or occupational structures over
time by disaggregating them into three sets of factors:
national growth effects (N), sectoral or industry mix
effects (M) and regional shares effects (S):

The measurement of these effects can be illustrated by examining changes in the employment structure
of the Bicol River Basin between 1970 and 1975, the
five-year period just before the UFRD project began.

The first step is to compare changes in employment
distribution by sector for the region and the nation,
as illustrated in Table 3-5 by:

1. Listing the numbers of people employed in
    each sector or industry for a "base year"
    and a later year;
2. Calculating the absolute change in
    employment over the period in each sector
    or industry; and
3. Calculating the percentage change in
    employment over the period in each sector
    or industry;

Table 3-5 indicates that while national employment
grew by nearly 5.5 percent over the period of analysis,
employment in the Bicol River Basin declined by about
4.7 percent. Only in the utilities sector did employment in the Bicol River Basin grow faster than in the
Philippine economy. While agricultural employment grew
by nearly 6.5 percent in the Philippines, the BRB's
employment declined by nearly 2 percent. Manufacturing
employment in Bicol declined at a rate almost three
times higher than the decline in manufacturing employment in the Philippines, and while national employment
increased in commercial activities by nearly 20 percent, Bicol's commercial employment dropped by almost
12 percent.

The next step in mix-and-share analysis attempts
to answer the question: "How much would have employment in the region grown if it had expanded in each
sector at the same rate as national employment?" The
national growth effect (N) can be computed as in Table
3-6 by:

1. Listing the number employed in each
    sector of the regional economy for the
    base year;
2. Multiplying the numbers of people
    employed in each sector or industry by
    the national employment growth rate (from
    upper half of column 4 of Table 3-5);
3. Listing the absolute growth of employment
    in each sector or industry in the region;
    and

TABLE 3-5

DISTRIBUTION OF EXPERIENCED WORKERS BY SECTOR
PHILIPPINES AND BICOL RIVER BASIN

Philippines	Employment (000s) 1970 (1)	1975 (2)	Employment Change 1970-1975 Absolute Numbers (2)-(1) (3)	Percent (3)/(1) (4)
Agriculture, Forestry	6,334.7	6,743.5	+408.8	+6.5
Mining and Quarrying	52.7	62.1	+9.4	+17.8
Manufacturing	1,398.5	1,328.8	-69.7	-4.9
Elec. Gas, Sanitation	33.8	37.3	+3.5	+10.4
Construction	461.3	422.2	-39.1	-8.5
Commerce Transport,	861.8	1,030.8	+169.0	+19.6
Communication	512.5	521.6	+9.1	+1.8
Services	1,926.0	2,098.8	+172.8	+8.9
Other	194.0	173.9	-20.1	-10.4
Total	11,775.3	12,419.0	+643.7	+5.5
Bicol River Basin				
Agriculture, Forestry	303.5	297.7	-5.8	-1.9
Mining and Quarrying	.6	.5	-0.1	-16.7
Manufacturing	68.3	58.2	-10.1	-14.8
Elec. Gas, San.	1.1	1.5	+0.4	+36.4
Construction	14.9	12.7	-2.2	-14.8
Commerce	32.6	28.8	-3.8	-11.7
Transp., Comm.	13.7	13.7	0	0
Services	68.4	66.9	-1.5	-2.2
Others	9.6	8.8	-0.8	-8.3
Total	512.7	488.8	-23.9	-4.7

TABLE 3-6

NATIONAL GROWTH EFFECT ON EMPLOYMENT IN BICOL RIVER BASIN 1970-1975

Sector	Employment 1000s in Bicol River Basin 1970 (1)	National Growth Effect N=(1) X National Growth Rate (.055) (2)	R = Actual Regional Employment Growth (3)	M+S = R-N Net Regional Change to be Accounted for (3)-(2) (4)
Agriculture, Forestry	303.5	16.69	-5.8	-22.49
Mining and Quarrying	0.6	0.03	-0.1	-0.13
Manufacturing	68.3	3.76	-10.1	-13.86
Elec. Gas, Sanitation	1.1	.06	+0.4	+0.34
Construction	14.9	.82	-2.2	-3.02
Commerce	32.6	1.79	-3.8	-5.59
Transporation, Communications	13.7	.75	0	-0.75
Services	68.4	3.76	-1.5	-5.26
Others	9.6	.53	-0.8	-1.33
Total	512.7	28.19	-23.9	-52.09

    4.   Subtracting the national growth effect
        (column 2) from rate of employment growth
        of the regional economy (column 3).

Table 3-6 indicates that had employment in each sector grown in the Bicol River Basin at the same rate as in the Philippine economy, the total employment of the Basin would have <u>increased</u> by 28,190 jobs, whereas in reality it <u>decreased</u> by 23,900. Employment in agriculture would have grown by 17,000 jobs, manufacturing by nearly 4,000 jobs, commerce by almost 1,800 jobs and services by nearly 3,800 jobs. Table 3-6 seems to indicate that it is the characteristics of the regional economy that probably explain the shortfall of 52,000 jobs in the Bicol River Basin compared to the potential number of jobs that could have been available had the Basin's sectors grown at the same rate as the nation's.

    Calculation of the <u>industry mix effect</u> (M) attempts to determine to what extent the deviation of the growth of employment in the Bicol River Basin from that of the Philippines was attributable to the fact that workers were distributed more heavily in industries that grew below the national average. The regional mix effect is calculated as in Table 3-7 by:

    1.   Listing the <u>percent of workers</u> in each
        sector or industry in the base year for
        the nation and the region;
    2.   Calculating the <u>deviation</u> by subtracting
        the national growth rate from the sector
        or industry growth rate (from upper half
        of column 4 of Table 3-5);
    3.   Listing the <u>number of workers</u> in each
        sector of the regional economy in the base
        year; and,
    4.   Calculating the regional mix effect by
        multiplying the deviation (column 3) by
        the number of experienced workers in each
        sector (column 4).

Table 3-7 indicates that a negative industry mix in Bicol offset the national growth effect by 113,760 jobs. The percentage of experienced workers in agriculture in Bicol was higher than in the national economy, but employment in Bicol grew far less than in the Philippines. Indeed, while employment in Philippine agriculture grew by 6.5 percent, it declined in Bicol by 1.9 percent. The high proportion of workers in agriculture in Bicol could not offset the relatively lower proportion of workers in other sectors nor the relatively slow rate of employment growth in Bicol compared to that of the national economy.

    Finally, the <u>regional shares effect</u> (S) can be computed to determine what part of the net relative change in employment in the Bicol River Basin--61,670 jobs--was

TABLE 3-7

INDUSTRY EFFECT ON EMPLOYMENT IN THE BICOL RIVER BASIN, 1970-1975

Sector	Percent Distribution of Employment, 1970 in Philippines (1)	Bicol River Basin (2)	Deviation: Industry Growth Rate Minus National Growth Rate (3)	Regional Employment, 1970 (4)	Industry Mix M=(3)X(4) (5)
Agriculture, Forestry	53.8	59.2	6.5 -5.5 = +1.0	303.5	+303.50
Mining and Quarrying	0.5	0.1	17.8 -5.5 = +12.3	0.6	+7.38
Manufacturing	11.9	13.3	-4.9 -5.5 = -10.4	68.3	-710.32
Electric, Gas, sanitation	0.3	0.2	10.4 -5.5 = +4.9	1.1	+5.39
Construction	3.9	2.9	-8.5 -5.5 = -14.0	14.9	-208.60
Commerce	7.3	6.4	19.5 -5.5 = +14.1	32.6	+459.66
Transport., Communic.	4.3	2.7	1.8 -5.5 = -3.7	13.6	-50.69
Services	16.4	13.3	8.9 -5.5 = +3.4	68.4	+232.56
Others	1.6	1.9	-10.4 -5.5 = -15.9	9.6	-152.64
	100.0	100.0		512.7	-113.76

not accounted for by regional mix effect. Regional
shares effect is a residual and can be calculated as in
Table 3-8, by:
1. Calculating the change in employment in
    the region for each sector between the
    base year and the later year (R); and,
2. Subtracting the national growth effect and
    the industry mix effect from the change in
    the number of workers in each sector.

Table 3-8 provides an indication of the effects of
national employment growth, industry mix and regional
shares on various industries in Bicol and on regional
employment. For example, had agricultural employment
in the Philippines grew at the national employment
growth rate and had employment in agriculture grown in
Bicol at the national rate, experienced agricultural
workers in Bicol would have increased by 16,690 from
303,500 in 1970 to 320,190 in 1975. But regional
employment in agriculture declined by 5,800 jobs to
297,700 in 1975. The net change of minus 22,490 jobs
over the period can be accounted for by the fact that
national agricultural employment grew faster than total
employment, and that Bicol's employment growth rate in
agriculture during the same period declined.

For the regional economy, Table 3-8 indicates that
the net impact of the negative industry mix in Bicol
(-113,760 jobs) was far greater than the positive
national growth effect (+28,190 jobs) and the regional
shares effect (+61,670) to leave a net decline of
23,900 jobs.

The mix-and-share analysis raises a number of
other questions, of course, that must be examined carefully before final conclusions are made. Mix-and-share
analysis, like all other methods used in the UFRD
approach, is less likely to yield definitive answers to
policy questions than to allow planners and policy-
makers to ask more refined and better directed questions.[17] Descriptive statistics and mix-and-share analysis can be combined with location quotients to indicate relative concentration or specialization in the
region. Inter-regional indexes and other methods can
be used to determine the relative position of the
region within the national economy.

INTRA-REGIONAL PROFILES

A second aspect of the regional profile is to compare administrative or economic areas within the region
by their share of resources, socio-economic characteristics and levels of development. Descriptive statistics, location quotients, measures of concentration,
deconcentration and association, indexes, scales and
weighted rankings are most useful for this task.

TABLE 3-8

EMPLOYMENT AND COMPONENTS OF EMPLOYMENT CHANGE IN BICOL RIVER BASIN, 1970-1975
(THOUSANDS OF PERSONS EMPLOYED)

Sector	Employment in Bicol River Basin 1970 (1)	1975 (2)	Regional Employment Change (R) 1970 and 1975 (3)	National Growth Effect N (4)	Industry Mix Effect M (5)	Regional Shares Effect S=R-N-M (6)
Agriculture, Forestry	303.5	297.7	-5.8	16.69	+303.50	-325.99
Mining and Quarrying	0.6	0.5	-0.1	0.03	+7.38	-7.51
Manufacturing	68.3	58.2	-10.1	3.76	-710.32	+696.46
Elec., Gas and San.	1.1	1.5	0.4	0.06	+5.39	-5.05
Construction	14.9	12.7	-2.2	0.82	-208.60	+205.58
Commerce	32.6	28.8	-3.8	1.79	+459.66	-465.25
Transport., Commun.	13.7	13.7	0	0.75	-50.69	+49.94
Services	68.4	66.9	-1.5	3.76	+232.56	-237.82
Others	9.6	8.8	-0.8	0.53	-152.64	+151.31
	512.7	488.8	-23.9	28.19	-113.76	61.67

Descriptive Statistics

Intra-regional analysis attempts to identify the
distinguishing characteristics of administrative or
economic sub-units within the region. The information
gathered at this stage of the analysis can also be used
later to supplement the settlement and linkage analyses, to assist planners with interpreting data on
accessibility and to help assess the productive potential of each area within the region. As in inter-
regional analysis, simple descriptive statistics--aver-
ages, percentages, ratios and frequency distributions-
-are often the most useful methods of determining differences in levels of development within the region and
of providing a clearer description of the region's
strengths and weaknesses.

Ideally, the analysis should take into account the
distribution of population and of major economic activities and physical resources, and especially data on
water resources, soil types, land use patterns, crop
cultivation and other information related to the
region's economic base. Social welfare data that indicate levels of development and differences in standards
of living should also be reflected in the profile.
Obviously, the types of data that are included in the
profile depend heavily on those that are available or
that can be easily and quickly collected. These can
later be supplemented with information collected
through field surveys or special studies.

The intra-regional profile for the Department of
Potosi, Bolivia, for example, was composed of the demographic and income data listed in Table 3-9 and social
service, education, and health indicators listed in
Table 3-10. The results offer a detailed profile of a
downward-transitional region with underdeveloped peripheral areas and a weak core. Evans points out in his
analysis of Potosi that socio-economic conditions
differ rather drastically even in a poor region.[18]
Housing indicators show that few homes in the Department were connected to modern infrastructure and that
in the most rural provinces--Saavedra, Chayanta,
Charcas, Ibanez, Sud Lipez, and Linares--less than 10
percent of the households had access to piped water,
sewers, and electricity. Even in the urban areas less
than 60 percent of the households had access to these
basic services. People in most provinces had low rates
of literacy and opportunities for education, but again
those living in provinces with towns and urban centers
were generally better off than people living in rural
provinces. More than half of the population was illit-
erate in six of the provinces, more than half of the
school age children had dropped out in nine of the provinces, and the vast majority of people had never
attended high school.

TABLE 3-9

SOCIO-ECONOMIC PROFILE OF PROVINCES IN THE DEPARTMENT OF POTOSI, BOLIVIA

Province	Population	Percent of Department	Pop. Per Sq. Km.	Income Per Capita	Percent Annual Net Migration	Percent Annual Population Growth	Percent of Workforce Fully or Partially Employed
Bilbao	9,683	1.5	15.1	678	-0.51	0.15	93.0
Ibanez	22,635	3.6	10.9	609	-0.30	0.27	96.0
Charcas	32,302	4.9	10.9	861	-0.54	0.52	94.0
Bustillos	91,418	13.9	40.9	688	-0.47	1.61	91.0
Chayanta	88,969	13.5	12.7	580	-0.51	1.10	96.0
Frias	122,810	18.8	35.9	410	-0.28	1.86	93.7
Saavedra	54,113	8.2	22.8	389	-0.17	0.64	96.0
Linares	53,481	8.1	10.4	156	-1.10	0.55	97.0
Quijarro	38,723	5.9	2.7	231	-0.85	0.26	92.0
Nor Chichas	47,965	7.3	5.3	207	-0.23	0.02	95.0
Sud Chichas	51,115	8.4	6.5	270	-0.76	1.38	94.0
Omiste	20,651	3.1	9.1	473	+1.22	0.70	94.0
D. Campos	5,567	0.8	0.5	384	-0.85	0.80	97.0
Nor Lipez	9,162	1.4	0.4	217	-0.89	0.95	90.0
Sud Lipez	4,149	0.6	0.2	191	-0.33	1.28	84.0
Department	657,743	100.0	5.6	--	-0.64	0.99	

Source: H. Evans, Urban Functions in Rural Development: The Case of the Potosi
Region in Bolivia, Washington: USAID, 1982.

TABLE 3-10

SOCIAL INDICATORS FOR PROVINCES IN THE DEPARTMENT OF POTOSI, BOLIVIA

Provinces	Housing				Education			Health			
	A1	A2	A3	A4	B1	B2	B3	C1	C2	C3	C4
Frias	59.2	29.5	48.9	67.4	65.9	55.7	20.5	13.15	0.8	2.4	8.0
Bustillos	53.1	8.2	42.6	63.0	60.6	54.5	15.0	6.71	0.7	4.0	11.0
Saavedra	9.6	1.0	5.4	36.1	34.0	35.1	1.9	6.31	0.1	0.5	10.9
Chayanta	7.2	0.4	3.5	12.0	25.0	28.0	1.5	0.85	0.1	0.8	4.5
Charcas	2.8	0.1	0.9	7.0	26.0	35.0	1.7	0.34	0.0	0.0	10.8
Nor Chichas	16.1	1.5	12.9	28.0	50.0	47.0	4.3	1.34	0.3	3.0	19.2
Ibanez	4.1	0.2	0.1	7.0	36.7	35.4	2.8	0.92	0.0	0.8	11.2
Sud Chichas	48.1	8.7	42.5	59.0	70.4	30.7	14.4	0.82	1.1	7.1	14.8
Nor Lipez	25.2	1.8	1.5	21.0	72.7	52.0	5.8	0.34	0.2	3.5	11.8
Sud Lipex	0.0	0.5	8.8	15.8	68.0	43.8	4.0	0.05	0.0	0.5	18.7
Linares	4.8	0.9	2.8	26.0	43.0	43.6	3.0	1.36	0.1	1.1	11.7
Quijarro	39.0	7.0	26.0	40.0	67.4	55.0	11.0	1.01	0.5	3.3	13.2
Bilbao	60.0	0.8	0.5	13.0	43.5	42.0	1.3	1.60	0.0	0.0	15.4
D. Campos	43.0	4.5	18.0	43.0	88.0	64.0	17.0	0.41	0.2	0.9	24.5
Omiste	42.0	22.0	34.0	52.0	69.0	54.0	14.0	3.10	0.1	1.5	9.7

A1 = % households with direct connection to water

A2 = % households with direct connection to sewer

A3 = % households with electricity

A4 = % homes with at least 2 of 3 elements (wall, floor, roof) build from permanent materials

B1 = % population that is literate

B2 = % school age children attending school

B3 = % population with some high school education

C1 = # of health facilities per 1000 square kms

C2 = # of doctors per thousand inhabitants

C3 = # of hospital beds per thousand inhabitants

C4 = infant mortality, measured as % live births ending in death within first year

D1 = % workforce employed full or part-time

Source: CORDEPO, Functiones Urbanas en el Desarrollo Rural: Resultados del Estudio en Potosi, Vol. 1, CORDEPO, Potosi, 1981; Hugh Evans, Urban Functions in Rural Development: The Case of the Potosi Region in Bolivia, Washington: USAID, 1982.

Unemployment was estimated to be less than 10% in most provinces but this disguised the fact that many people had only part-time work. Health indicators varied widely, showing one doctor for every 900 inhabitants in Sud Chichas, but no doctors at all in the provinces of Sud Lipez and Bilbao. Infant mortality rates in Bolivia were among the highest in Latin America, reaching their peak in the Department of Potosi: in all but three of the provinces more than one out of every ten children died before their first birthday, and in three provinces more than one out of six.[19]

The highest per capita income levels were found in those provinces with the highest proportion of people living in urban areas and with the highest degree of access to social services. The five most urbanized provinces, Frias (with the city of Potosi), Omiste (with the city of Villazon), Bustillos (with mining towns around Llallagua/Uncia), Sud Chichas (with the town of Tupiza) and Quijarro (with the town of Uyuni) had the highest income levels.

In the Bicol River Basin of the Philippines the intra-regional profile consisted of social, economic, physical and demographic data disaggregated by municipality, which is the major administrative level below the province. The profile consisted of data on population size, density, and composition; percent of children under 14 years old; levels of literacy and educational attainment; conditions of dwelling units; size of municipal revenues; land area; crop production; value of production; and size of the work force. The statistical compendium on muncipalities also included information about population changes in villages (barangays), number and percent of households with lighting and sanitary facilities, strength of building materials used in housing construction, distribution of market receipts, and distribution of agricultural production. Types, numbers and distribution of commercial, service and business establishments, and the numbers and distribution of hospitals, educational institutions and health facilities and services were also included in the profile.

In Bicol the data were derived from national census reports, key informants within muncipalities, special studies conducted by Ministries operating within the Basin, and from project feasibility analyses commissioned by the Bicol River Basin Development Program. In both Potosi and Bicol, these data were used not only to provide a statistical description of differences among administrative units within the region, but also later to formulate a development index.

Measures of Distribution and Association

Measures of concentration, deconcentration and association also provide useful insights about the degree to which activities and characteristics are distributed among communities in the region, and about the activities and characteristics that tend to be concentrated together in the same areas.

The measure of concentration indicates the degree to which activities or characteristics are dispersed widely among, or highly concentrated within, subareas of a region. The measure is expressed in the formula:

$$C = \frac{\sum |X - Y|}{2}$$

or, the sum of the absolute values of X, which is the percent of the region's physical area in each territorial unit, and Y, which is the percent of an activity or characteristic in each territorial unit. The measure has utility in a comparative sense, indicating the status of one region or subarea relative to another, or for areas at different points in time 0. Values of C vary from 0 to 100. The higher the value of C, the more unevenly distributed or highly concentrated the activity or characteristic is within the region.

The measurement of concentration is calculated by:
1. Listing the physical area (in square kilometers, hectares, miles, etc.) of each territorial unit with the region;
2. Calculating the percentage of physical area (X) of the region in each territorial unit;
3. Listing the number of activities or magnitude of characteristics to be measured in each of the territorial units of the region;
4. Calculating the percentage of each activity or characteristic (Y) in each territorial unit;
5. Subtracting the value of Y from the value of X and recording its absolute value;
6. Dividing the sum of the absolute values of X-Y by 2.

The calculation of the degree of concentration of manufacturing establishments in Albay Province in the Bicol River Basin, for example, is shown in Table 3-11. It shows that manufacturing activities are not highly concentrated in the Province; indeed, they are quite widely distributed among municipalities. This should not be surprising, given the characteristics of manufacturing in the Basin: it is primarily cottage and very small-scale industry which does not require highly urbanized locations or economies of scale.

Moreover, a <u>distribution quotient</u> can be calculated by dividing the percentage of manufacturing establishments by the percentage of land area for each municipality:

$$D.Q. = \frac{Y}{X}$$

Relatively higher degrees of concentration of manufacturing activity can be found in those municipalities with distribution quotients greater than unity, such as Daraga, Legaspi City, Malilipot, Polangui, Santo Domingo and Tabaco (last column of Table 3-11).

By comparing measures of concentration over time it is possible to determine whether manufacturing or other economic and social characteristics of an area have become more or less concentrated. The <u>measure of deconcentration</u> is calculated by subtracting the value of C for an earlier date (1) from the value of C for a later date (C_2):

$$D = C_2 - C_1$$

The values of D can range between -100.0 and +100.0. Positive numbers indicate deconcentration and negative numbers greater concentration.

Another useful measure is the degree of association between selected activities in a region. The <u>measure of association</u> is expressed by the following formula:

$$La = 100.0 - [\Sigma|X-Y|/2]$$

where X and Y are percentages of two types of activities or characteristics located in each territorial unit. Values of La range from 0.0 to 100.0. The higher the value of La, the stronger the locational association between the two activities within the region. For example, the degree of association between manufacturing and wholesale and retail trade establishments in Albay Province of the Bicol River Basin is shown in Table 3-12. It shows a relatively high degree of association between manufacturing and trade establishments in municipalities of the province. A time series of measures of association can also be constructed to show changes in the locational association of activities over a number of years.

Location Quotients

Location quotients are easily calculated indices of relative specializations of areas in particular activities or characteristics. They are especially useful for determining relative industrial or occupational specialization using employment as a surrogate for production. A location quotient is basically a

TABLE 3-11

CONCENTRATION OF MANUFACTURING ESTABLISHMENTS AMONG MUNICIPALITIES IN ALBAY PROVINCE, BICOL RIVER BASIN

Municipality	Total Area in Sq. Kilometers	Percent of Area (X)	Number of Mfg. Est.	Percent of Mfg. Est. (Y)	X-Y	Distribution Quotient
Bacacay	112.2	4.7	50	3.1	1.6	0.66
Camalig	130.9	5.5	73	4.6	0.9	0.84
Daraga	118.6	4.9	189	11.9	7.0	2.43
Guinobatan	203.0	8.5	64	4.0	4.5	0.47
Jovellar	105.4	4.4	27	1.7	2.7	0.39
Legaspi City	153.7	6.4	132	8.3	1.9	1.30
Libon	185.4	7.8	95	6.0	1.8	0.77
Ligao	246.4	10.3	159	10.0	0.3	0.97
Mililipot	53.6	2.2	112	7.1	4.9	3.22
Malinao	107.5	4.5	13	0.8	3.7	0.18
Manito	107.4	4.5	7	0.4	4.1	0.09
Oas	271.3	11.3	116	7.3	4.0	0.64
Pio Duran	133.7	5.6	27	1.7	3.9	0.34
Polangui	145.3	6.1	206	13.0	6.9	2.13
Sto. Domingo	76.6	3.2	104	6.6	3.4	2.06
Tabaco	116.4	4.9	150	9.5	4.6	1.94
Tiwi	123.4	5.2	64	4.0	1.2	0.77
Albay Province	2,390.8		1,588		57.4	

$$C = \frac{\sum |X-Y|}{2} = \frac{57.4}{2} = 28.7$$

TABLE 3-12

ASSOCIATION BETWEEN MANUFACTURING AND WHOLESALE AND RETAIL
TRADE ESTABLISHMENTS IN ALBAY PROVINCE, BICOL RIVER BASIN

Municipality	No. of Manufacturing Establishments	Percent (X)	No. of Wholesale and Retail Est.	Percent (Y)	|X-Y|
Bacacay	50	3.1	373	5.5	2.4
Camalig	73	4.6	289	4.2	0.4
Daraga	189	11.9	794	11.6	0.3
Guinobatan	64	4.0	514	7.5	3.5
Jovellar	27	1.7	143	2.1	0.4
Legaspi City	132	8.3	1,285	18.8	10.5
Libon	95	6.0	483	7.1	1.1
Ligao	159	10.0	410	6.0	4.0
Malilipot	112	7.1	103	1.5	5.6
Malinao	13	0.8	180	2.6	1.8
Oas	116	7.3	298	4.4	2.9
Pio Duran	27	1.7	250	3.7	2.0
Polangui	206	13.0	495	7.3	5.7
Santo Domingo	104	6.5	171	2.5	4.1
Tabaco	150	9.5	711	10.4	0.9
Tiwi	64	4.0	225	3.3	0.7
Albay Province	1,588		6,825		47.4

$$La = 100.0 - [\textstyle\sum |X-Y|/2] = 100.0 - 47.4/2 = 76.3$$

"ratio of ratios." It compares, for example, the ratio of employment in a given industry or occupation in a municipality to employment in all industries in that municipality, to the ratio of employment in that industry in a larger reference area, such as a region, to all industrial employment in that region. The formula is as follows:

$$LQ = \frac{M_i/M}{R_i/R}$$

where: M_i = employment in industry i in muncipality;
     M = total industrial employment in muncipality;
     R_i = employment in industry i in the region;
     R = total industrial employment in the region.

A location quotient with a value greater than 1.0 indicates that the municipality is more specialized in that activity than the region, and implies that the municipality may be engaged in an "export" activity, that is, that it is satisfying the needs of other areas, settlements or regions. A location quotient of less than 1.0 implies that the municipality is less specialized in that activity than the region, and may be "importing" goods and services to satisfy local needs, or that local people must go to other areas in order to obtain them.[20]

Planners in the Bicol River Basin used employment data to construct location quotients for municipalities in order to create a regional profile of municipal specializations. Table 3-13 shows location quotients calculated for selected municipalities in Camarines Sur Province. It indicates that the municipalities of Naga City, Camaligan, Gainza and Magarao, for example, are specialized in professional, technical, and managerial workers serving the province. It is assumed that those municipalities that have location quotients at or near unity are sufficiently specialized in those occupations to serve local needs.

In the Department of Potosi in Bolivia, location quotients of major economic activities differentiated the economic bases of provinces quite clearly (see Table 3-14). Some provinces have economies heavily dominated by mining—Bustillos, Frias, Nor Chichas, Sud Chichas and Sud Lipez—for example; while others—such as Bilbao, Ibanez, Charcas, Chayanta, Saavedra, and Linares—are relatively specialized in agriculture. Only a few provinces were relatively specialized in manufacturing—Bilbao and Omiste, for example—and further investigations revealed that their manufacturing base was composed almost entirely of handicrafts and small-scale processing. Location quotients calculated for employment in various sectors in the Department of Potosi

TABLE 3-13

LOCATION QUOTIENTS FOR SELECTED MUNICIPALITIES IN CAMARINES SUR PROVINCE

Municipality	Experienced Workers by Occupation Group			
	Prof., Tech. Managerial, and Administrative	Farmers, Fishermen, Miners, and Related Workers	Craftsmen, Production Process Workers and Laborers	Service, Commercial and Related Workers
Naga City	1.31	0.81	0.73	1.08
Bombon	0.58	0.89	1.29	1.48
Bula	0.49	1.42	0.46	0.71
Calabanga	0.91	1.06	1.01	0.81
Camaligan	1.12	0.55	1.35	1.15
Canaman	0.61	1.16	1.24	0.82
Gainza	1.78	1.07	0.54	0.33
Magarao	1.32	0.85	1.06	1.54
Milaor	0.57	1.13	1.09	0.88
Minalabac	0.66	1.48	0.38	0.29
Pamplona	0.09	1.44	0.51	0.31
Pasacao	0.15	1.46	0.20	0.67
Pili	1.09	1.12	0.59	1.09
San Fernando	0.37	1.48	0.49	0.32

Source: Bicol River Basin Urban Functions in Rural Development Project; and D. Rondinelli, "Spatial Analysis for Regional Development: A Case Study in the Bicol River Basin of the Philippines," Resource Systems Theory and Methodology Series, No. 2 (Tokyo: United Nations University, 1980.

Table 3-14

SECTORAL LOCATION QUOTIENTS OF EMPLOYMENT FOR PROVINCES

IN THE DEPARTMENT OF POTOSI, BOLIVIA

Province	Agriculture	Mining	Manufacturing	Energy	Construction	Commerce and Finance	Transport & Communications	General Services
Frias	0.53	1.54	1.16	1.68	1.87	2.00	1.54	1.94
Busillos	0.73	2.03	0.82	1.00	0.82	0.98	0.89	1.41
Saavedra	1.31	0.41	1.21	0	0.70	0.55	0.38	0.33
Chayanta	1.44	0.19	1.31	0.27	0.18	0.27	0.15	0.17
Charcas	1.49	0.01	1.20	0	0.13	0.16	0.04	0.25
N. Chichas	1.06	1.47	0.48	0.47	1.05	0.50	0.57	0.71
Ibanez	1.59	0.04	0.13	0	0.13	0.08	0.08	0.30
S. Chichas	0.46	1.97	0.66	2.51	2.29	1.55	2.13	2.01
N. Lipez	1.08	0.61	0.36	0	0.94	0.31	3.12	1.19
S. Lipez	1.02	1.72	0.12	0.81	0.90	0.70	0.78	0.74
Linares	1.40	0.24	0.89	0	0.63	0.38	0.29	0.39
Quijarro	0.81	1.19	0.61	6.36	1.04	1.09	3.73	1.31
Bilbao	1.30	0	2.81	0	0.29	0.14	0.05	0.26
Campos	1.10	0.87	0.12	0.56	0.41	0.36	1.54	1.12
Omiste	0.48	0.27	1.85	0.61	2.85	5.10	2.38	1.71
Department	0.64	3.00	0.27	1.00	0.50	1.05	0.88	1.11

Source: H. Evans, Urban Functions in Rural Development: The Case of the Potosi Region in Bolivia, Washington: USAID, 1982.

compared to Bolivia indicate quite clearly that Potosi, from a national perspective, was highly specialized only in mining. It was relatively deficient in employment in agriculture, industry and construction.[21]

A variety of socio-economic data can be analyzed using the location quotient to determine relative specialization. Location quotients can be calculated to determine relative specializations in the region compared to the entire country. Moreover, a time-series of location quotients can be calculated to show changes in specialization among settlements or areas over a period of time. Location quotients are very rough indicators, however, and must be carefully inter-preted and refined using other analytical techniques.

Level of Development Index

Finally, the UFRD approach attempts to discern and explain differences in levels or degrees of development among territorial units within the region based on a composite of social and economic indicators. Weighted or composite rankings are used to distinguish between those areas that have a greater number and higher level of social and economic resources and those that have a relatively lower or higher standard of living or wel-fare.

In the Bicol River Basin, for example, municipali-ties were ranked by level of development based on three sets of indicators--socio-economic and demographic char-acteristics; share of industrial, commercial and agri-cultural production and establishments; and degree of transportation access based on the length and condition of roads passing through the municipality. Among the socio-economic indicators used were: population size, percentage of settlements with more than half of the population living in urban areas, percentage of literate population, level of educational attainment, percentage of labor force employed, per capital municipal revenues, per capita market receipts, number of enterprises or commercial establishments, percentage of workforce in farming occupations, number of hospital beds per 1,000 population, number of households served by water and sanitary facilities. Share of production and productive establishments was determined directly and through sur-rogate indicators. Among the indicators used were: total amount of land in agricultural production; value and yield of rice, coconut and other major crops per hectare; number of establishments in all industries in the municipality; numbers of wholesale and retail trade, transportation and communications, manufacturing, busi-ness, service, financial and real estate establishments; and percentage of population employed in personal

service occupations. The third set of indicators--
transportation access--consisted of measures of road
lengths and types and rankings of road conditions.

The indicators were weighted according to local
planners' perceptions of their importance in determining
the level of socioeconomic development within the Basin.
Municipalities were scaled from 1 to 4, depending on
their share of those indicators within their boundaries.
A composite ranking was developed to classify all municipalities into three categories: relatively high ranking areas that were considered to be developing, transitional or less developed municipalities, and relatively
underdeveloped or declining areas.

The analysis showed that although the entire Bicol
River Basin was relatively poor and underdeveloped,
municipalities differed significantly in their socio-
economic characteristics. The distribution of services,
facilities, infrastructure and productive and social
organizations among municipalities was highly skewed.
Table 3-15 summarizes some of the characteristics of
municipalities in the three categories of development
that were determined by the composite rankings.[22]

1. Developing municipalities included the six most
"urbanized," encompassing the two provincial centers of
Naga and Camaligan, and Legaspi and Daraga, the city of
Iriga and the town of Tobaco. Services, facilities and
productive activities were highly concentrated in these
six municipalities, especially in Naga and Legaspi
cities. The developing municipalities contained about
one-quarter of the population (386,000 people or 22 percent) but accounted for more than 40 percent of the
"urban" population, raised 45 percent of the Basin's
municipal revenues, and had significantly higher percentages of households served by piped water and electricity. Most of the Basin's educational and vocational
training institutions were concentrated within them as
were most of the major health care institutions. The
developing municipalities contained nearly a third of
all high school and 45 percent of all college graduates
in Bicol. They were the financial centers of the Basin,
with nearly half of all financial institutions and more
than 85 percent of deposit and loan assets. More than
one-third of all corn mills, agricultural warehouses,
farm supply stores and farm machine and tool establishments, and nearly half of the cottage industries, and
commercial, financial and service establishments were
located within their boundaries.

2. Less Developed or Transitional Municipalities
were ten that lay at or near the Manila South Road
within the central plain of the river basin. They were
closer in socio-economic and physical characteristics
to the underdeveloped municipalities than to the developing ones. But they were distinguished from the

TABLE 3-15

SOCIOECONOMIC PROFILE OF MUNICIPALITIES BY LEVELS OF DEVELOPMENT, BICOL RIVER BASIN, PHILIPPINES

	Developing Municipalities (N=6)	Less Developed or Transitional Municipalities (N=10)	Underdeveloped and Peripheral Municipalities (N=38)
Population	22.4	26.4	51.2
Educational Attainment			
High School Graduates	31.2	26.3	42.4
College Graduates	44.8	23.2	32.0
Dwelling Units of Strong Construction	32.6	26.9	40.4
Municipal Revenues	44.5	18.6	36.9
Financial Institutions	48.1	13.4	38.2
Deposits and Loan Assets of Financial Institutions	86.9	4.7	8.4
Agro-processing, Storage and Commercial Establishments	24.9	31.4	36.7
Rice and Corn Mills	23.9	32.8	43.3
Warehouses	36.5	33.0	30.4
Agro-Supply Stores	41.7	30.6	27.7
Farm Machine and Tool Stores	64.5	9.7	25.8
Manufacturing, Commercial and Service Establishments	45.4	29.8	24.8
Health Facilities			
Hospitals	51.2	25.5	23.8
Hospital Beds	58.9	11.7	29.3

Source: Government of the Philippines, National Census and Statistics Office, Unpublished reports, 1970.

former primarily by the fact that their access to the
Manila South Road or provincial arteries connecting
them to the major cities of Naga and Legaspi had generated some diversification of economic and social activities in the poblacions, and that they contained the
potentially richest agricultural land in the Basin.
This group of municipalities accounted for slightly
more than 26 percent of the population and had concentrations of services, cottage industries, infrastructure and facilities slightly larger than its share of
population. Rural areas of these municipalities were
largely underdeveloped: less than 20 percent of households were served by piped water, they had few educational or health institutions, and commercial establishments were rare and scattered. Perhaps because of
their physical proximity to the major provincial centers, these areas had not become highly specialized and
seemed to depend on the larger centers for marketing
and trade.

    3. Underdeveloped Municipalities included 38 pre-
dominantly rural, subsistence agricultural areas form-
ing the periphery of the Basin. Slightly more than
half of the population of the Bicol River Basin lived
in these municipalities, which, by all socioeconomic
characteristics, were the poorest and least developed.
These 38 municipalities had a far smaller proportion of
facilities, services, educated manpower, financial resources, and productive economic activities than their
share of population. Their residents were scattered in
rather small barangays. Only eight percent of households received water and less than six percent had
electrical power. Only five of the 38 municipalities
had post-secondary educational or vocational training
institutions; nearly 40 percent had no markets of any
kind, and 8 contained no financial institutions. These
municipalities collected less than two-fifths of all
municipal revenues and, on the average, depended on the
national government for nearly a third of their municipal income. Some of the municipalities obtained more
than half of their revenues from the national government and had few sources of internal income. The
financial institutions in these underdeveloped municipalities had less than 10 percent of the deposit and
loan assets in the Basin. As a group, these municipalities contained less than one-quarter of the manufacturing, commercial, financial and service establishments, only a little more than a third of agro-
processing, storage and commercial establishments and
one-fourth of the health facilities.

    Thus, the analyses revealed that a majority of the
population in the Bicol River Basin lived in municipalities with few services or facilities needed to meet

basic human needs or to increase agricultural production and expand nonagricultural employment opportunities. Moreover, they were generally isolated from or had extremely poor access to the municipalities in which services, facilities and markets were most highly concentrated.

In the Department of Potosi in Bolivia a somewhat different set of indicators were used to construct a development index. Evans notes in his study of Potosi that a series of development indicators were calculated for the fifteen provinces, including housing conditions and services provided to dwellings, education, health, employment, transport and communications. These were either derived from data in the population and housing censuses or were based on information collected in a survey of towns as part of the settlement system analysis. Information used in the development index is listed in Table 3-10.[23]

To arrive at a development index a ranking method was used. For each indicator the difference between the top and bottom score was divided into three equal parts. Since the number of indicators for each category of data varied from one to four, they were assigned different weights by the local planners in order to balance their importance in the overall rankings. Provinces were classified as more developed, less developed, and least developed based on their composite weighted rankings (see Table 3-16). Those with from 29 to 35 points (34 was the highest number of points scored by any province) were considered to be the more developed; those with 22 to 28 points, less developed; and those with from 15 to 21 points, the least developed.

In addition, estimates were made of the per capita income levels in each of the provinces. These estimates were based on output per unit of labor in each sector at the departmental level, and sectoral employment in each province. This assumed that productivity levels were constant across all provinces, which is obviously not true, but in the absence of alternative data it provided at least a first approximation.[24]

Income per capita in province i, Y_i, is calculated as follows:

$$Y_i = \frac{1}{P_i} \sum_{j=1} N_{ij} \times Y^*_j; \quad \text{with } Y^*_j = Y_j/N_j$$

where: P_i = population of the province i;
N_{ij} = labor in sector j in province i;
Y^*_j = estimated output per labor in sector j in province i;
Y_j = output in sector j in the Department;
N_j = labor in sector j in the Department.

TABLE 3-16

RANKINGS OF PROVINCES BY LEVELS OF DEVELOPMENT, DEPARTMENT OF POTOSI, BOLIVIA

Levels of Development and Provinces in Each Level	Housing						Employ-ment	Health				Transpor-tation and Comm.		Total
	A1	A2	A3	B1	B2	B3	C1	D1	D2	D3	D4	E1	E2	
More Developed														
Frias	3	3	3	2	3	3	2	3	3	1	1	2	2	34
Omiste	3	3	3	3	3	2	2	1	1	1	1	2	3	31
S. Chichas	3	1	3	3	1	2	2	1	3	2	2	2	3	32
Bustillos	3	1	3	2	3	2	1	2	3	2	1	1	2	29
Less Developed														
Quijarro	2	1	2	2	3	2	2	1	2	2	2	1	1	25
N. Chichas	1	1	1	2	2	1	3	1	1	3	3	1	1	22
Campos	3	1	2	3	3	3	3	1	1	3	3	1	1	28
Least Developed														
Saavedra	1	1	1	1	1	1	3	2	1	1	1	2	3	21
Linares	1	1	2	1	1	1	3	1	1	2	2	2	2	21
Bilbao	1	1	1	1	1	1	2	1	1	2	2	3	3	21
N. Lipez	2	1	1	3	3	1	1	1	1	2	2	1	2	20
Ibanez	1	1	1	1	1	1	3	1	1	2	2	1	1	18
S. Lipez	1	1	1	2	2	1	3	1	1	3	3	1	1	18
Chayanta	1	1	1	1	1	1	1	1	1	1	1	1	1	16
Charcas	1	1	1	1	1	1	2	1	1	1	1	1	1	15

Indicators:
A1 – % of houses with water
A2 – % of houses with sewers
A3 – % of houses with electricity
A4 – % of houses of strong building materials
B1 – % of population literate
B2 – % of population that attended school
B3 – % of population with elementary education

C1 – % of population employed
D1 – number of health facilities
D2 – physicians per thousand population
D3 – hospital rooms per thousand population
D4 – mortality rate
E1 – condition of roads
E2 – telegraph facilities

Source: H. Evans, Potosi Urban Functions in Rural Development field research data.

The results are listed in column 5 of Table 3-9.
     The index of development tended to confirm the
findings of other elements of the regional profile. It
indicated that the provinces that were most urbanized
and that had strong mining activities tended to have
the highest levels of social and economic services and
facilities. The rural agricultural provinces tended to
be the least developed and to have the lowest levels of
services and facilities. The index of development provided planners a broader framework in which to conduct
a more detailed analysis of discrete settlements within
the region.
     Thus, the regional profile can be useful in con-
firming or documenting the relative strengths and weaknesses of the regional economy and in determining the
distribution and levels of development of human, social
and physical resources among areas within the region.
In most developing countries, however, detailed information is usually only available for major administrative subdivisions or for principal economic areas, and
not for discrete settlements. Relatively little data
are usually available for most towns and villages.
Thus the UFRD approach makes use of simple and rapid
methods of collecting and organizing information on the
distribution of functions among settlements and the
functional characteristics of different types of settlements within a region. These are described in
Chapter Four.

NOTES

1.   United Nations Economic and Social Commission for Asia and the Pacific, Guidelines for Rural Centre Planning, New York: United Naitons, 1979.
2.   John Friedmann, Regional Development Policy: A Case Study of Venezuela, Cambridge, Mass.:   MIT Press, 1966.
3.   John Friedmann, Urbanization, Planning and National Development (Beverly Hills: Sage Publications, 1973), pp. 302-303.
4.   United Nations Economic and Social Commission for Asia and the Pacific, op. cit., p. 109.
5.   Dennis A. Rondinelli and Barclay G. Jones, "Decision-Making, Managerial Capacity and Development: An Entrepreneurial Approach to Planning," African Administrative Studies, No. 13 (1975), pp. 105-118.
6.   Avrom Bendavid-Val, Regional and Local Economic Analysis for Practitioners, New York: Praeger, 1983.
7.   Kenneth Ruddle and Dennis A. Rondinelli, Transforming Natural Resources for Human Development: A Resouce Systems Approach Development Policy, Tokyo: United Nations University Press, 1983.
8.   Bendavid-Val, op. cit., pp. 23-28.
9.   F.E. Croxton, D. Cowden and S. Klein, Applied General Statistics, Englewood Cliffs, N.J.: Prentice-Hall, 1967.
10.   Bicol River Basin Development Program, Urban Functions in Rural Development: A Research Project in Spatial Analysis and Planning (Pili, The Philippines: BRBDP, 1978), Chapter 1.
11.   See Dennis A. Rondinelli, "Spatial Analysis for Regional Development: A Case Study in the Bicol River Basin of the Philippines," Resource Systems Theory and Methodology Series, No. 2, Tokyo: United Nations University Press, 1980.
12.   Dennis A. Rondinelli, Bicol River Basin Urban Functions in Rural Development Project: Summary and Evaluation, Washington: U.S. Agency for International Development, 1978.
13.   Ibid.

4
Analysis of the Settlement System

Although intra-regional analysis provides a good
deal of information about territorial units within a
region, it does not offer much insight into the characteristics of the communities in which people live and
carry out the social and economic activities that contribute to local and regional development. The major
sources of information about those activities in most
countries are national censuses and specialized demographic surveys that usually do not disaggregate data
to the level of discrete communities or settlements.
Usually this information is only available for larger
administrative units such as provinces, districts or
municipalities, which may contain many settlements of
different types and characteristics.

Geographers, demographers and planners have usually used three methods to analyze settlement systems:[1]
1.   Morphological classifications that attempt to
distinguish urban and rural communities on the basis of
demographic and physical characteristics;
2.   Population size classifications that seek to
categorize settlements into metropolitan areas, cities,
towns, villages and hamlets based on the number and
density of residents within their boundaries; and
3.   Functional classifications that attempt to
distinguish among settlements on the basis of the
types, combinations and diversity of social and economic activities located in them.

The UFRD approach to regional planning is concerned primarily with the social and economic functions
that discrete communities perform and how in combination they form a pattern or system that can influence
economic and social development. Thus, this stage of
the analysis focuses heavily on the functional characteristics of communities and describes a region as a
pattern of human settlement defined by both population
and functional features.

The objectives of this stage of the analysis are to:

1. Identify the discrete elements or components of the regional settlement system--that is, the number and location of communities in which people live and interact with each other in performing significant economic and social activities;

2. Determine the functional characteristics of communities and the degree to which the settlements serve populations living outside of their boundaries--that is, the degree to which settlements in the system are central places;

3. Delineate the pattern of settlement within the region--that is, its levels of hierarchy and diffusion and the centrality of places within it; and,

4. Determine the distribution of and patterns of association among social and economic functions--services, infrastructure, organizations and facilities--within settlements that are important for local and regional development.

This information, together with the analysis of spatial linkages, can assist planners and policy-makers in understanding how the pattern of settlement and the level of development within the region are related. It can help them determine the degree of access that people in different communities and parts of the region have to various services, facilities, infrastructure and organizations; in determining where functions are adequate or deficient; and in judging where the location of new investments will increase the capacity of communities to provide the access that people living in rural areas need to town-based services, facilities and infrastructure. Moreover, the information can be useful in making location decisions about new investments and about the potential for clustering services and facilities in new ways to increase the capacity of settlements to stimulate development in their areas.

MORPHOLOGICAL AND POPULATION SIZE ANALYSES

The most frequently used methods of analyzing settlements in developing countries are morphological and demographic, primarily because population data are the most commonly available. As noted earlier, the morphological approach attempts to determine which communities are "urban" or "rural" based usually on a definition that sets a minimum population size and a few easily observed physical characteristics as the distinguishing criteria. Demographic analyses usually use population size to determine the pattern of settlements--that is, the degree of hierarchy or diffuseness, the rank-order, and the degree of urbanity. Although these approaches yield little information about the social and economic characteristics of communities, they do provide an initial and easily determined profile of the settlement pattern that can be analyzed in more detail and cross-checked with functional analyses.

In the Bicol River Basin of the Philippines, for example, the UFRD analysis began with an examination of the morphological and demographic characteristics of the region's settlements. Settlements were divided into "urban" and "rural" areas by using the national census definition of urban areas: (1) all settlements or municipalities having a population density of at least 1,000 persons per square kilometer; (2) central districts of municipalities or places having a population density of at least 500 persons per square kilometer; (3) central districts not included in criteria 1 and 2, regardless of population size, that have (a) a street pattern, i.e., network of streets in either parallel or right-angle orientation, (b) at least six commercial, manufacturing, recreational or personal services, and (c) at least three of the following functions: a town hall, church or chapel with religious services at least once a month, a public plaza, park or cemetery, a market place or building where trading activities are carried on at least once a week and a public building such as a school, hospital, health center or library; and (4) those settlements with at least 1,000 inhabitants that meet conditions set out in criterion 3, and where the occupation of the inhabitants is predominantly non-farming or non-fishing.[2]

Using this definition, barangays (administrative subunits of municipalities) could be categorized as either urban or rural places and the percentage of population in each municipality and in the Bicol River Basin living in urban and rural settlements could be roughly estimated. Table 4-1 indicates that few municipalities in the region had a large percentage of population living in urban areas. Only Naga City was considered totally urbanized; even other larger municipalities in the region, such as Legaspi City, Camaligan, and Magarao had substantial numbers of residents living in rural places. More than 87 percent of Albay's and 79 percent of Camarines Sur's residents lived in rural places. Overall, less than 18 percent of the Bicol River Basin's population was urbanized.

The morphological and demographic data also provided some indication of the size classes of settlements in the Bicol River Basin and the average population size of barangays. The analysis showed, for example, that less than 5 percent of all barangays in the Basin had populations of 3,000 or more, about one-third of the barangays had populations of between 1,000

TABLE 4-1

URBAN AND RURAL SETTLEMENTS IN THE BICOL RIVER BASIN

Municipality	Population (1975)	No. of Barangays	Urban Settlements			Rural Settlements		
			No. of Barangays	Urban Population	Percent of Municipal Population	No. of Barangays	Rural Population	Percent of Municipal Population
Bacacay	39,500	46	4	4,187	10.6	42	35,313	89.4
Camalig	41,702	45	1	3,210	7.7	44	38,492	92.3
Daraga	63,265	54	2	4,011	6.3	52	59,254	93.7
Guinobatan	49,724	46	2	1,080	2.2	44	48,644	97.8
Jovellar	14,121	23	9	2,335	16.5	14	11,786	83.5
Legaspi City	88,378	65	35	37,724	42.7	30	50,654	57.3
Libon	47,890	41	1	6,645	13.9	40	41,254	86.1
Ligao	61,549	55	1	1,741	2.8	54	59,808	97.2
Malilipot	20,497	14	-	-	-	14	20,497	100.0
Malinao	24,889	26	-	-	-	26	24,889	100.0
Manito	13,647	14	-	-	-	14	13,647	100.0
Oas	50,293	53	1	281	0.6	52	50,012	99.4
Pio Duran	31,188	29	-	-	-	29	31,188	100.0
Polangui	52,541	44	2	5,085	9.7	42	47,456	90.3
Sto. Domingo	17,562	17	4	5,550	31.6	13	12,012	68.4
Tabaco	65,254	47	7	13,955	21.4	40	51,269	78.6
Tiwi	24,350	25	1	2,040	8.4	24	22,310	91.6
Albay	706,350	644	70	87,844	12.4	574	618,485	87.6
Baao	30,219	30	7	8,641	28.6	23	21,578	71.4
Balatan	13,159	17	1	1,808	13.7	16	11,351	86.3
Bato	28,492	33	6	9,501	33.3	27	18,991	66.7
Bombon	7,494	6	-	-	-	6	7,494	100.0
Buhi	44,226	38	6	9,848	22.3	32	34,378	77.0
Bula	36,904	31	-	-	-	31	36,904	100.0
Cabusao	10,110	9	2	1,369	13.5	7	8,741	86.5
Calabanga	40,274	48	8	6,413	15.9	40	33,861	84.1

TABLE 4-1 (continued)

Camaligan	9,853	13	7	4,058	41.2	6	5,795	58.8
Canaman	14,522	24	5	4,014	27.6	19	10,508	72.4
Caramoan	31,399	49	3	2,587	8.2	46	28,812	91.8
Del Gallego	13,754	32	3	1,914	13.9	29	11,840	86.1
Gainza	5,931	7	–	–	–	7	5,931	100.0
Garchitorena	16,438	20	–	–	–	20	16,438	100.0
Goa	34,049	34	10	7,133	20.9	24	26,916	79.1
Iriga City	75,885	37	3	13,938	18.4	34	61,947	81.6
Lagonoy	33,297	38	6	4,469	13.4	32	28,828	86.6
Libmanan	66,601	75	1	2,041	3.1	74	64,560	96.9
Lupi	19,682	38	1	1,274	6.5	37	18,408	93.5
Magarao	11,846	15	8	7,984	67.4	7	3,862	32.6
Milaor	13,167	14	–	–	–	14	13,167	100.0
Minalabac	27,089	25	4	2,817	10.4	21	24,272	89.6
Naboa	48,635	40	9	7,611	15.6	31	41,024	84.4
Naga City	83,337	27	27	83,337	100.0	–	–	–
Ocampo	19,283	25	3	2,068	10.7	22	17,215	89.3
Pamplona	18,350	17	1	3,123	17.0	16	15,227	83.0
Pasacao	21,809	19	3	4,350	19.9	16	17,459	80.1
Pili	36,676	26	6	5,984	16.3	20	30,692	83.7
Presentacion	13,555	18	–	–	–	18	13,555	100.0
Ragay	32,798	38	2	2,686	8.2	36	30,112	91.8
Sangay	18,013	18	4	2,854	15.3	14	12,259	84.7
San Fernando	15,524	22	4	3,317	21.4	18	12,207	78.6
San Jose	21,859	29	6	3,329	15.2	23	18,530	84.8
Sipocot	39,457	45	–	–	–	45	39,457	100.0
Siruma	10,435	22	1	430	4.1	21	10,005	95.9
Tigaon	25,282	23	1	2,912	11.5	22	22,370	88.5
Tinambac	34,415	44	6	3,908	11.4	38	30,507	88.6
Camarines Sur	1,023,819	1,046	154	215,618	23.1	892	805,201	78.9
Grand Total (Basin)	1,730,169	1,690	224	303,462	17.5	1,466	1,423,686	82.5

Source: Center for Policy and Development Studies, Urban Functions in Rural Development, Bicol River Basin Development Program, Vol. II-B (College, Laguna: University of the Philippines, Los Banos, 1978).

and 3,000, and that about 62 percent of the barangays had populations of less than 1,000. The average size of all barangays in the Bicol River Basin was about 1,100 people. The analysis seemed to confirm that the Bicol River Basin suffered from many of the adversities described in Chapter One of a settlement system with very small populations. Relatively few settlements in Bicol had large enough population size, it would seem, to be able to support a wide variety of central functions. The demographic data would only allow planners to surmise that population levels were too low for most settlements to offer central functions, however, and they would have to be cross-checked by a functional analysis of settlements to determine the types and ranges of functions supported by communities of different size groups.

Morphological and demographic analyses, in addition to helping planners to distinguish quickly between urban and rural settlements, also provides some insights into size classes of settlements and changes in them over time. Similar studies in the Department of Potosi in Bolivia revealed a pattern of settlement similar to that in Bicol. Table 4-2 indicates that there were only 2 settlements in the region with more than 13,000 population; only 6 with between 5,000 and 13,000 residents, only about a dozen settlements with between 2,000 and 5,000 people; and the large majority-- more than 40 towns and villages--had between 500 and 2,000 residents when the last census was taken in 1976.

The settlement pattern in the Department of Potosi showed a high degree of primacy, measured by the four-city primacy index, or the ratio of the population of the largest city to the combined populations of the next three largest cities.

$$Pr = \frac{P_1}{P_2 + P_3 + P_4}$$

The city of Potosi, the largest settlement in the Department, had more than three times the population of the next largest town in the region, and a primacy index of 1.65, indicating that it was more than one and a half times the size of the next three largest towns.

The population size data indicate that the primacy of the city of Potosi among settlements in the Department declined slightly from about 1.91 in 1950 and that the number of settlements with more than 500 population increased from the 32 that existed in 1950 to 60 in 1976. Moreover, a rank ordering of the settlements with more than 500 people shows a substantial number of shifts in the population rank among towns in the region over the quarter of a century (see Figure 4-1). In

TABLE 4-2

CHANGES IN POPULATION SIZE OF SETTLEMENTS IN THE DEPARTMENT
OF POTOSI, BOLIVIA

Population Size Category	Towns Population 1950		Towns Population 1976	
20,000 or more	Potosi	43,306	Potosi Llallagua	77,334 23,361
10,000-20,000			·Villazon Siglo XX Tupiza	12,536 10,766 10,682
5,000-10,000	Tupiza Pulacayo Uyuni Llallagua Villazon	8,235 7,735 6,671 6,626 6,175	Uyuni C.M. Catavi Uncia	8,639 7,593 7,396
2,000- 5,000	Uncia	4,454	Atocha R. Tazna Chayanta Animas Colquechaca S. Barbara Siete Suyos Pulacayo Tatasi Telamayu Betanzos B. Retiro	4,677 3,171 2,937 2,694 2,686 2,556 2,523 2,398 2,380 2,332 2,205 2,052
1,000- 2,000	10 towns		11 towns	
500- 1,000	15 villages		29 villages	

Source: H. Evans, Urban Functions in Rural Development: The
Case of Potosi Region of Bolivia, Washington: USAID,
1982.

1950 only the city of Potosi had more than 10,000
residents; by 1976 there were six cities in the region
of that size or larger, and about 20 with more than
2,000 people compared to 7 a quarter of a century
earlier. However, as Figure 4-1 indicates, more than
half of the towns with more than 500 residents in 1950
lost population over the next 26 years. More extensive
investigations later found that nearly all of the
settlements that lost population were farming communities and nearly all that gained were mining centers.
The explanation is clearly found in the economic characteristics of the region and economic policy of the
government, which emphasized mining to the detriment of
agriculture in investment allocations. Evans points
out that the population growth of settlements in the
Potosi region was closely related to the economic base
of the area in which they were located.[3] The few farming settlements that grew were closely linked to larger
centers of consumption, underlining the importance of
demand and market outlets in stimulating and sustaining
rural production. Mining towns such as Pulacayo, which
lost over 70 percent of its population between 1950 and
1976, declined as profitable mineral deposits were
gradually exhausted.

FUNCTIONAL ANALYSIS OF THE SETTLEMENT SYSTEM

Although morphological and population size analyses provide some useful information about the settlement system in a region, they do not offer insights
into the functional characteristics of communities or
provide a satisfactory description of the regional
settlement hierarchy. The UFRD approach uses a combination of methods to determine the functional characteristics of the settlement system, including: Guttman
scales, manual scalograms, threshold analyses, weighted
centrality indexes, and frequency distributions.

Scale Analyses

A Guttman scale is a means of analyzing the underlying characteristics of particular items. In regional
analysis the items are functions--services, facilities,
infrastructure, organizations and economic activities--
which give settlements (cases) centrality in the
spatial system. In order to construct a scale, the
measures must be unidimensional, that is, measurement
must be toward or away from a single underlying objective for each case. The scale must be ordinal--items
can be divided into two portions, that is, "yes" or
"no" or "present" or "absent". Moreover, the scale
must be cumulative, so that items can be ordered by
their degree of complexity, such that each higher order

Figure 4.1

107

POPULATION GROWTH AND RANK SIZE CHANGES OF SETTLEMENTS
IN THE DEPARTMENT OF POTOSI, BOLIVIA

RANK, 1950

RANK, 1976

RANK, 1950	RANK, 1976
1. Potosi	1. Potosi
2. Tupiza	2. Llallagua
3. Pulacayo	3. Villazon
4. Uyuni	4. Siglo XX
5. Llallagua	5. Tupiza
6. Villazon	6. Uyuni
7. Uncia	7. Catavi Mina
8. Sacaca	8. Uncia
9. Ocuri	9. Atocha
10. Vitichi	10. Rosario Tazna
11. Cotagaita	11. Chayanta
12. Chayanta	12. Animas
13. Toropalca	13. Colquechaca
14. Betanzos	14. Santa Barbara
15. S.P. Buena Vista	15. Siete Suyos
16. Colquechaca	16. Pulacayo
17. Macha	17. Tatasi
18. Panacachi	18. Telamayo
19. Ravelo	19. Buen Retiro
20. Chairapata	20. Betanzos
21. Puna	21. Cancaniri
22. Pocoata	22. Chilcobiji
23. Caiza "D"	23. Sacaca
24. Arampampa	24. Santa Ana
25. Porco	25. Catavi Civil
26. Tinguipaya	26. Puna
27. Aymaya	27. Cala Cala
28. Caripuyo	28. Caracota
29. Acasio	29. Ravelo
30. Andavilque	30. Llica
31. Llica	31. Caiza "D"
32. Colcha "M"	32. Sacaca Ocuri
- Siglo XX	33. Macha
- Catavi Mina	34. Cotagaita
- Santa Barbara	35. Vitichi
- Rosario Tazna	36. Colavi Mina
- Buen Retiro	37. Miraflores
- Siete Suyos	38. Porco
- Animas	39. Pucro
- Telamayu	40. Candelaria
- Atocha	41. Quechisla
- Tatasi	42. Chaqui
- Cancaniri	43. Palca y S. Juan
- Catavi Civil	44. Sala Sala
- Cala Cala	45. S.F. de Colavi
- Santa Ana	46. Killpani
- Chilcobija	47. Rio Mulatos
- Caracota	48. Chuafaya
- Chiracoro	49. Tinguipaya
- Miraflores	50. Pocoata
- Entre Rios	51. Agua Castilla
- Pucro	52. Colcha "K"
- S.F de Colavi	53. Chiracordo
- Colavi Mina	54. Entre Rios
34. Chaqui	55. Colchani
- Mojotorillo	56. Aymaya
- Chuafaya	57. Andavilque
- Sala Sala	58. Mojotorillo
- Quechisla	59. S.P. Buena Vista
- Juntavi	60. Juntavi
- Palca y S. Juan	61. Acasio
- Candelaria	62. Arampama
- Rio Mulatos	63. Caripuyo
33. Killpan	64. Toropalca
- Agua Castilla	- Panacachi
- Colchani	- Chairapata

item is composed of lower order ones. In a perfectly
hierarchical scale of settlements, for example, each
settlement would be expected to possess all functions
(items) of those of places of lower order (functional
complexity), but would not be expected to possess those
functions of places ranking higher in the scale. Each
deviation from the "expected pattern" is considered an
"error." That is, when functions are missing from a
higher order settlement that are found in lower order
ones, or when functions are present in lower order settlements that are not found in higher order ones, this
constitutes a statistical error that requires further
investigation for an adequate explanation. Statistical
measures, based on analysis of errors, can also help
determine the validity of the scale. A coefficient of
scalability determines whether or not the scale is unidimensional and cumulative.[4]

Obviously, there are few regions in which settlements would be perfectly ordered in a hierarchical
scale. Because of distance and other factors there are
usually many "unexpectedly present" and "unexpectedly
absent" functions in a settlement hierarchy. In both
cases, other means of analysis must be employed to
determine whether the presence or absence of functions
in particular communities constitutes a problem or an
opportunity for investment.

Guttman Scale is a relatively easy way of examining both the functional complexity of settlements and
the distribution of functions among communities within
a region. But as with all methods of analysis
described here, it provides only rough approximations
that must be cross-checked and further analyzed by
other methods. Assuming that a settlement's "level of
development" is reflected in the number and diversity
of functions located within it, relative levels of
development and hierarchy for all settlements in a
region can be determined by the array of Guttman scale
scores.

Combined with other analyses the Guttman scale can
be used to group settlements into different levels of a
hierarchy or categories of development and to depict
relative levels of development within a region by plotting scale scores of each place on a map. Voelkner has
used the scale scores, for instance, to classify
settlements by degree of "modernization"--ranging from
traditional villages with few functions through early
transitional, late transitional, early modern, and
modern, depending on the diversity and types of functions found within them. Scalogram analysis also indicates the centrality of settlements, assuming that centrality is the ability of a settlement to provide
varied goods and services to people living in other
areas.

As will be seen later, data need only be collected on the presence or absence of functions in settlements and can usually be gathered quickly through simple surveys. In some cases aerial photography can be used to determine the presence or absence of physical facilities or activities with distinguishable physical structures, as well as to determine locations and distances of facilities from population concentrations. Indeed, aerial photographs that clearly show the number of dwelling units in settlements can be used to approximate the number of people living in the community, as a check on or to substitute for census data.

The most important aspect of the scale analysis is that it gives planners and policy analysts the ability to process a great diversity of qualitative data concerning development when quantitative data are either not available or cannot be quickly and economically acquired. It is also useful in situations where more sophisticated statistical analysis cannot conveniently be applied. Scale methodologies discern detailed differences in quality among the units of analysis, such as settlements, administrative areas, districts or regions. But they also go beyond the capacity of such statistical techniques as factor analysis, which measure quantitative variances or differences among cases. Scales can delineate specific qualitative differences among settlements and the cumulative sequence of attributes or characteristics within them. As Voelkner points out, scale analysis can be used as a substitute for quantitative analysis, but ideally it is "complementary to quantitative analysis and vice-versa in measuring development. The strength of quantitative analysis lies in the measurement of efficiency and correlations between variables. It does poorly in identifying sequence and multiple interdependencies of development factors. The strength and weaknesses of scalogram analysis are the opposite."[5]

Scale analyses can be done in two ways--using a computerized statistical program or a manual method. Both were tested in the UFRD pilot projects in the Philippines and Bolivia. In the Bicol project, planners initially attempted to extend a statistical application of scale analysis that had been done earlier for municipalities in Camarines Sur Province to the rest of the Basin.[6] The approach used in Camarines Sur province clearly illustrates the procedure for applying Guttman scales in regional analysis. First, a survey identified existing institutions, services, facilities and establishments in town centers (poblacions) and other communities (barangays) in each municipality.[7] Among the information collected were the name, administrative level and administrative class of the place, the number of barangays, land area, population size, number of dwelling units and population densities of each town center and <u>barangay</u>. In addition, information was gathered about the presence or absence of and the number of communities possessing the following functions:

1. <u>Public utilities and facilities</u>--including telephone company, telegraph office, post office, messenger service, radio station, TV station, printing press, newspaper or magazine publisher, police force, fire department, sewage system, electric utility, security agency, street lights, water supply, paved streets, paved sidewalks, national highway, and irrigation system.

2. <u>Transportation services</u>--including <u>calesas</u> (horse-drawn carts), tricycles, buses, jeepneys, taxis, motorboats, aircraft, trains, airports, train stations, bus terminals, or commercial ports.

3. <u>Commercial establishments</u>--including <u>sari-sari</u> (neighborhood) stores, groceries, department stores or bazaars, drugstores, gas stations, auto repair shops, bakeries, banks, hardware stores, lumber yeards, rice or corn mills, furniture shops, applicance stores, agrochemical stores, insurance or real estate offices, and factories.

4. <u>Health facilities</u>--including public and private hospitals or clinics, child health care centers, family planning clinics, and optical, dental or chest clinics, or rural health stations.

5. <u>Recreational facilities</u>--including theaters, cock-fighting pits, bowling alleys, basketball courts, tennis, volleyball and raquetball courts, nightclubs, bars, reading centers, recreation halls or centers, resort facilities, golf courts and dancing pavilions.

6. <u>Extension services</u>--agricultural, local government, family planning, plant industry, and national grain authority agents, social work, forestry, fishery or animal industry agents, welfare services and malaria control units.

7. <u>Community organizations</u>--school and church-related activities, civic groups, professional organizations, marketing, consumer or irrigation cooperatives, credit groups, compact farm groups, labor unions, women's clubs, cultural organizations and youth clubs.

8. <u>Educational institutions</u>--including kindergarten and nursery schools, primary, intermediate and secondary schools, vocational schools, public and private colleges and universities, technical and business schools.

9. <u>Health services</u>--physicians, nurses, licensed midwives, dentists, pharmacists, healers, herbalists, optometrists, opticians, faith healers, medical technologists, and health paraprofessionals.

10. <u>Professional services</u>--lawyers, engineers, accountants, architects, building contractors, survey-ors, chemists, teachers, licensed electricians and plumbers and others.

11. <u>Personal services</u>--including barber shops, beauty parlors, tailor shops, dressmaker shops, shoe-repair shops, hotels and lodging places, cafeterias, restaurants, laundaries, funeral parlors, photo studios, sauna baths and others.

Once these data were collected for the 33 munici-palities in Camarines Sur Province, the items or func-tions were coded as being either present or absent and scaled by the Guttman method. A computer program arranged the towns in a scale, with those having the least number of functions scoring "low" and those with the most scoring "high." The municipalities were then arrayed in a hierarchy of functional complexity, and based on scale scores, were regrouped into scale steps (see Table 4-3). The 30 scale steps were condensed to nine and plotted on a map. Using the condensed steps as indicators of development levels of municipalities, cumulative isopleth lines were drawn around municipali-ties of equal levels of development (see Figure 4-2).

The analysis clearly identified Naga City and Iriga as the most functionally complex centers in the province, delineated their apparent "areas of influ-ence" and pinpointed the satellite or supplementary centers within those influence areas. The analysts found a strong correlation between transport access in settlements and their functional complexity, concluding that "accessibility coupled with complexity is a major factor in the evolution of a center" in the Bicol River Basin.

The Urban Functions in Rural Development project sought to extend the methods used in Camarines Sur to all 54 municipalities in the Bicol River Basin, employ-ing 64 functions in eight categories--economic, social services, physical facilities, communications, recrea-tional facilities, personal services, community organi-zations and extension and protective services--identified in the Camarines Sur municipal inventory. The validity of using these items in Albay province was later verified by a sample survey of municipalities in that province.

Although this exercise provided useful information concerning the functional complexity and concentration of various services and facilities in municipalities---and strongly confirmed the findings of the descriptive statistics and indexes of development in the regional profile concerning levels of development among municipalities--its most important deficiency was that the municipalities in the Philippines are administra-tive areas and not necessarily discrete settlements. A

TABLE 4-3

GUTTMAN SCALE OF FUNCTIONAL COMPLEXITY OF MUNICIPALITIES IN
CAMARINES SUR PROVINCE, BICOL RIVER BASIN, 1975

Rank	Municipality	Scale Score		Scale Step	
		Number of Functions Discriminated in Scale	Percentage of Functions in Municipality Relative to Number of Functions in most "Developed" Municipality	N	Condensed
33	Gainza	29	19	1	1
32	Del Gallego	48	32	2	2
31	Lupi	53	35	3	2
30	Tinambac	55	36	4	2
28	Balatan	55	36	4	2
28	Minalabac	57	38	5	2
27	Pasacao	59	39	6	2
26	Bula	61	40	7	2
25	Bombon	63	41	8	2
24	Camaligan	63	41	8	2
23	Cabusao	65	43	9	2
22	San Fernando	66	43	10	2
21	Milaor	66	43	10	2
20	Ocampo	67	44	11	2
19	Magarao	68	45	12	2
18	Canaman	70	46	13	2
17	Sangay	71	47	14	2
16	San Jose	73	48	15	2
15	Lagonoy	74	49	16	2
14	Pamplona	81	53	17	3
13	Ragay	88	58	18	4
12	Bato	93	61	19	5
11	Sipocot	96	63	20	5
10	Calabanga	97	64	21	5
9	Baao	99	65	22	5
8	Buhi	104	68	23	6
7	Tigaon	109	72	24	6
6	Nabua	111	73	25	6
5	Libmanan	117	77	26	7
4	Pili	119	78	27	7
3	Goa	122	80	28	7
2	Iriga City	134	88	29	8
1	Naga City	152	100	30	9

Source: S. Roco, Jr. and F. Lynch, "Development Levels in
Bicol River Basin," SSRU Research Report Series,
No. 17, unpublished draft, 1975.

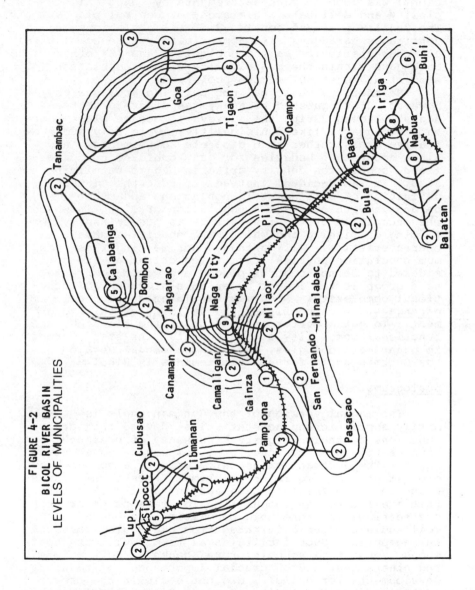

FIGURE 4-2
BICOL RIVER BASIN
LEVELS OF MUNICIPALITIES

second scale, of urbanized or "built-up areas" (poblacions) was done to rank settlements by functional complexity and delineate a hierarchy of central places.
The "built-up areas" consisted of (1) poblacions and
contiguous barangays with approximately the same land
use characteristics as the poblacion, and (2) other
barangays within the municipality with a population
size of at least 50% of the poblacion.

Neither the municipal nor built-up area scales,
however, distinguished barangays as discrete settlements. Indeed during the surveys it became clear that
many barangays, like municipalities, were only administrative areas rather than discrete settlements. And
since accurate boundaries for many could not be determined, population density criteria had to be eliminated. It was decided, instead, to test the Census
definition of settlements: poblacions and other
barangays with at least a population of 1,000 in which
the occupation of the inhabitants is predominantly non-
farming or fishing and which have specified physical
characteristics. All barangays not meeting these minimum population-physical facilities criteria were considered to be non-central places and would be treated
as a group at the lowest order in a hierarchy of functional complexity. A survey was later done of all
barangays, which confirmed the validity of this judgment. To get a better indication of the hierarchy and
functional complexity of settlements, the staff turned
to other methodologies, including a manual version of
the Guttman scale for all settlements in Bicol.[8]

Scalograms

The manual version of the Guttman scale is primarily a graphic and nonstatistical device that arrays
functions by their ubiquity (frequency of presence) and
ranks settlements by functional complexity on a matrix
chart. The Guttman scales calculated by a computer
program present two major problems. First, some functions that are fairly widespread in rural villages but
that are located in communities for reasons other than
the settlements' threshold population size do not scale
well and are often eliminated from the scale scores by
the computer. Such facilities as farm equipment repair
shops, vocational schools, rural banks, credit unions,
and others that are of crucial importance for rural
development, for example, did not scale in the program
applied in the Bicol River Basin. Second, the computer
output is often very difficult to understand, especially by policy-makers and technical officials who are
not familiar with social science methodologies.

A graphic scale used successfully in India and Indonesia was adopted for the Bicol study and subsequently applied in the Potosi project in Bolivia. Both the data collection and calculation requirements for constructing a scalogram are minimal. The only information required is:

1. A list of all settlements in the region (hamlets, villages, market towns, small cities, larger urban centers);
2. The population size of each settlement;
3. A map pinpointing the location of the settlements; and,
4. An inventory showing the presence or absence of functions (services, organizations, facilities, infrastructure, economic activities) in each settlement.

The procedure for constructing a scalogram is as follows:

1. On the left side of a worksheet, list settlements as rows in descending order of their population;
2. Across the top of the worksheet, list the functions found in the region in their descending order of ubiquity (frequency of presence);
3. Draw row and column lines so that the worksheet becomes a matrix in which each cell represents a function that may appear in the settlement;
4. Fill in with a dark color, an "X", or a "1" all cells in which a function is actually found in a settlement, leave cells for which a function does not appear in a settlement blank, or fill in a "0";
5. Reorder the rows and columns so as to visually minimize the blank cells appearing in the dark pattern found in the upper left section of the matrix, or in decreasing order of presence of functions;
6. The scalogram is complete when no shifting of a settlement row or function column can reduce the number of blank cells in this pattern;
7. The final order of settlement rows identifies a ranking of settlements which can be interpreted as an ordinal centrality score.

The exercise results in a matrix such as that depicted in Figure 4-3, for the Bicol River Basin.

The number and types of functions that are included in the analysis will vary from region to

116

FIGURE 4-3

PORTION OF A SCALOGRAM FOR SETTLEMENTS IN THE BICOL
RIVER BASIN

region depending on planners' judgments about which are
most important for determining the centrality and hierarchy of settlements and for allocating investments
among communities. In Bicol, planners included both
"central functions" and other indicators. Sixty-four
functions, listed in Table 4-4, were selected by analysts to reflect both levels of development and centrality.[9]

In Bolivia, two versions of the scalogram were
prepared. The first included a complete inventory of
information collected from a survey of towns, covering
more than 120 functions in 112 settlements. This was a
useful reference base, but included a large number of
noncentral functions. In order to define the hierarchy
of central places, a second scalogram was prepared.
Only 58 functions that were considered to be the best
indicators of functional complexity were included.[10]
This scalogram is shown in Figure 4-4.

Scale analysis has a number of important uses in
regional development planning. As Fisher notes, "the
scalogram provides a visual description of the...set-
tlement and institutional hierarchy that is easy to
read and useful as a reference in analyzing numerous
issues for planning."[11] This observation was confirmed
in the presentations at technical workshops in Bicol,
where both technically-trained personnel and local
political leaders examined an initial version of the
scalogram prepared for the 120 settlements at the "top"
of the hierarchy. Moreover, as Voelkner observes of
the application of scalogram analysis in Thailand, the
Philippines and Sri Lanka, it can "systematically process and measure qualitative data which previously permitted only intuitive analysis."[12] It can also process
quantitative data that are error-prone or not statis-
tically reliable by using only their qualitative con-
tent, for which the error margin is low, and can serve
as a substitute for quantitative analysis when reliable
statistical data cannot be collected quickly or economically.

Among the potential uses of the scalogram in
regional planning are the following:
1. It can be used to categorize settlements
    into levels of functional complexity and
    determine the types and diversity of ser-
    vices and facilities located in central
    places at various levels of a hierarchy;
2. The scalogram shows rough associations
    among services and facilities in specific
    locations and potential linkages among
    them;
3. The scalogram indicates the sequence in
    which settlements accumulate functions
    and the implications for sequencing com-
    plementary or catalytical investments;

TABLE 4-4

FUNCTIONS ANALYZED IN BICOL RIVER BASIN UFRD PROJECT

Category	Functions
Economic Activities	Shopping center or supermarket Public market Appliance store Farm supply or agro-chemicals store Banks and financial institutions other than rural banks Rural bank Manufacturing or processing plant other than cottage industry Cottage industry
Social Services and Facilities	Nursing school College Vocational school High school Private hospital Government hospital (operational) Private clinic Drugstore
Transport and Communications Services and Facilities	Airport Port Train station Bus station Newspaper publisher Radio station Telephone exchange Telecommunications office
Infrastructure and Maintenance Services	Functioning power plant Piped water system Hardware supply store Farm equipment repair shop Housing estate or subdivision Surveyor's office Construction supply store Auto repair shop

TABLE 4-4 (continued)

Category	Functions
Recreational Activities	Bowling alleys Gymnasium or auditorium Cinema with daily showings Nightclub Playground with facilities Cock-fighting pit Cinema with periodic showings Concrete-paved basketball court
Personal Services	Optometrist or optical shop Xerox copying services Photo studio Restaurant Cemetery Funeral parlor Hotel Lodging house
Community Organizations	Credit union or cooperative Other cooperative "Paluwagan" (welfare society) Labor union Professional organization Civic organization Sports association Farmers association

Extension and Protective
  Services
	Security agency (private)
	Philippine Constabulary station
	Red Cross office
	Firetruck
	Bureau of Animal Industry agent
	Bureau of Agricultural Extension
	  agent
	Bureau of Plant Industry agent
	Department of Local Government
	  and Community Development
	  office

FIGURE 4-4
SCALOGRAM OF SETTLEMENTS IN POTOSI, BOLIVIA

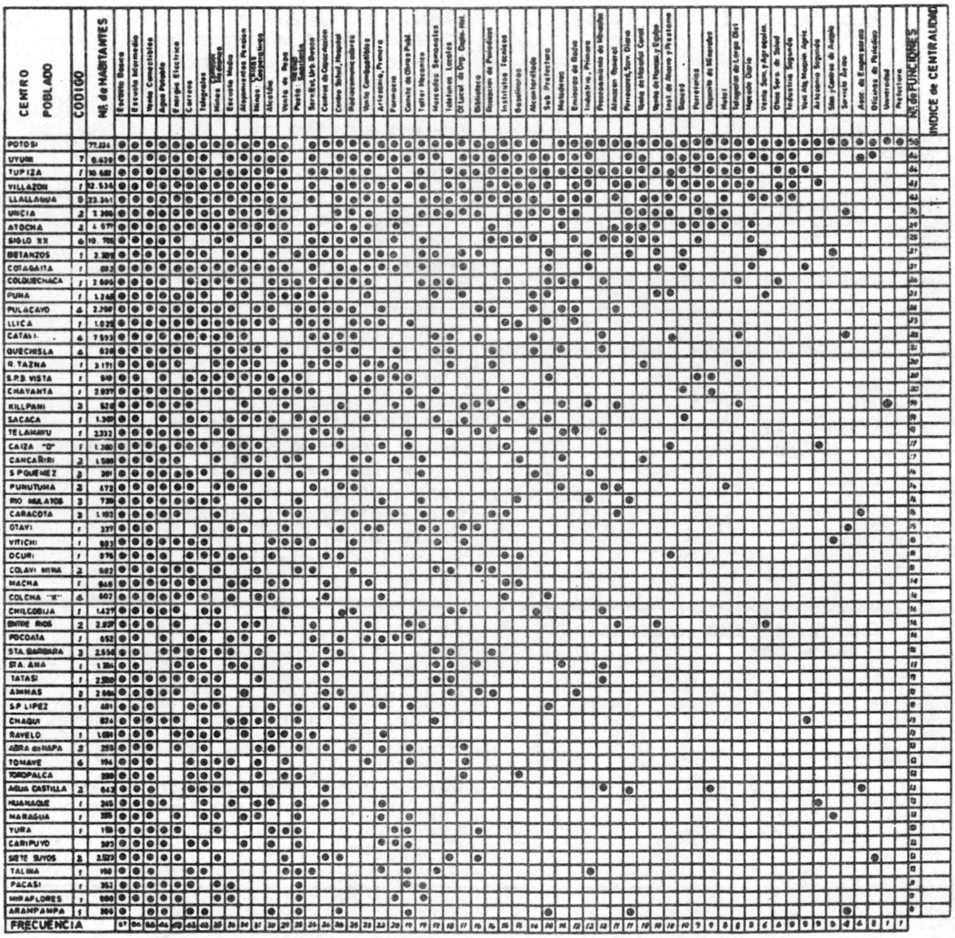

Source: Evans 1982.

4. By reading any column the ubiquity of a service or facility, and its distribution among settlements, can be easily seen;

5. The array of items in the scalogram, analyzed in conjunction with a map showing locations of functions and their distribution and with population-service criteria, can be used to make determinations about the adequacy of services and facilities in the region;

6. "Missing" or unexpectedly absent functions are clearly identified and investigations can be made into the reason that settlements at that scale level do not have the services or facilities, and decisions can be taken about the appropriateness of investing in those functions;

7. Unexpectedly present functions are also identified, and the reason for the appearance of services and facilities in those settlements can be determined;

8. Rough indicators of population threshold size needed to support various services and facilities can be determined from scalograms that show the population sizes of settlements in which functions currently appear; and,

9. The scalogram can be used to make decisions about appropriate "packages" of investments for settlements at different levels in the spatial hierarchy.[13]

Thus, a manual scalogram has definite advantages over the computarized Guttman scale for application by rural planners, since it is easy to construct and interpret, requires no sophisticated training or equipment, and can be easily updated and revised using either "windshield surveys" or good aerial photography. Systematic reporting schemes can be designed to obtain information about changes in services and facilities in settlements of a region.

Threshold Analysis

Another means of assessing the functional characteristics of settlements in a region is through an analysis of the population sizes required to support those services, facilities and infrastructures that already exist within an area. In the Bicol River Basin planners used Marshall's approach to threshold analysis.[14] Marshall explains that "the threshold is that size of center which divides the ranked list of centers in such a way that the number of centers lacking the function above the division is equal to the number of centers possessing the function below the division." The method is especially appropriate for analysis of rural regions using data already collected for scalogram analysis, in that it requires only a ranked listing of settlements and the presence or absence of functions. Marshall suggests a modification on the general rule: "Once a threshold has been determined, this threshold (and the function to which it applies), will subsequently be disregarded unless at least half of all the centers above the threshold size possess the function in question."

The planners in Bicol adapted a procedure which is illustrated in Table 4-5:

1. Construct a table with a rank listing of centers according to population, a corresponding list of population data and the presence (1) or absence (0) of every function in each of the centers listed;

2. Apply Marshall's rule and identify each function's population threshold; and

3. Apply Marshall's supplementary rule and disregard functions eliminated by this process.[15]

Another method--the Reed-Muench approach--can also be used to determine the approximate threshold level of functions.[16] This process calculates the median population for a function by comparing the proportion of settlements that have the function at different population levels, using the formula:

$$Th = \frac{100 \times Ps}{Ps \times Ag}$$

where: Ps = number of settlements below a certain population level having the function; and,

Ag = number of settlements above this population level not having the function.

The median can also be obtained by graphically plotting values of Ps and Ag for different population levels as depicted in Figure 4-5.

There are strong limitations on the use of these methods, however. They tend to underestimate the population needed to support a function by using only the population size of the settlements rather than that of their service areas. Moreover, current thresholds may not realistically reflect the potential for settlements of various sizes to support services and facilities in an unintegrated and poorly developed settlement system. Indeed, they may reflect location decisions based on criteria other than economic efficiency. These methods do, however, offer a quick way of getting rough estimates of population threshold sizes for currently available services and facilities and can provide useful information if cross-checked or supplemented by other types of analyses.

TABLE 4-5

CALCULATION OF THRESHOLD LEVELS FOR CENTRAL PLACE FUNCTIONS

Central Places in Descending Order of Rank	Population Size	Function		
		1	2	3
A	10,000	1	1	1
B	8,000	0	1	1
C	6,000	0	1	1
D	5,500	0	0	1
E	3,000	0	0	1
F	2,700	1	1	0
G	1,900	0	1	1
H	1,700	0	0	1

Figure 4-5

REED–MUENCH GRAPHIC METHOD
OF PLOTTING THRESHOLD LEVELS
OF FUNCTIONS

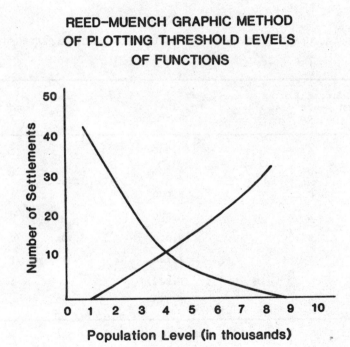

Weighted Centrality Indexes

Another exercise was used in both the Bicol River Basin and the the Potosi Region to obtain an indication of the centrality of settlements. This index measures functional complexity in terms not only of the number of functions in a place, but also their frequency of occurrence. Functions are assigned a weight in inverse proportion to the frequency with which they occur. Thus, a technical school or general hospital, which are found in only a few places, are weighted more heavily than an elementary school or health clinic, which are more widespread. The centrality index for a place is therefore the sum of the weights of the functions found there; the higher the index the greater its functional complexity.[17]

The procedure for calculating the weighted centrality index is as follows:[18]

1. Reproduce the Guttman scale in an inverted form with cases arranged vertically and items horizontally;
2. Total each row and column;
3. Using the assumption that the total number of functional attributes in the entire system has a combined centrality value of 100, determine the weight or "location coefficient" of the functional attribute by applying the formula:

$$C = t/T$$

where C = the weight of functional attribute t;
t = combined centrality value of 100;
T = total number of attributes in the system;

4. Add one block to the table and enter the weights computed;
5. Reproduce another table similar to that in step "1" displaying the weights calculated in step "3" and the total centrality values;
6. Sum the weights of each row to produce the indices of centrality.

Tables 4-6 and 4-7 illustrate the calculation of the centrality index. The centrality index allowed use of attributes or functions that appear as "errors" in the Guttman scale, based on the assumption that the presence of "rare" functions in an otherwise lower scale center does contribute to its centrality.

TABLE 4-6

CALCULATING WEIGHTS OF FUNCTIONS

Places	Functions										Total
	1	2	3	4	5	6	7	8	9	10	
A	1	1	1	1	1	1	1	1	1	1	10
B	1	1	1	1	1	1	1	0	1	0	8
C	1	1	1	1	1	1	0	0	0	0	6
D	1	1	1	1	1	1	0	1	0	0	7
E	1	1	1	1	1	0	0	0	0	0	5
F	1	1	1	1	0	0	0	0	0	0	4
G	1	1	1	0	0	0	0	0	0	0	3
H	1	1	1	0	0	0	0	0	0	0	3
Total Functions	8	8	8	6	5	4	2	2	2	1	46
Total Centrality	100	100	100	100	100	100	100	100	100	100	
Weights	12.5	12.5	12.5	16.6	20.0	25.0	50.0	50.0	50.0	100.0	

TABLE 4-7

CALCULATING CENTRALITY INDEXES

Places	Functions										Total
	1	2	3	4	5	6		8	9	10	
A	12.5	12.5	12.5	16.6	20.0	25.0	50.0	50.0	50.0	100.0	349.1
B	12.5	12.5	12.5	16.6	20.0	25.0	50.0		50.0		199.1
C	12.5	12.5	12.5	16.6	20.0	25.0					99.1
D	12.5	12.5	12.5	16.6	20.0	25.0					149.1
E	12.5	12.5	12.5	16.6	20.0	25.0		50.0			74.1
F	12.5	12.5	12.5	16.6	20.0						54.1
G	12.5	12.5	12.5	16.6							37.5
H	12.5	12.5	12.5								37.5
Total Centrality	100	100	100	100	100	100	100	100	100	100	1,000.0*

*Total does not add due to rounding.

DISTRIBUTION OF FUNCTIONS AND DELINEATION OF SETTLEMENT HIERARCHIES

The information collected for the scalogram analysis can also be used to determine the distribution of
functions among settlements in a region and to delineate
a hierarchy of settlements based on functional complexity. The distribution analysis indicates not only the
number of settlements that have a particular function,
but also the frequency with which a function appears
among settlements in the region. Together with a linkage analysis—which is described in Chapter Five—
estimates can be made of the accessibility of functions
for people living in different areas of the region. The
distribution of functions for the Bicol River Basin is
shown in Table 4-8.

The distribution of functions can also be used to
determine, along with the scalogram analysis, the functional hierarchy of settlements. In the Philippines,
for example, analysis suggested that the Bicol River
Basin was a region in which the services and facilities
that were needed for fulfilling basic human needs and
generating economic development were not only inadequate
but also highly concentrated in a few of the larger
central places. Those places were not easily accessible
to people living outside of their boundaries. The hierarchical distribution of settlements was strongly skewed
and the spatial system was neither well articulated nor
tightly integrated. Of the 1,419 discrete settlements
located in the basin—120 "built up" areas and more than
1,200 barangays—little more than half contained any of
the 64 functions. Nearly 90 percent of all functions
appeared in less than 20 percent of the settlements.
Most of the other functions that appeared in more than
20 percent of the settlements were either highly localized services or social organizations with little or no
productive capacity. And even among the built-up areas
functions were unevenly distributed. Nearly 60 percent
of all central functions appeared in less than 20 percent of the built-up areas, with one-fifth of these
places containing no functions at all.

Using the scalogram analysis, centrality indexes
and functional distributions, together with their knowledge of most of the settlements in the Basin, planners
were able to distinguish among four levels of settlements within the region. The four levels were determined by the following criteria:

Level I —all centers having at least 60 of the 64
facilities and services used in the
scalogram, centrality and functional
distribution analyses. At least half of
these functions should be central services and facilities serving a wide area.

TABLE 4-8

DISTRIBUTION OF FUNCTIONS AMONG SETTLEMENTS IN BICOL RIVER BASIN

Range of Settlements with Functions	Number of Functions	Type of Functions (Percent of Settlements with Function)
80 -100%	0	--
60 - 79%	0	--
40 - 59%	1	Agro-Processing Facility (41.1)
20 - 39%	3	Farmers Association (38.9) Cottage Industry (26.7) Civic Organization (26.7)
10 - 19%	3	Sports Association (13.6) Paved Basketball Court (13.5) Piped Water Supply (12.5)
5 - 9%	2	High School (7.8) Agricultural Extension Station (6.1)
2 - 4.9%	18	Photo Studio (4.8) Professional Organiza- tion (4.1) Plant Industries Exten- tion Office (4.3) Private Medical Clin- ic (3.8) Farm Supply-Agro- Chemical Store (3.4) Regular Public Mar- ket (3.2) Farm Equipment Repair Shop (2.9) Rural Bank (2.8) Ministry of Local Gov- ernment Office (4.1) Animal Industries Ex- tension Office (3.9) Auto Repair Shop (4.1) Cockfighting Pit (3.6) Construction Supply Store (3.4) Hardward Supply Store (3.1) Playground with Facili- ties (2.9) Housing Subdivision (2.8)

TABLE 4-8 (continued)

Range of Settlements with Functions	Number of Functions	Type of Functions (Percent of Settlements with Function)
1 - 1.9%	19	Labor Union (2.3), Cooperative Organization (2.2), Drugstore (1.8), Restaurant (1.8), Credit Union (1.8), Police Constabulary Station (1.8), Nightclub or Bar (1.7), Train Station (1.7), Surveyor (1.7), Appliance Store (1.6), Gymnasium/Auditorium (1.6), Bus Station with Repair Facilities (1.5), Private Hospital (1.5), Lodging Place (1.3), Vocational School (1.3), Power Plant or Station (1.2), Telecommunications Station (1.1), College (1.1), Bank or Financial Establishment (1.1), Optometry/Optical Shop (1.1), Funeral Parlor (1.0)
Less than 1.0%	18	Telephone Exchange (0.9), Xerox Copy Service (0.9), Cinema with Daily Run (0.8), Paluwagen (Welfare Society (0.7), Operational Government Hospital (0.7), Fire Station with Trucks (0.7), Shopping Center (0.6), Cinema with Less than Daily Run (0.7), Cemetery (0.6), Port or Pier (0.5), Radio Station (0.4), Nursing School (0.4), Newspaper Publisher (0.3), Security Agency (0.3), Red Cross Office (0.2), Hotel (0.3), Airport (0.1), Bowling Alley (0.2)

Level II --all centers at having at least 30 of the
64 functions; at least eleven of these
should be central functions.
Level III--all settlements having at least 10 of
the 64 facilities and services. At
least two of these should be non-
residentiary in nature.
Level IV --all places with less than 10 of the 64
facilities and services.

The hierarchy and the characteristics of its four
levels is shown in Table 4-9 and Figure 4.6. Only two
central places--the Naga-Camaligan and Legaspi-Daraga
urban areas, which contained most of the functions found
in the Basin--tended to serve as provincial centers and
offered a wide range of services and facilities. These
two places accounted for less than one percent of all
communities and contained about 10 percent of the
Bicol's population. Legaspi-Daraga had a centrality
index of 422 and Naga-Camaligan an index of 383, the two
highest in the region. At a second level were 11 settlements which as a group seemed to function as local
service centers, with from 31 to 54 functions. These
centers performed a few area-wide and a larger number of
local commercial and administrative functions. Almost
all had markets and were connected by the Manila highway
or provincial roads to smaller places in their immediate
hinterlands. Most had a few cottage industries, a
moderate range of commercial and service activities;
almost all had elementary and secondary schools, health
clinics and administrative offices of the municipality.
Their level of centrality ranged from 298 (Iriga) to 98
(Guinobatan). A third level of about 43 settlements,
representing about 3 percent of all communities and
about 10 percent of the Basin's population seemed to act
as small rural service centers in which 10 to 28 functions appeared. About half of these communities had
public markets, although the majority were no more than
collection points for agricultural produce that was
shipped to Naga or Legaspi for processing and sale.
Most had general stores, small groceries and sari-sari
stores. Very few of these settlements had cottage
industries; some had shops that turned out abaca craft,
candies and pastries. In a few there were warehouses,
copra storehouses, and trading establishments, sawmills
and furniture upholstery shops. Most had rice or corn
mills and about half contained a rural bank. Their
characteristic features were that most had rural extension services supplied by the national departments of
agriculture, plant industry, animal industry and local
government. Farmers associations, credit services and
cooperatives were found in many and most had either elementary or secondary schools. About half had private
health clinics or public health stations.19

TABLE 4-9

FUNCTIONAL COMPLEXITY OF LEVELS OF SETTLEMENTS IN BICOL RIVER BASIN,

Level of Hierarchy	Functional Character- istics	Number of Settlements	Settlements	Range of Functions	Percent of All Settlements	Percent of Basin Population	Average Popula- tion Size
I	Provincial Service Centers	2	Naga Camaligan	60-61	0.14	10.6	89,892
II	Local Service Centers	11	Iriga, Tabaco, Goa, Tigaon, Pili, Nabua, Baao, Guinobatan, Libmanan, Ligao	31-54	0.77	7.3	11,107
III	Rural Service Centers	43	37 Poplacions 6 Barangays	10-28	3.03	10.5	4,196
IV	Non-Central Places	1,363	2 Poblacions 1,361 Barangays	0- 9	96.06	71.6	922

132

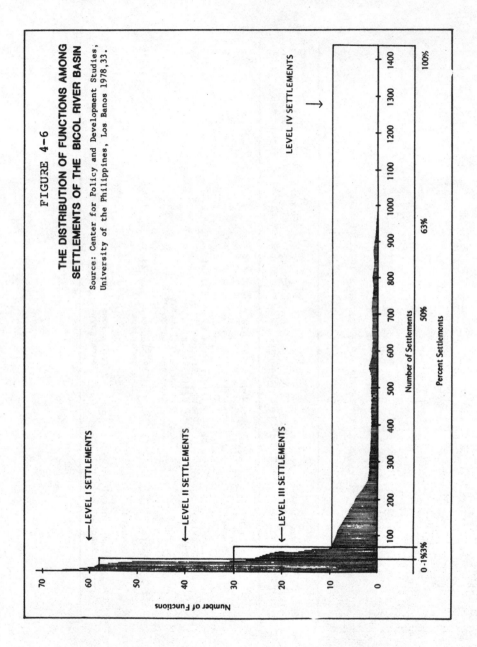

FIGURE 4-6

THE DISTRIBUTION OF FUNCTIONS AMONG
SETTLEMENTS OF THE BICOL RIVER BASIN

Source: Center for Policy and Development Studies,
University of the Philippines, Los Banos 1978,33.

The overwhelming majority of settlements in the
Bicol River Basin, however, were found to be non-
central places. Over 1,300, or about 96 percent of the
total--were villages of a few hundred or less families
engaged in subsistence or near subsistence agriculture
or working as tenants or on small family owned plots.
All communities in this category had less than 9 functions; most contained only a few or none at all. Those
that had a few functions usually only contained farmers
associations, a chapel or primary school, a sari-sari
store and sometimes an extension worker or small rice
or corn mill. More than 70 percent of the Basin's
population were found to be living in places that provided no central functions.

The scale analysis of the Bicol River Basin showed
very little functional distinction among most settlements, except for the Level I communities and a few in
Level II. The eleven settlements in Level II did not
differ from each other significantly in the range of
functions they provided nor did they differ greatly
from many of the settlements found in Level III. In
reality, then, there was little functional differentia-
tion or specialization among most settlements in the
Bicol River Basin, due primarily to the predominance of
subsistence agricultural economy and the low levels of
household income throughout the region.

A similar analysis done in the Department of
Potosi in Bolivia yielded the results summarized in
Table 4-10. At one end of the scale was the city of
Potosi, which contained all but two of the 58 functions
included in the scalogram: the office of a Sub-prefect
which occurred only in provincial capitals, and a medical post which was usually located in villages and
small towns. At the other end of the scale were the
smallest villages with very few amenities, perhaps a
junior school, piped drinking water or a small grocery
store. Between these two extremes, there appeared to
be two clear intervals, both of them at the upper end.
The first fell between the city of Potosi with 56 functions and the second ranked Uyuni with 46 functions.
The second interval was between sixth placed Uncia with
35 and seventh placed Atocha with 29. Further down the
list no such obvious breaks occurred. But Evans suggests that this may indicate that there is only one
city in the first tier of the hierarchy, the city of
Potosi, followed by a group of five at the second
level--Uyuni, Tupiza, Villazon, Llallagua and Uncia.
The latter two were within five kilometers of each
other and were therefore treated as a single urban
area. Together they had 45 functions, which emphasizes
the gap between the second and third group beginning
with Atocha.[20]

TABLE 4-10

FUNCTIONAL CHARACTERISTICS OF SETTLEMENTS IN POTOSI, BOLIVIA

Level and Settlement Type	Number of Functions	Centrality Index	Number of Functions of Level i or Higher
I Regional center	56	675	6
City of Potosi			
II Sub-regional center	(min 35)	(min 200.0)	(min 10 max 18)
Uyuni	46	372.7	17
Tupiza	46	299.4	15
Villazon	43	294.6	16
Llallagua	42	253.3	11
Uncia .	35	209.3	10
III Rural center	(min 20)	(min 100.0)	(min 10 max 38)
Atocha	28	149.2	14
Betanzos	27	155.0	16
Siglo XX	27	153.3	15
Cotagaita	26	131.5	13
Colquechaca	24	121.7	11
Catavi	23	126.7	10
Quechisla	23	101.2	11
Rosario Tazna	23	104.7	11
Puna	22	123.6	10
Llica	22	87.0	10
Killpani	20	100.0	12
IV Local center	(min 13)	(min 50.0)	(min 7 max 43)
Pulacayo	23	92.2	12
San Pedro de Buena Vista	19	79.4	12
Chayanta	19	75.4	9
Sacaca	18	79.6	11
Telamayu	18	71.8	10
San Pedro de Quemez	17	61.0	8
Tatasi	17	72.5	9
Cancaniri	17	68.2	10
Punutuma	17	71.9	10
Rio Mulatos	17	64.5	9
Caiza "D"	16	60.3	8
Caracota	16	95.3	9
Otavi	15	81.0	9
Colcha "K"	15	53.5	7
Vitichi	15	70.7	7
Ocuri	15	59.9	8
Chilcobija	15	65.5	7
Colavi Mina	15	52.2	7
Macha	15	52.8	9
Entre Rios	14	72.8	8
Pocoata	14	47.2	8
Animas	14	57.5	8
Santa Barbara	14	46.7	7
Huanaque	14	87.7	7
San Pablo de Lipez	13	45.6	9
Santa Ana	13	48.8	9

The scalogram, centrality and functional distribution analyses suggested that the hierarchy of settlements of Potosi consisted of five levels[21] (see Table 4-11). At the top was the regional center, the City of Potosi, with a population of about 77,000 and a centrality index of 675, the highest in the region. The city had almost a full range of the 58 functions, including several that appeared only once in the region: a university, the Prefecture office, editorial offices of a newspaper, a television station and regular air service.

At a second level were four towns with an average population of 12,500: the urban area of Llallagua/Unica in the north, Uyuni in the west, Tupiza in the south, and Villazon on the border with Argentina. Centrality indices ranged from 373 for Uyuni to 209 for Uncia. Treating Llallgua/Uncia as a single entity, this group of towns possessed a similar range of between 43 and 46 functions, typical of which were hospitals, daily markets, manufacturing industry, commercial banks, rail service, long distance telephone service, and depositories of the central Mining Bank, where independent mining concerns could sell their output to the government.

There was a wide gap in functional complexity between the second and third tiers of the hierarchy. The rural service centers consisted of only eleven settlements with a mean population of 3,200. These centers had centrality indices ranging from 87 to 149, and between 20 and 28 functions. At the fourth level were 26 places, having centrality indices of 45 to 95 and containing anywhere from 13 to 23 functions, most typically a post office, high school, doctor's clinic and clothing store. The remaining seventy settlements fell into the fifth category of villages or non-central places, having twelve functions or less, such as drinking water, electricity, or a food store, most of which served only the residents of the immediate vicinity.

The scalogram revealed a weak relationship between the size of the settlement, measured by population, and its functional complexity. Uyuni, for example, with barely a quarter of the 30,000 population of the Llalagua/Uncia urban area, had the same number of functions, while Llica and Cotagaita with around 1,000 inhabitants each, had more functions than Catavi, which had seven times the number of residents. Location provides part of the explanation: the distance of center to its nearest larger-sized neighbor influences the kinds of functions it can support. Thus, Uyuni had no competition for miles around, while Catavi was only a five-minute bus ride from Llallagua. Another explanation stems from the favored treatment of the mining centers, which were often equipped with basic infrastruc-

TABLE 4-11

FUNCTIONAL ATTRIBUTES OF SETTLEMENTS AT EACH LEVEL OF THE HIERARCHY, POTOSI, BOLIVIA

Level	Function Range	Index Range	Typical Functions	Average Population	Percent of Departmental Population
I Regional Center	56	657	Prefecture university air service television station newspaper office	7,334	11.7
II Sub-regional center	35-46	209-381	rail service long distance telephone daily market hospital manufacturing industry banks farm supply stores	1,252	9.5
III Rural center	20-28	87-156	inter-urban bus service newspaper delivery radio communication weekly market health center pharmacy vehicle repair workshop gas station	3,238	5.4
IV Local	13-23	46-92	post and telegraph office doctor's clinic high school clothes store	1,371	5.2
V Villages (non-central places)	0-12	0-84	junior school grocery store drinking water	457	4.8

Source: H. Evans, Urban Functions in Rural Development: The Case of the Potosi Region in Bolivia, Washington: USAID, 1982.

ture, health and education services, subsidized provision stores and other facilities, usually financed by the semi-autonomous state mining corporation, COMIBOL, or occasionally by large private mining companies. A further factor is the low level of urbanization in the region. With the majority of Potosinos scattered in small villages and rural areas, the population size of a settlement was a poor guide to the number of rural people who used its services and facilities.[22]

In both the Bicol River Basin and the Department of Potosi, the UFRD project's settlement system analysis gave planners and policy-makers the first statistical profile of towns and villages within their regions. In some cases it documented for the first time general knowledge about settlements in those regions. In other cases it provided new information about the distribution of services and facilities, infrastructure, productive activities and local resources. In both regions, for the first time, planners had methods and techniques for identifying, collecting and organizing information about the settlement system, the distribution of functions among settlements and the settlement hierarchy. Although this information is useful in creating a profile of settlements within the region, a better understanding of the patterns of interaction among settlements is also needed to understand the dynamics of regional development or underdevelopment. This requires an analysis of spatial linkages, one method of which is described in the next chapter.

138

NOTES

1. See P. Haggett, A.D. Cliff and A. Frey, _Location Analysis in Human Geography_, New York: Wiley, 1977.
2. Republic of the Philippines, _Census of Population and Housing_, Manila: National Census and Statistics Office, 1974.
3. Hugh Evans, _Urban Functions in Rural Development: The Case of the Potosi Region in Bolivia_, (Washington: U.S. Agency for International Development, 1982), pp. 37-38.
4. H.E. Voelkner, _Shortcut Methods to Assess Poverty and Basic Needs for Rural Regional Planning_, Geneva: United Nations Research Institute for Social Development, 1978.
5. _Ibid_., p. 43.
6. Agapito M. Tria III, _SSRU Municipal Inventory_. Naga, The Philippines: Social Survey Research Unit, Bicol River Basin Development Program, 1974.
7. Bicol River Basin Development Program, _Urban Functions in Rural Development: A Research Project in Spatial Analysis and Planning_, Pili, The Philippines: BRBDP, 1978.
8. See Dennis A. Rondinelli, "Spatial Analysis for Regional Development: A Case Study in the Bicol River Basin of the Philippines," _Resource Systems Theory and Methodology Series_, No. 2, Tokyo: United Nations University Press, 1980.
9. Tria, _op. cit._, lists the functions surveyed.
10. Bicol River Basin Development Program, _op. cit_.
11. H. Benjamin Fisher, "Methods of Identification of Agro-Urban Centers at the Kapubaten and Provincial Levels," (Jakarta: Ford Foundation, 1975) mimeographed.
12. H.E. Voelkner, "The Structural Complexity Growth Model and Scalogram Analysis of Development and Human Ecosystems," unpublished paper, (Washington: World Bank, 1974), p. 16.
13. See Rondinelli, "Spatial Analysis for Regional Develop-ment." _op. cit._ for a more detailed description.
14. See John U. Marshall, _The Location of Service Towns_, Toronto: University of Toronto Press, 1969.
15. Junio M. Ragragio, "The Design for the Identification of the Hierarchy, Centrality and Threshold of the Central Place System in the Bicol River Basin," Project Discussion Paper, (College, Laguna: Center for Policy and Development Studies, University of the Philippines--Los Banos, 1977.
16. See Haggett, Cliff and Frey _op. cit._ for a more detailed explanation.

17. Evans, op. cit.
18. Ragragio, op. cit.
19. Dennis A. Rondinelli, "Applied Policy Analysis for Integrated Regional Development Planning in the Philippines," Third World Planning Review, Vol. i, No. 2 (Autumn 1979), pp. 150-178.
20. Evans, op. cit., pp. 39-45.
21. Ibid., pp. 45-48.
22. Ibid., pp. 77-88.

5
Spatial Linkage Analysis

A region is not only a system of functionally
diversified settlements but also a network of social,
economic, and physical interactions. The processes of
interaction are shaped by linkages among settlements.
They are the means through which people living in rural
areas and small villages obtain access to services,
facilities, infrastructure and economic activities
located in towns and cities. Through these linkages
rural people receive many of the inputs needed to
increase agricultural productivity and market the goods
they produce. Therefore, regional planners and policy-
makers must be concerned about the effectiveness of
these processes of interaction and the degree to which
settlements are linked to each other in ways that provide a maximum amount of access to people living in all
parts of the region.

THE ROLE OF LINKAGES IN REGIONAL DEVELOPMENT

Regional development occurs through the growth and
diversification of settlements and the creation of new
and stronger linkages among them.[1] In some cases the
extension of physical linkages such as road, rail or
river transport promotes growth and diversification in
existing settlements; in others it stimulates the
growth of new central places. New linkages usually
promote greater interaction between settlements and
their rural hinterlands. Moreover, the linkages that
integrate a settlement system are themselves inextric-
ably linked. Creating one new linkage can produce a
"cascade effect," making other activities and linkages
possible. Once a new set of linkages is introduced
into a rural market system, for example, it can trigger
a set of "circular and cumulative" changes that promote
further growth and change. Simply improving transportation among villages often leads to reorganization and
expansion of existing periodic markets. Displacement

141

of weak or unsuccessful markets and redistribution of
commerce and trade can create entirely new markets and
increase demands on the transportation system.[2] New
physical linkages between urban centers and rural
villages can change the flow of economic resources, the
social pattern of interaction and the movement of
people and goods. Closer interaction among villages,
market towns, intermediate cities and major metropolitan centers can make it more convenient and less
expensive to integrate technology at each level of the
spatial hierarchy and to distribute more widely services that are needed for regional development.

In its manual on rural service center planning,
ESCAP points out that analysis of urban and rural linkages can provide planners with important information
about the following questions concerning regional
development:[3]

-- What is the pattern of flows of agricultural products from rural areas to
   demand centers?
-- Which areas provide the raw materials for
   manufacturing activities?
-- To which centers do farmers go to obtain
   the agricultural inputs they need, such as
   fertilizers, farm implements, improved
   seed and credit?
-- What changes can be made in the road network to improve the marketing of rural
   products?
-- Does the regional resource base provide
   the potential to support additional production and processing activities?
-- What new activities can be supported?
   What linkages are needed to implement
   these activities?
-- What is the pattern of key communications
   linkages?
-- What are the daily, weekly and seasonal
   commuting patterns of off-farm labor?
-- What are the key bottlenecks in the existing linkage system?

A complete set of linkages can be found in more
developed regions[4] (see Table 5-1). These include:

1. Physical Linkages. The spatial integration of
communities results primarily from physical linkages
through man-made or natural transportation networks.
New roads, water channels and rail systems can reduce
travel time, lower shipping costs, widen marketing,
commuting and migration opportunities, allow greater
access to non-agricultural employment, improve communications and extend areas of service delivery. Farm-
to-market roads have promoted the creation of new
markets in rural areas, increased interaction among

TABLE 5-1

MAJOR LINKAGES IN SPATIAL DEVELOPMENT

TYPE	ELEMENTS
Physical Linkages	Road Networks River and Water Transport Networks Railroad Networks Ecological Interdependencies
Economic Linkages	Market Patterns Raw Materials and Intermediate Goods Flows Capital Flows Production Linkages--Backward, Forward and Lateral Consumption and Shopping Patterns Income Flows Sectoral and Interregional Commodity Flows "Cross Linkages"
Population Movement Linkages	Migration--Temporary and Permanent Journey to Work
Technological Linkages	Technology Interdependencies Irrigation Systems Telecommunications Systems
Social Interac- tion Linkages	Visiting Patterns Kinship Patterns Rites, Rituals and Religious Activities Social Group Interaction
Service Delivery Linkages	Energy Flows and Networks Credit and Financial Networks Education, Training and Extension Linkages Health Service Delivery Systems Professional, Commercial and Technical Service Patterns Transport Service Systems
Political, Admin- istrative, and Organizational Linkages	Structural Relationships Government Budgetary Flows Organizational Interdependencies Authority-Approval-Supervision Patterns Inter-jurisdictional Transaction Patterns Informal Political Decision Chains

villages, linked agricultural production areas to crop
collection and distribution centers and made new crops
economically viable. Those areas of a region without
easy physical access to central places are usually
characterized by low social mobility, localized and
subsistence agriculture, and low levels of trade.

    2. Economic Linkages. Economic interaction also
promotes spatial integration. The most important linkages are market networks through which commodities, raw
materials, and manufactured products flow among settlements; capital and income flows; and forward and backward production linkages among manufacturing and agricultural processing activities. The expansion of
market linkages is a primary force in commercializing
agriculture, diversifying production and expanding the
spatial system of exchange.[5] Since the market town is
the main channel through which rural people obtain
basic goods and services in return for their agricultural products, the impact of vertical coordination of
marketing systems can have widespread effects and provide substantial benefits to the farmer. It can increase farmers' bargaining powers by improving price
information and market competitiveness, reduce trans-
action and physical distribution costs by standardizing
marketing procedures and allowing farmers to use more
efficient means of transporting their goods. Vertical
linkages can also reduce losses and improve quality by
establishing incentives for standardized grading, processing and packaging.[6]

    The combination of increased transportation and
marketing linkages within a region can encourage the
growth of nested and integrated markets, expand patterns of exchange for agricultural commodities and
ensure broader access for rural people to basic goods
and services.[7]

    3. Population Movement Linkages. Short-term and
permanent migration is a ubiquitous characteristic of
development and an important form of urban-rural linkage. Temporary migration and journey-to-work, more
strongly than other forms of spatial interaction,
depend on transportation and communication linkages
between urban and rural areas, and on the location of
industrial activities in intermediate cities and
smaller towns. More permanent migration depends on a
wider range of economic and social determinants,
including the availability of jobs in towns and cities;
wage, public service and educational opportunity dif-
ferentials between cities and villages; and the distance, cost and convenience of moving. Rural people,
given potential job opportunities and convenient means
of travel, are more likely to migrate to a city where
they have friends or kin.[8]

4. <u>Technological Linkages</u>. Developing regions
need a variety of technologies, appropriate to different social, economic, technical and administrative
capacities of communities of different sizes and stages
of development. Technology--equipment, procedures and
methods of production--must also be integrated spatially and functionally, since no single technological
innovation will promote social and economic transformation in a region unless it is appropriate to local
needs and conditions, and linked to both higher and
lower levels of technology and related inputs. Spatial
and organizational linkages are especially crucial for
capital-intensive industrial technologies. To have an
impact on development, capital technologies must be
introduced into industries with strong backward and
forward production linkages and in countries where
there are strong connections between government scientific programs and private sector activities. As
Parent points out, each branch of a major industry
" . . . produces linkage effects which spread to other
apparently quite unconnected industries," and the
impact of the new technology in a leading industry will
then depend " . . . on several factors including the
importance of the originating industry in total industrial production and the number of its direct connections with other industries. If the supporting industries are missing, attempts to establish leading industries will fail."[9] Similarly, if elements of the spatial structure which allow industry to disperse geographically are missing, technological linkages and
channels of innovation will not promote widespread
growth.

5. <u>Social Linkages</u>. Market towns and intermediate cities do more than generate physical and economic activities, they are the focal points for a wide
variety of social linkages among settlements and
between central places and their rural hinterlands.
Market centers perform many social roles in rural
areas. The types and frequency of economic activities
are often closely linked to social events. Traditional
markets provide an important locus of social interaction; marketplaces are often used for games and
dances; they contain a variety of social facilities--
restaurants, bars, baths, churches, temples, and
cinemas--attracting people from the villages not only
to exchange goods and services but also to engage in
recreation and to meet friends, acquaintances, and
kin.[10] The growth of market towns in many countries
has a profound effect on rural social interaction.
Market centers provide a spatial focus for social
interaction within a broad trading area. Because
people make regular visits to the market throughout
their lifetime, even the poorest farmers come to know

almost every other adult in the marketing area; marriage arrangements are often made from within the
trading boundaries; credit and lending decisions are
based on people's reputations formed through frequent
market transactions; and the acceptance of common criteria of exchange, such as standard weights and measures, evolve from the need to maintain social harmony
among disparate villages and groups within a trading
area.[11] With market expansion and increasing commercialization of agriculture, periodic markets evolve
into permanent places of exchange, daily markets dis-
place smaller, infrequent exchange points, and diffuse
social linkages promote increasing social and spatial
integration. Widening market areas extend the spatial
range of social interaction for marriage arrangements,
steadily integrating smaller clans, communities and
villages, promoting new kinship ties and visiting
patterns, transforming social group and organizational
relations.[12]

6. _Service Delivery Linkages_. Increasing the
physical, economic and technological linkages among
central places is critical to expanding service delivery networks in developing nations. Urban centers and
rural areas must be closely linked in order to distribute social and commercial services more widely and to
increase the access of rural residents to urban amenities. Nearly all services require the support of a
minimum number of people concentrated in a limited geographical area, a "threshold population" of sufficient
size and density to attract enough customers to earn
profits for suppliers of commercial and professional
services and to allow public services to reach the
largest number of people at the lowest cost. Threshold
levels for services vary widely. Because each service
has a specific threshold, the types, degree of specialization and delivery range of services found in any
given community depends on the size and density of its
population, its occupational profile and income distribution, transportation access and economic diversification. All other things being equal, the "hierarchy" of
services in a region is closely related to the hierarchy of central places. Larger population size and
higher density create economies of scale that allow
services to be offered at lower cost.

Services also have different "ranges of influence," the distance over which they can be extended or
that people will travel to purchase or use them. The
larger the area of influence and the more densely concentrated the users within that area, the more efficiently services can be provided, especially those
requiring physical facilities or infrastructure for
delivery such as water, sanitation, energy and health.
The World Bank points out that per capita costs of

supplying water and sanitation services increases substantially in smaller communities: " . . . sector
characteristics change markedly as one progresses from
large urban centers, through medium sized cities, small
towns and villages, to the dispersed population. The
administrative structure becomes more diffuse, income
levels decline, and per capita costs for equivalent
levels of service tend to increase."[13] In areas with
widely scattered populations and small central places
there exists less institutional, financial and technological capability to deliver services efficiently.

Most developing regions require a hierarchy of
services with a range of facilities appropriate to the
needs and support capacity of different levels in the
spatial system. Public health services, for instance,
can usually be efficiently provided to widely scattered
villages and hamlets only in the form of small clinics
that offer basic preventive treatment, first aid,
maternity care, and perhaps family planning information, staffed by a nurse or paramedic. Small hospitals
with basic treatment and diagnostic facilities, and
with either a visiting or part-time physician, a nurse
or paramedic requires a larger service area and usually
is found only in large market towns or small cities. A
full services general hospital with a small staff of
doctors and more extensive diagnostic and treatment
equipment is most often found in intermediate cities or
regional centers. Diversified, specialized medical
centers with a staff of full-time physicians and tech-
nicians, containing more sophisticated diagnostic and
treatment equipment, can usually only be supported by
major metropolitan areas.

7. _Political, Administrative and Organizational_
Linkages. Finally, spatial systems are integrated and
transformed through a set of political and administrative linkages reflected in formal government structural
relationships, flows of public budget resources, administrative authority, supervision and approval patterns,
transactions among government jurisdictions, informal
political influence, and interdependencies among spatially dispersed specialized organizations.

Linkages among settlements evolve because in
nearly every developing nation government functions,
services and resources are fragmented among organizations and jurisdictions. Linkages among government
organizations not only extend services, facilities, and
budget resources throughout the spatial system, but
also act as channels for obtaining political support
and authority to undertake activities that are essential to integrated development. As Uphoff and Esman
conclude from their reivew of case studies of rural
development in Asia, " . . . organization for rural
development must be seen as a system of institutions

performing various functions in the rural sector . . .
and effectiveness of linkages between and among institutions, horizontally with other organizations at the
same level and especially vertically between local
organizations and structures at the center of government which set policy and allocate resources [is]
essential to the success of rural development."14

As urban centers grow and new central places
emerge, political and administrative linkages change
and functions are transformed within each center. The
number of social functions performed by government
tends to increase as communities grow. A variety of
health, education, security, welfare and other services
that are usually offered in rural areas and villages by
extended families are provided by government in cities
and metropolitan areas.

An analysis of these linkages can provide information with which planners and policy-makers can determine the degree to which settlements within the region
are integrated, the degree to which people living in
various parts of the region have access to town-based
services and facilities, and the approximate service
areas of central place settlements.

The linkage analysis methodologies used in UFRD
may not address all of these issues directly; they are
intended, instead, to provide a profile or overview of
the system of linkages in a region that will lead planners to design more detailed studies. But the methods
described here can provide planners and policy-makers
with sufficient information about the nature and extent
of linkages to begin refining their investment patterns
to strengthen the network of linkages and to identify
projects that are needed immediately to increase the
interaction among strategic settlements and the access
of rural people to central places.

The Urban Functions in Rural Development approach
uses a number of methods to identify and assess the
strength of linkages among settlements: market center
studies, transport and physical access analyses, goods
and services flow analyses, service area analyses, and
social interaction studies.

MARKET CENTER STUDIES

The UFRD analyses of market centers and market
linkages are heavily based on methodologies suggested
by Bromley.15 Bromley defines a market as a "public
gathering of buyers and sellers of commodities meeting
at an appointed or customary location at regular intervals ranging from daily to monthly."16 A market center
is a nucleated settlement with one or more markets each
week. Its size and importance are related to the
amount of market activity taking place there each time

the market meets. Markets can be divided into daily markets meeting every day of the week, and periodic markets meeting less frequently.

A wide variety of other commercial activities are usually associated with larger market places. As noted in Chapter One, most market places offer opportunities for small farmers to trade their produce, vegetables, grains, rice and other staples; for stock raisers to sell cattle, goats, sheep and dairy products; for gatherers to exchange firewood, lumber, charcoal, lime, and other uncultivated products; for fishermen to sell their catches; for artisans to sell or trade textiles, pottery, baskets, woven materials, iron, brick- or wood-work, household utensils and an enormous variety of households goods. Services located near the market place can reach large numbers of consumers more efficiently. Carpenters, masons, bakers, butchers, barbers, midwives, blacksmiths, tailors, seamstresses, stonecutters, traditional healers and herb vendors, and marriage brokers ply their trades in or near the markets along with mechanics, repairmen, doctors, druggists, agricultural suppliers, and others whose permanent shops or offices are located near the marketplace. Moreover, larger daily markets often support traveling vendors, storekeepers, agents, brokers, middlemen, and truckers, moneylenders, commission agents, warehouse owners and others who facilitate market trade.[17] Because people often come from many miles around to trade or participate in market centers, market trade patterns are important integrating linkages and indicators of the "service area" of a central place. In regions where market systems are well developed, the hierarchy of settlements often conforms quite closely to the hierarchy of market centers.

Market center analysis involves four major activities: (1) compiling a list of market centers and market days within the region; (2) mapping market centers and classifying them by size and periodicity; (3) measuring market activity; and (4) determining market centers' areas of influence.[18]

1. Compiling a list of market centers and market days. In countries where gazeteers or agricultural censuses have already compiled information on markets, their meeting days and types of activities and stalls, the data needed for regional market analysis can simply be derived from those reports and cross-checked or updated through sample field surveys. Where such information has not already been collected, the list of market centers must be complied through key informant interviews and field surveys. Field visits are usually needed to determine where market places are located, the days of the week on which they meet, their size and importance in terms of numbers of participants and the

volume and types of goods traded. In compiling lists
of market centers through field surveys, Bromley suggests that planners attempt to produce as detailed a
list of nucleated settlements and concentrations of
commercial activities as possible. Attempts should be
made to specify for each settlement: its population,
location of "competing" settlements, information about
the road network, administrative status, number and
types of transportation services, and the presence or
absence of the types of services, facilities, organizations, infrastructure and other functions that are
described in the scalogram analysis.[19]

    2. <u>Mapping market centers and classifying them by
size and periodicity</u>. When a list is compiled it
should be transferred to a map. Size classifications
can be made using the number of stalls or amount of
market fees collected by local authorities as rough
indicators. The map should be coded by the day of the
week and the number of times a week the market oper-
ates.

    3. <u>Measuring market activity</u>. Bromley suggests a
number of direct and indirect methods of measuring
market activity.[20] Indirect measures include the
levels of market taxes collected, the number of
licenses issued, numbers of market stalls, the square
footage of the market occupied by traders, the size of
permanent market buildings and other data often collected by local or national governments. These may be
incomplete or inaccurate, however, both because of the
inefficiency of administrative procedures and because
much marketing activity takes place outside of permanent market buildings, on sidewalks or roads surrounding
the formal market place.

More direct measures attempt to estimate market
turnover by counting numbers of traders and types of
merchandise. Counting sheets can be used on which
surveyors note the number of traders in and around the
market place and the categories of goods they sell.
The surveyors can use a checklist of categories of
goods, including perishables such as fruits, vegetables, grains, root crops, preserves, flour, bread,
sugar, salt, fats, meat, fish, eggs, milk, cheese, food
and drink for ready consumption, fuel and animal
fodder, and live domestic animals such as chickens.
They should also count durables and services, such as
textiles, clothing, footwear, metal, plastic and glass
products, medicines, artisanal goods, tailor, cobbler
or repair services, and other types of goods or services traded in the market place. The counts should be
taken over a number of weeks to account for variations
in market activity.

4. __Determining market centers' areas of influ-
ence.__ Bromley points out that rough approximations can
be made of a market's area of influence by examining
administrative divisions, natural barriers, transport
networks and services, and physical terrain features in
the area around market centers to judge how far people
are likely to travel to participate in the center's
marketing activities.[21] Where registers are kept of
ferry traffic, road toll collections or police check-
point traffic, these may provide data that allow planners to construct traffic volume and flow patterns in
and out of a market center. Bus companies or those
that offer other forms of transportation to and from
market places also provide information useful for esti-
mating the service area of a market center.

A more detailed and precise estimate of market
activity must rely on field surveys. Bromley suggests
"quota sampling" questionnaires for rapid market activity analyses. He describes the method as follows:

Quota samples are based on a count of stalls or
traders taken earlier the same day, and involve
interviewing a specific portion of all traders in
each of the classificatory categories used in the
count. For example, a 5% (one in 20) sample may
imply interviewing 12 female vegetable sellers,
two male vegetable sellers, five female clothing
sellers, and 11 male clothing sellers.

Interviewers then go out into the marketplace
interviewing traders in each category until their
quota of successful interviews is completed.
'Refusals' or 'idiotic responses' and other negative interviews are simply replaced by another
interview so as to ensure that the target is
achieved.

Within each category interviewers are instructed
to ensure a reasonably broad spatial distribution
of cases, bearing in mind the overall distribution
of traders in that category, and to avoid concentrating on specific types of traders within a
category (e.g., old vegetable sellers, rather than
interviewing a mixture of old and young roughly
proportional to their distribution in the total
population of vegetable sellers).[22]

The quota sample techniques can be used to gather
information about the distance from which traders come
to participate in market activities, their places of
residence, supplementary occupations, working routes
and stopover points, means of transportation, number
and location of marketplaces in which they trade, and
sources of the goods in which they trade.

The activity data can be mapped, and the influence
or service-area of the market centers can be delineated

based on the distances from which participants come,
the flows of goods into and out of the market place and
the routes or networks of markets that traders use.
The data can also be used to trace the linkages among
settlements in a market center's network and the interactions among them in the market system.

A more detailed form of analysis can be used for
periodic markets in rural areas, one that Bromley calls
market movement surveys.[23] These are simultaneous
counts and origin-destination surveys of vehicles and
pedestrians going into each entrance of a market center
during peak periods of a market day. The surveys can
be done using volunteer high school students or paid
young-adult assistants. Bromley suggests that detailed
plans and arrangements be made over a two week period
prior to the actual survey. They should be organized
to achieve five major goals:[24]

a. To secure local collaboration from police,
   army detachments and, most important of all,
   from secondary schools or other potential
   sources of census-takers;

b. To map the perimeter of the market center, and
   all the roads and paths leading into the settlement;

c. To observe the flow of people into the market
   center on, and before, the major market day,
   in order to determine the starting and finishing times of pedestrian and vehicle flows into
   the market center;

d. To prepare a detailed plan of action, including timings of commencement and termination of
   work, dropping off the survey takers at their
   posts, serving refreshments, changing shifts,
   checking on efficiency, picking everyone up at
   the end of their jobs, and collecting the results; and

e. To hold one or more briefing sessions for the
   6-100 people participating in the work.

Actual survey work usually begins prior to the
time when significant numbers of people begin coming
into the market center on market day. It continues
until the flow begins to drop off significantly. Two
pairs of surveyors are stationed at each entrance to
the market center. One counts pedestrians, the other
counts vehicles. Those counting vehicles must have the
assistance of a policeman or soldier to control the
flow of traffic.

Pedestrians (including people on bicycles, motorcycles and animal-pulled carts) are asked where they
come from. Motor vehicles are classified by type--
buses, trucks, cars, jeeps or others--and drivers are
asked where the journey originated and where it will

end. Rough counts are made of passengers, and information is requested on the types and amounts of products and livestock carried into the market.

Market movement data can be used to estimate the linkages among settlements, and also the service area of market centers, the volume and flow of different types of goods traded, and the origins and destinations of market participants.

The market center studies carried out in the UFRD projects in the Philippines and Bolivia used different combinations of methods suggested by Bromley.

In the Bicol River Basin of the Philippines, a sample market center study was done of six large regular markets and six small periodic markets, which were considered by local planners to be the most important and most representative. A comprehensive market centers study was to be carried out later during a planned agricultural marketing study of the region. A survey of the six major market centers in Camarines Sur and Albay Provinces was conducted to trace the origin and destination of agricultural and manufactured commodities and to determine the service areas of these markets. Naga, Iriga, Goa, Legaspi, Tabaco and Ligao were selected as the leading market centers based on their strategic location, population size and their estimated volume of market activity.

The number of respondents was determined by proportional allocation--i.e., the population by type of commodity was first determined and the samples were taken by choosing every nth trader or producer. Using prepared questionnaires, one hundred traders and middlemen and fifty producers from each market center were interviewed. These respondents were drawn from the registered traders in the market.

The information that was gathered included: (a) source and destination of commodities; (b) type of buyer and seller; (c) place of sales and purchases; (d) type and cost of transport; (e) frequency of disposal and purchases; (f) packing and storage practices; (g) mode of payment; (h) problems encountered; and (i) other related information.

The commodities included were: (a) rice and palay; (b) corn; (c) sugar; (d) copra and coconut; (e) vegetables; (f) poultry and livestock; (g) fish; (h) manufactured goods; (i) agricultural and veterinary products; (j) farm implements; and (k) cottage industry products.

The six small markets, which operate once or twice a week, were studied to determine the degree to which they are linked to larger markets and to the rural areas in which they are located. The sample included three centers in Camarines Sur Province (Payatan, San Gabriel, and San Ramon) and three in Albay Province

(Pili, Paulba and Sinungtan). Interviewers sought information on the historical factors that brought the market into existence, the origin and destination of commodities traded in the market place, the linkages between these market centers and other periodic markets and between them and their rural hinterlands, marketing practices and conditions, marketing problems and potential solutions, and related information.

The sample surveys yielded a great deal of information not only about particular market centers but also about the nature of the marketing center system in the Basin. The Bicol planners found that:25

1. Markets in the Bicol River Basin were primarily local trading centers. The analysis of commodity flows in the six major regular markets showed that they functioned largely as local centers of trade. Nearly half of the commodity transactions in the Basin's largest market at Naga City were local; the remaining half were either with Manila or with periodic markets in the immediately surrounding area of the city. The same pattern of trade was characteristic of the second largest market, in Legaspi. Nearly 70 percent of the transactions occurring in the Tabaco market were among people who lived within a 5 km. radius of the town. For all six major markets, well over two-thirds of their transactions were among people living within a 10 km. area. Only about 12 percent of the transactions in Naga and Legaspi markets were with centers outside of the region, and nearly all were with the national capital, Manila. Figure 5-1 shows the degree to which the major markets in the Basin were linked to other market centers.

2. Market centers in the Basin had narrowly circumscribed service areas and provided limited access to people living outside of them. Planners found that the service areas of even the largest market centers in the Basin--Naga and Legaspi--did not encompass large portions of their provinces. They discovered that Naga's service area encompassed only 28 of the 37 municipalities in its province, while Legaspi's covered only 12 of the 17 municipalities in its province. Transactions between Naga and 13 of the 28 municipalities with which it had linkages were less than one percent of the total trading activity. Significant transactions between traders in the Legaspi market took place with those in only 10 of Albay's municipalities. Moreover, the trading linkages between Naga and Legaspi were minimal, accounting for only 3 percent of Naga's transactions and 2 percent of Legaspi's. The degree of interaction between the major markets in the Basin are depicted in Figure 5-2.

The service areas of the periodic markets, as might be expected, were even more constrained. Trans-

FIGURE 5-1

ORGANIZATIONAL LINKAGES AMONG SIX MAJOR MARKETS IN BICOL RIVER BASIN

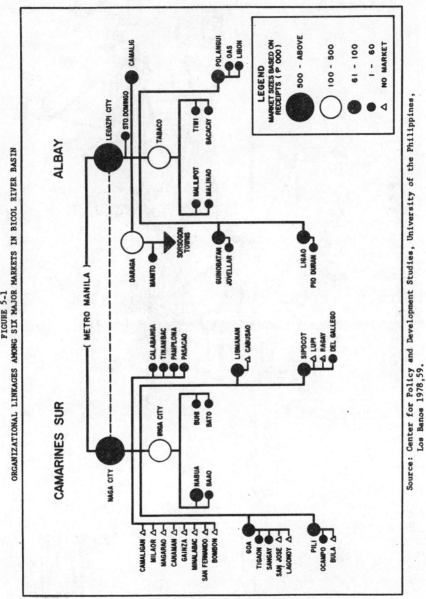

Source: Center for Policy and Development Studies, University of the Philippines,
Los Banos 1978,59.

FIGURE 5-2

LINKAGES AMONG SIX MAJOR MARKETS IN BICOL RIVER BASIN, PHILIPPINES

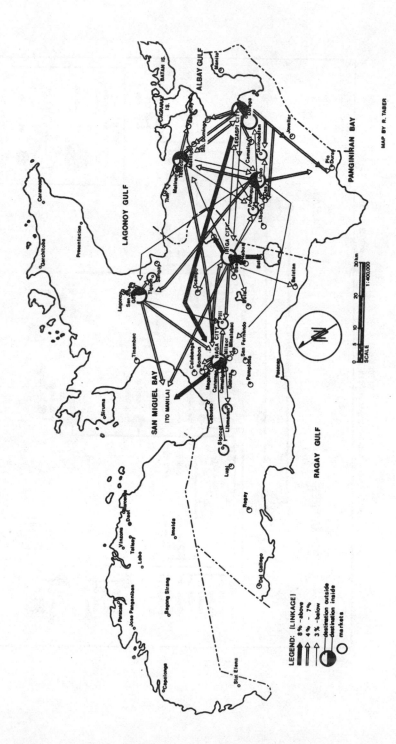

port service to them was infrequent. During the rainy
season, the roads became impassable and the periodic
markets became nearly inaccessible (see Figure 5-3).
In two of the six periodic markets more than 90 percent
of the participants travelled by foot. The trading
areas of periodic markets were found to be 5 kilometers
on average; while the average range of the larger
markets was only about 14 kms. Naga obtained 73 percent of its agricultural commodities from with a 20 km.
range and sold 73 percent of its goods within a 10 km.
range (see Table 5-2).

   3. Market centers in the Basin were predominantly
agricultural trading places. Planners found that
except for Iriga, the major markets in the Basin traded
more in agricultural than in manufactured goods. The
most frequently traded goods were palay, rice, copra,
coconut, fresh and dried fish, poultry and livestock.
None of the major markets were specialized in any particular commodity. All manufactured or processed goods
came from outside of the region; mostly from Manila.
The processed goods most frequently found in the market
included agricultural and veterinary products, groceries, small appliances, household utensils, personal
wear, drugs and medicine. In these goods, the major
markets in Bicol acted only as transfer points; the
periodic markets traded predominantly in agricultural
products grown in the immediately surrounding area and
had few manufactured goods available.

   From these market center studies planners in the
Bicol River Basin were able to obtain, quickly and
inexpensively, an initial profile of economic and trade
linkages among settlements in the region and in-depth
information about the functions and characteristics of
a sample of market centers.

   In the Department of Potosi in Bolivia, information about market functions and linkages was gathered
as part of a general survey of settlements. Interviewers requested information about the existence of
markets in the towns, the type of market, when it was
established, and the frequency with which it operated.
Key informants were asked to identify the principal
products traded in the market; the distances from which
principal products and participants came, where the
town's inhabitants went to trade if no market existed
in that town, and major marketing problems. Information about supporting services and facilities, transportation access to the market center from other towns
and rural areas, and flows of goods from the market
were determined through household and settlement surveys done in connection with the scalogram analysis.

   The surveys found that in the Potosi region, where
more than half the population was engaged in agricul-

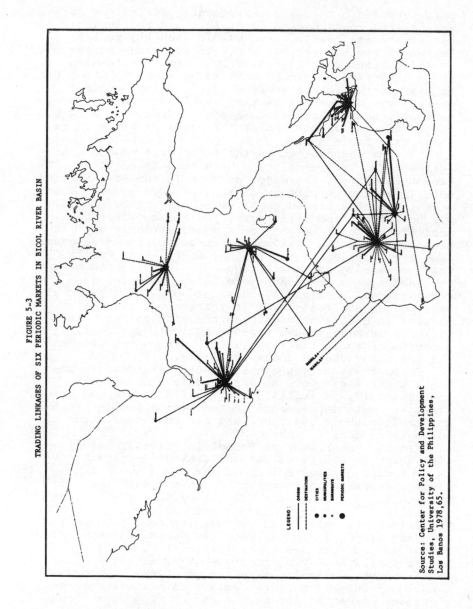

FIGURE 5-3

TRADING LINKAGES OF SIX PERIODIC MARKETS IN BICOL RIVER BASIN

Source: Center for Policy and Development
Studies, University of the Philippines,
Los Banos 1978,65.

TABLE 5-2

TRADING DISTANCES OF SIX MAJOR MARKETS IN BICOL RIVER BASIN

Agricultural

Market Center	No. of Places	Sources of goods traded				No. of Places	Destination of goods traded			
		0-10 km.	11-20 km.	21-50 km.	51+ km.		0-10 km.	11-20 km.	21-50 km.	50+ km.
Naga City	89	38.2	34.8	34.8	10.1	102	73.5	3.9	3.9	17.2
Legaspi City	110	44.5	11.8	24.5	19.1	110	58.2	3.6	16.4	4.2
Iriga City	46	65.2	26.1	8.7	--	62	61.3	11.3	16.1	7.3
Tabaco	111	74.8	4.5	2.7	18.0	112	71.4	12.0	1.8	12.2
Ligao	114	78.9	0.9	14.0	6.2	117	70.1	0	15.4	55.9
Gao	120	86.7	0.8	2.5	10.0	191	--	--	--	14.5

Manufactured

Market Center	No. of Places	Sources of goods traded				No. of Places	Destination of goods traded			
		0-10 km.	11-20 km.	21-50 km.	51+ km.		0-10 km.	11-20 km.	21-50 km.	50+ km.
Naga City	69	37.7	1.4	2.9	58.0	87	67.8	4.6	10.3	17.2
Legaspi City	60	11.7	10.0	5.0	73.3	96	61.5	30.2	3.1	4.2
Iriga City	16	32.9	14.8	16.2	36.1	438	48.9	25.8	18.0	7.3
Tabaco	64	28.1	3.0	25.0	43.8	82	54.9	28.0	4.9	12.2
Ligao	31	6.5	0	32.3	61.2	34	44.1	0	0	55.9
Gao	25	52.0	0	0	48.0	62	85.5	0	0	14.5

Source: UFRD Market Research, 1977

tural activities, market centers were extremely important as outlets for the sale or trade of surplus commodities and as sources of basic consumer goods and
inputs for agricultural production.[26] The information
collected in the surveys of settlements allowed planners to describe the basic structure of market interaction in the region. The studies found that the most
important market centers were the larger towns in which
other commercial and service activities were located.
Smaller markets were usually located in rural service
centers within areas of higher agricultural production.

The studies found that the largest settlement in
the region--the City of Potosi, with five markets--
played an important role in structuring the pattern of
market interaction in that part of the Department in
which the city was located. The strong volume of activity in Potosi, its relatively good access by road, and
its interaction with a larger market in the city of
Sucre, stimulated interaction with periodic markets in
several nearby small towns as well--Betanzos, Puna,
Otavi, and Ckullco--most of which were located in the
main areas of agricultural production and accessible
from the main road that ran through the Department.

The studies indicated that in the southern part of
the region, daily markets were found mainly in centers
of consumption--Tupiza, Villazon and Atocha--and that
several mining centers had weekly markets. The more
sparsely populated western part of the region had
markets located mostly in mining towns. The lack of
markets in the west and north, and the lack of roads
connecting rural villages to them, created strong dis-
incentives for farmers to increase production and
encouraged them to make longer market trips to larger
towns when they did engage in market trade.[27]

TRANSPORTATION LINKAGE STUDIES

Transporation linkages--roads, rail and water networks as well as transportation services--are among the
most important means of connecting settlements within a
region and of providing access for rural people to
town-based services and facilities.

In its manual on rural service center planning,
ESCAP suggests that the following types of transport
information be collected:[28]

1. Density of road systems--number of kilo-
    meters of road per square kilometer of
    land in the region;
2. Access needs of rural population;
3. Quality of the road system--extent to
    which it provides access to services and
    markets in central place settlements;

4. Average distances among settlements
   within the region and of population to
   roads;
5. Classification of road hierarchies,
   including:[29]
   a. national roads--"serving inter-
      national, intercity and interregional
      demands, requiring superior mobility
      and structural strength for long
      distance trips and heavy vehicles and
      therefore high engineering standards
      and bitumen or similar surfacing;"
   b. regional roads--"providing continuous
      access to designated centers as well
      as internal area (province and dis-
      trict) circulation, requiring all-
      weather constructed roads;"
   c. local roads--"connecting minor centers
      and farms to market and service cen-
      ters, which are possibly suitable for
      labor-intensive construction and main-
      tenance methods."
6. Modes of transport and their suitability--
   ranging from pedestrian travel, animal or
   animal pulled conveyences, bicycles,
   motorcycles, automobiles, trucks, buses,
   water-borne conveyences, rail and other
   means and the degree to which they facilitate existing and projected traffic
   needs;
7. Road conditions and levels of mainten-
   ance--roads can be classified as paved,
   deficient-paved, sealed gravel, unsealed
   gravel and earthen, or some other cate-
   gorization that reflects road traffic and
   accessibility criteria;
8. Origin and destination of traffic, commodity and population flows and traffic
   volume flows.

Transport linkage studies played a prominent role
in the regional planning projects in both Bicol and
Potosi. In the Bicol River Basin planners compiled
information on transportation linkages among municipalities by mode, on road networks and road conditions,
and calculated interpoint distances among villages and
between villages and town centers. In addition, information on road traffic volumes, commodity flows, means
of transportation, and origins and destinations of
vehicles had already been collected through a major
transportation survey. Most of the data were mapped
and provided a detailed profile of physical linkages
among settlements within the Basin.

Transport studies showed that more than 70 percent
of all roads in the Basin were of poor quality and
needed upgrading. Only the national highway cutting
through the center of the Basin, and a few provincial
roads, were of all-weather construction and passable
during the rainy season. Farm-to-market roads were few
and poorly constructed. Many rural villages could only
be reached by small boat or on foot. The inadequacy of
regular transport linkages was reflected in part by the
use of non-motorized vehicles, animal-drawn wagons, use
of illegal "skates" along the railroad tracks and small
boats and barges, and in part by the fact that the
majority of trips taken within the Bicol River Basin
were on foot. The railroad provided limited service to
points outside the Basin and the major centers were
linked to Manila only by infrequent bus and air service.

Roads were used by 85 percent of the passengers
taking trips within the Bicol River Basin and to transport over 80 percent of the agricultural commodities.
But as physical linkages among communities, the roads
provided rather poor service (see Table 5-3). Most of
the rural population lived in settlements not easily
accessible by road, and transport was difficult and
expensive in most of the Basin. The costs of transporting commodities in interior rural areas was up to
six times more than in areas connected by roads passable by motor vehicles. Farmers from rural areas had
to walk for hours to the nearest road and carry their
produce on their backs or on slow-moving carabao or
horses. Even after they reached a provincial road, the
waiting times for a jeepney or bus were long and the
costs so high that marginal profits were sometimes
completely wiped out. Rural farmers had to wait an
average of 30 times longer for transportation at secondary roads than at places adjacent to the Manila South
Road and in some more remote sections of the Basin they
had to wait as long as three or four hours. Because of
the cost of transportation and difficulty of travelling, 85 percent of all trips taken within the Basin
were among places within the same municipality and 99
percent were within the same province. Relatively
little travel--for shopping, work, trade, social interaction, or any other purpose--took place among municipalities and there was little interaction on a regular
basis between the Basin's two provinces.[30]

In Bolivia, information about transportation linkages could be obtained from secondary sources through
national agencies engaged in transport planning and
management. The study found that the Department of
Potosi had a more extensive transport network in rela-
tion to its land area than other regions, although none
of the roads in the department were paved. Given the

TABLE 5-3

POPULATION AND SETTLEMENTS SERVED BY ROADS AND OTHER MEANS OF
TRANSPORTATION IN BICOL RIVER BASIN

	POPULATION SERVED[a]				SETTLEMENTS SERVED[b]			
	Albay % Albay popula-tion	Cam. Sur % Cam. Sur popula-tion	Total	% Basin popula-tion	Albay % Albay settle-ments	Cam. Sur % Cam. Sur settle-ments	Total	% Basin settle-ments
Road								
Concrete (MSR)	9	9	155,977	9	3	4	52	4
Asphalt (provincial road)	13	4	124,606	7	6	2	49	4
Gravel and earth (others)	46	35	677,751	40	48	39	600	42
Sub-total			958,334	56			701	49
Footpath[c]	30	42	629,942	37	39	41	580	41
Other Means								
Watercraft	–	7	71,827	4	–	11	104	7
Railway	2	3	39,966	3	3	2	34	2
Bicol River	–	(2)	(229,372)	(14)				
Total	100	100	1,700,069	100	100	100	1,419	100

[a] Population served by river transport not added since these settlements are also served by road and other means.
[b] BUA's or barangays are computed.
[c] The total population and settlements served by footpaths were computed by subtracting the population and settlements served by all types of road and other means from the Basin population and settlements for the two provinces.
Source: UFRD Research, 1977, based on BRBDP Transport Study, 1976, DPH and PEO of Camarines Sur and Albay.

mountainous terrain, travelling was slow and difficult, especially during the rainy season.

The national highway service classified roads into three categories: the supposedly all-weather basic network that connects departmental capital cities; the complementary network that links capital cities with larger towns; and the local network that includes all other roads.[31] In reality, none of these roads in Potosi was of all-weather construction. Roads in the basic network connected the city of Potosi with nearby departmental capitals and La Paz, but often the journey was long and slow. Several roads in Potosi were part of the complementary network although only the link between Potosi and Tupiza and Villazon to the south approached all-weather status. Local feeder roads reached most of the settlements with more than a few hundred residents, but except on flat terrain they were tortuous and rarely permitted vehicles to travel more than 15 kilometers an hour.

The transport linkage surveys in Potosi found that there was bus service only to cities and towns connected by roads in somewhat better condition. Buses ran a few times a week from Potosi to the second and third largest towns in the Department, but there was no regular service to the fourth largest town or smaller settlements. The main means of transport to towns and villages that were located off the main highway was by truck where there were local feeder roads, and by mules and llamas elsewhere. The rail system was built mainly to export minerals to seaports in Chile, Peru and Argentina and passenger service remained inferior even to road transport. The railroad offered connections between Potosi and other Bolivian cities only once or twice a week.[32]

The transport study made apparent the physical isolation of many parts of the region, and how few physical linkages existed among settlements within the region or between larger towns in the region and others in Bolivia.

SOCIAL INTERACTION LINKAGE STUDIES

To the extent that the integration of settlements within a region occurs through social interaction among residents--through kinship ties, visiting among kin and friends, intervillage marriages, and for recreation and ritual--social linkages reflect the degree to which people perceive a region as a coherent and unified unit of society. One means of finding out about the extent of social interaction among settlements in a region is to include questions about the purposes of journeys in origin and destination surveys. To obtain adequate information, however, the studies must be conducted

over a period of time and include weekends and holi-
days, when people are free to travel for social purposes.

Another means of obtaining a profile of social
linkages in regions where much of the interaction is
expected to take place among kin, is to study the spatial patterns of courtship and marriage. Under appropriate cultural conditions, the spatial patterns of
spouse selection reveal a great deal about social
interactions among communities both prior to and after
marriage linkages are forged.

Such a study was considered to be an important
indicator of social interaction in the Bicol River
Basin, and the planners were able to map spouse selection patterns by compiling data in each municipal hall
from a 10 percent sample of the marriage record files
over a five year period. The records showed the residence of both the bride and the groom at the time of
marriage. The study confirmed the findings of the market and transport linkage analyses that there was
little linkage or interaction among municipalities in
the Basin. Only an average of 19 percent of the marriages during the period studied were between people
from different municipalities. Thus, more than 80 percent of the marriages occurred among men and women from
the same locality; and of these only about 4 percent
were among partners from different villages. Those
marriages that were between spouses from different
settlements tended to take place mostly in the municipalities around Naga City, the largest market center in
the region.[33]

SOCIAL SERVICE LINKAGE STUDIES

Another means of determining both the degree of
interaction that takes place among settlements and the
service or influence area of central places is to study
the origins of consumers or clients for important services, and especially for social services. Two studies
were made of service linkages in the Bicol River Basin:
one of the origin of students in secondary and post-
secondary schools and the other of patients in clinics
and hospitals.

The specific objectives of the studies were:
1. To determine the degree of centrality, if
    any, of schools and hospitals in the
    Basin;
2. To find out whether schools and hospitals
    were effective linkages between or among
    areas;
3. To identify the service areas of schools
    and hospitals; and

4. To determine what possible factors (spatial or non-spatial) create or maintain
linkages.

A list of secondary and post-secondary schools was
made from records of the Department of Education and
Culture and samples of students were drawn from two
educational levels: secondary schools; and post-
secondary schools such as colleges, trade and agricultural schools, technical schools and vocational training institutions. A sample of the eight largest secondary schools and 29 post-secondary schools was used to
draw a list of students from whose records information
could be obtained about their permanent residence.

The origin of patients was determined from a 10
percent sample of those registered over a one-year
period in the 43 hospitals in the region having more
than 10 beds. Data were collected on the permanent
residence of the patients and their types of ailment.

These studies confirmed that most of the education
and health services were located in larger settlements
and that their linkages to and accessibility from rural
areas were weak. Two-thirds of all higher education
facilities were located in Naga and Legaspi cities.
About 60 percent of the students in the higher educational institutions came from outside of the town in
which the facility was located, but the service areas
were quite small and extended on average only about 37
kilometers. Analysts found a close relationship
between the size of settlements and their centrality
for higher education and health services. More than
half of all larger schools in the Basin were found to
be concentrated in the largest settlements—Naga,
Legaspi, Daraga and Iriga. The studies of the service
areas of hospitals found that less than one percent of
the patients came from more than 36 kilometers from the
facilities' location (see Tables 5-4 and 5-5).

Similar studies conducted in Potosi, Bolivia,
found that although there were high schools in all
larger and a few smaller towns, those in the smaller
settlements did not offer a complete curriculum. A
complete high school education was offered only in
bigger cities and children from rural areas had to move
from home in order to attend. It was found that in
Potosi the size and degree of specialization of social
service institutions determined the degree to which
they served broad geographical areas. The largest
higher education institution, the University of Tomas
Frias, for example, had students from the entire country. But high schools and elementary schools tended to
serve only the towns in which they were located.

Patients in need of specialized medical treatment
had to go to La Paz or to one of the larger cities outside of the Department. The city of Potosi and the

TABLE 5-4

SERVICE AREAS AND LINKAGES OF SCHOOLS IN BICOL RIVER BASIN

School Location	No. of Schools	% of Students from Outside	Distribution of Origins					
			0-5%		5-10%		10% and above	
			No. of Places	Ave. % per Place	No. of Places	Ave. % per Place	No. of Places	Ave. % per place
Naga	9	58	205	1.9	30	6.2	7	17.9
Legaspi	7	69	82	2.1	12	6.7	6	14.6
Daraga	3	55	13	2.3	3	7.2	1	29.3
Guinobatan	2	54	16	2.5	7	7.3	3	16.2
Iriga	2	48	40	2.1	3	8.6	2	13.7
Tabaco	1	56	16	2.6	3	6.9	2	18.6
Pili	1	44	24	4.0	3	6.5	2	13.5
Sipocot	1	28	2	5.2	–	–	2	14.7
Polangui	1	42	–	–	3	8.3	1	16.7
Batob	1	6	3	1.7	–	–	–	–
Goa	1	46	6	2.2	2	6.3	1	21.9
Nabua	1	11	1	3.4	1	6.8	–	–
Pasacao	1	51	9	2.8	–	–	1	13.9
Ragayb	1	4	1	3.4	–	–	–	–
Tiwi	1	25	–	–	–	–	1	25.0

aOnly schools of higher education but not secondary schools, are included here. They include those that offer general, agricultural and trade, technical, and other higher specialized education.
bRagay is a railroad town and is inaccessible to the rest of the Basin towns; the school in Bato with very low centrality is a small local college whose capacity is not even enough to fill local demand.
Source: UFRD Primary Research, 1977.

TABLE 5-5

SERVICE AREAS AND LINKAGES OF HOSPITALS IN BICOL RIVER BASIN

Hospital Location	No. of Hospitals	% of Patients from Outside	Distribution of Origins					
			0-5%		5-10%		10% and above	
			No. of Places	Ave. % per Place	No. of Places	Ave. % per Place	No. of Places	Ave. % per Place
Legaspi	7	43	37	1.0	5	7	3	14
Tabaco	5	36	20	0.9	6	7	3	17
Naga	4	45	64	1.0	2	7	-	-
Polangui	4	33	18	1.0	2	6	4	19
Ligao	4	23	13	1.0	1	8	2	18
Daraga	3	40	35	0.5	2	6	2	37
Iriga	3	36	25	0.8	4	7	2	13
Libon	3	6	4	0.7	-	-	1	15
Pio Duran	2	26	9	0.6	2	6	2	11
Camalig	1	0	0	0.0	0	0	0	0
Guinobatan	1	9	4	2.0	0	0	0	0
Malilipot	1	77	13	0.5	1	9	3	20
Oas	1	20	12	0.8	0	0	1	10
Baao	1	23	7	0.6	0	0	1	17
Cabusao	1	49	29	0.7	1	5	1	17
Libmanan	1	14	12	0.4	1	9	0	0
San Jose	1	21	3	1.0	0	0	1	16
Tinambac	1	2	1	1.0	0	0	0	0

larger towns in the Department had general hospitals
that served mainly their own provinces; health centers
were available in most larger and intermediate towns,
and small clinics could be found in some villages,
although few of them functioned effectively because of
the lack of doctors, nurses, supplies and equipment.
Often, because those social services at the lower end
of the hierarchy were either missing of ineffective,
rural people had to go to larger cities to obtain
health and educational services or simply go without
them.[34] In both Bicol and Potosi, the analyses of
social service linkages provided a profile of the
service areas of educational and health facilities
located in central places and gave planners an overview
of the accessibility of different parts of the region
to those services.

POLITICAL, ADMINISTRATIVE AND ORGANIZATIONAL LINKAGE
STUDIES

        A related but somewhat different approach to
determining the degree to which settlements in a region
are integrated is to examine political, administrative
and organizational linkages among them. These linkages
are reflected in formal government structure, informal
decision-making relationships, flows of budget
resources from higher to lower levels of administration, transactions among political and administrative
jurisdictions, and the degree of administrative decentralization that exists within a region.
        In the Bicol River Basin various studies of gov-
ernment structure and decision-making patterns sought
to describe and assess the authority, relationships and
capabilities of government organizations located in
settlements of the region and to determine rural residents' access to the services and facilities offered by
public agencies.
        Six studies were done using field observation,
secondary data, case studies and structured interviews:[35]
        1. A case study of the provision of government
services in one area of the region, the municipality of
Minalabac in Camarines Sur province, was used to obtain
an in-depth profile of organizational structure and
interaction within a municipal unit of government. The
area contained both a town center and a rural hinterland. The municipality was located off the main highway and in an area that other studies indicated was
relatively weakly linked to the rest of the regional
economy. Interviews attempted to determine the avail-
ablility of educational, health, agricultural extension
and general government services. The questions sought
information on: (a) extent of use of services by the

respondents or other members of their households; (b) the cost and mode of transportation and the time required to obtain services; and (c) respondent's assessment of the quality of services available. Respondents were drawn from 25 barangays throughout the municipality.

2. Interviews with key personnel and data collected from secondary sources were used to study the extent to which agricultural extension services were available in the Bicol River Basin.

3. A study of rural health facilities was done in two municipalities--Minalabac and Malinao--using secondary data, interviews with key informants and field observation.

4. A study of local decision-making patterns was also done by interviewing key informants in the offices of provincial governors, city mayors, municipal mayors and barangay captains.

5. An in-depth case study of the conflict over the proposed transfer of the provincial capital in Camarines Sur from Naga City to the town of Pili provided information about formal and informal political interaction within the Basin.

6. A case study of locating an industrial estate in Bicol provided information about intergovernmental linkages, political decision-making and interaction between public and private decision-makers within the region.

These studies confirmed that formal government linkages among levels of administration in the Bicol were dominated by national ministries operating within the Basin and that formal structure was highly centralized. Most local officials were appointed by and responsible to national ministries. Municipal officials generally were not under the authority of the mayors, themselves holdover appointees under martial law, who had few resources to solve local problems. Most municipalities in the Basin were dependent on the national government for part of their revenues and most of their authority. Decisions were often made through personal relationships.

Studies of government structure and services in Bicol indicated that services provided by all levels were highly localized. Health, education, and other public institutions generally extended services only to populations living in the immediate vicinity of their sites or to the few who could afford to travel from rural barangays to obtain them in the larger cities. Even the post-secondary schools in the larger centers primarily served only the local area. Health, education and agricultural extension services were far below standards set by national ministries.[36]

In the Department of Potosi, Bolivia, it was decided to use a survey of the provision of basic infrastructure as a means of determining the degree to which government services reached towns and villages in the region. Infrastructure investment was the single most important activity in which government agencies were engaged in Potosi, and information about the distribution of infrastructure investments could provide a good indication of the degree to which settlements throughout the Department were linked into the governmental decision-making system.

Planners found that published statistics on connections to drinking water, sewerage and electricity were not disaggregated by towns and villages. Although these data were available on request, it was decided instead to use information collected in the survey of towns done for the scalograms. This was only a rough estimate, but it was more up to date than census data, and included in addition information on the provision of paved streets, street lighting and garbage collection. For each of the six aspects of physical infrastructure that were taken into account, communities were graded on a scale of 0 to 4, representing none to all, for example, of houses that were directly connected to drinking water, or of streets that were paved. Scores for the six categories were added together to arrive at a total for the community, and an average. Figures were summed for each of the four zones of the Department by simply calculating the average for all the communities in that zone. The city of Potosi was omitted from the calculation of the indices for the central area, since standards of provision there were so much higher than elsewhere and would distort the picture for the rest of the zone.[37]

Evans and his associates concluded from this analysis that the standard of provision of basic infrastructure was extremely low. The overall index for the entire Department (the city of Potosi excluded) was 1.15 on the scale of 0 to 4. Of the six elements considered, the provision of drinking water was furthest advanced, although this still represented only a small part of the total population. Next came electricity, paved roads, street lighting and garbage collection. Sewerage was rarely found outside the largest towns. The southern region emerged as best off--probably because infrastructure investments were made in mining towns by the national mining corporation, COMIBOL--but still with a low score of 1.65 (see Table 5-6).[38]

In brief, the spatial linkage analyses provide planners with abundant information about the degree to which people living in settlements of different sizes and functional characteristics and in different areas

172

TABLE 5-6

SUMMARY OF INFRASTRUCTURE INDICES FOR THE DEPARTMENT OF POTOSI

	Population of Survey Settlements	INFRASTRUCTURE							
		Water	Sewer	Garbage	Elec-tricity	Street Light	Paved Streets	Total	Average
North	72,071	2.33	0.33	0.30	1.48	0.63	1.00	6.07	1.01
Center*	26,812	1.61	0.07	0.10	1.85	1.22	1.07	5.93	0.99
South	51,482	2.93	0.73	1.32	2.86	1.73	1.32	9.89	1.65
West	18,157	2.38	0.05	0.48	1.19	0.67	1.05	5.81	0.97
Total	168,522	8.25	1.18	2.20	7.38	4.25	4.44	27.70	4.62
Average		2.06	0.29	0.51	1.85	1.06	1.11	6.92	1.15

*The central zone does not include the City of Potosi.
Source: Hugh Evans, Urban Functions in Rural Development: The case of the Potosi Region in Bolivia, Washington: USAID, 1983.

of the region are able to interact in economic and
social activities. They help determine the degree to
which services and facilities located in various settlements serve people living in rural areas and other
towns. They can also indicate the service areas of
important facilities located in towns and cities. The
information derived from linkage analyses can be used
in conjunction with other data to determine which parts
of the region are not served by central places and
where rural people have little or no access to important town-based functions.

NOTES

1.   Dennis A. Rondinelli and Kenneth Ruddle, Urbanization and Rural Development: A Spatial Policy for Equitable Growth, New York: Praeger, 1978.

2.   See R. Symanski and R. Bromley, "Market Development and the Ecological Complex," Professional Geographer, Vol. 26, No. 4 (1974): 328-388.

3.   United Nations Economic and Social Commission for Asia and the Pacific, Guidelines for Rural Centre Planning, (New York: United Nations, 1979): p. 186.

4.   For a detailed discussion see Rondinelli and Ruddle, op. cit., Chapter 7.

5.   See E.A.J. Johnson, The Organization of Space in Developing Countries, Cambridge, Mass.: Harvard University Press, 1970; G.W. Skinner, "Marketing and Social Structure in Rural China," Part 1, Journal of Asian Studies, Vol. 24, No. 1 (November 1964), pp. 3-43.

6.   See H.M. Riley and K.M. Harrison, "Vertical Coordination of Food Systems Servicing Large Urban Centres in Latin America," paper prepared for UN Food and Agriculture Organization, Conference on the Development of Food Marketing Systems for Large Urban Areas in Latin America, Rome: FAO, 1973.

7.   See Carol A. Smith (ed.) Regional Analysis, Vols. I and II, New York: Academic Press, 1976.

8.   U.S. Bureau of the Census, Planning for Internal Migration: A Review of Issues and Policies in Developing Countries, ISP-RD-4, Washington: US Government Printing Office, 1977.

9.   Jean Parent, "The Problem of Transferring Techology from Branch to Branch and the Multiplier," in Organization for Economic Cooperation and Development, Choice and Adaptation of Technology in Developing Countries, (Paris: OECD, 1974), p. 208.

10. See D.R.F. Taylor, "The Role of the Smaller Place in Development: The Case of Kenya," in S. ElShakhs and R. Obudho (eds.) Urbanization, National Development and Regional Planning in Africa, (New York: Praeger, 1974), pp. 142-160; Ronald G. Knapp, "Marketing and Social Patterns in Rural Taiwan," Annals of the Association of American Geographers, Vol. 61, No. 1 (March 1971), pp. 131-155; G. William Skinner, "Marketing and Social Structure in Rural China, "Part 2, Journal of Asian Studies, Vol. 24, No. 2 (February 1965), pp. 195-228.

11.   See Skinner, op. cit.; and Lawrence W. Crissman, "Marketing on the Chungua Plain, Taiwan," in W.E. Willmot (ed.), Economic Organization in Chinese Society, (Stanford: Stanford University Press, 1972), pp. 215-259.

12. Brian Schwimmer, "Periodic Markets and Urban Development in Southern Ghana," in Smith, op. cit., 123-146; Raymond J. Bromley, "Contemporary Market Periodicity in Highland Ecuador," Ibid, pp. 91-122.

13. World Bank, Village Water Supply, (Washington: World Bank, 1976), p. 29.

14. Norman T. Uphoff and Milton J. Esman, Local Organization for Rural Development: Analysis of the Asian Experience, (Ithaca: Cornell University Center for International Studies, 1974) p. xi; see also David K. Leonard, "Interorganizational Linkages for Decentralized Rural Development: Overcoming Administrative Weaknesses," in G.S. Cheema and Dennis A. Rondinelli (eds.), Decentralization and Development: Policy Implementation in Developing Countries, (Beverly Hills: Sage Publications, 1983), pp. 271-294.

15. Ray Bromley, "Market Centers in the Urban Functions in Rural Development Approach," Working Paper (Worcester, Mass: Clark University Settlement and Resource Systems Analysis and Management Project, 1983).

16. Ibid, p. 3.

17. See Ralph L. Beals, The Peasant Marketing System in Oaxaca, Mexico, Berkeley: University of California Press, 1975.

18. Bromley, "Marketing Centers in the UFRD Approach," op. cit. pp. 3-16.

19. Ibid., pp. 17-18.

20. Ibid., pp. 23-26.

21. Ibid., pp. 45-56.

22. Ibid., pp. 51-52.

23. Ibid., pp. 56-61.

24. Ibid., pp. 56-57.

25. Bicol River Basin Development Program, Urban Functions in Rural Development: A Research Project in Spatial Analysis and Planning, Pili, The Philippines: BRBDP, 1978.

26. Hugh Evans, Urban Functions in Rural Development: The Case of the Potosi Region in Bolivia, Washington: U.S. Agency for International Development, 1982.

27. See Dennis A. Rondinelli and Hugh Evans, "Integrated Regional Development Planning: Linking Urban Centers and Rural Areas in Bolivia," World Development, Vol. II, No. 1 (1983), pp. 31-54.

28. United Nations Economic Commission for Asia and the Pacific, op. cit., pp. 185-204.

29. Ibid., pp. 189-190.

30. Bicol River Basin Development Program, op. cit., pp. 99-100.

31. Evans, op. cit., pp. 51-52.

32. Idem.

33. Bicol River Basin Development Program, op. cit., pp. 72-73.
34. Ibid., pp. 74-78.
35. Ibid., pp. 89-98.
36. Ibid., pp. 97-98.
37. Evans, op. cit., pp. 58-61.
38. Ibid., pp. 47-49.

6
Applying Spatial Analysis
in Regional Planning

The first three stages of Urban Functions in Rural Development are primarily concerned with data collection, organization and preliminary analysis. The three following phases focus on presenting, interpreting and applying the information gathered for the regional profile, settlement system and spatial linkage analyses. In phases four through six of the UFRD approach, the information is summarized in maps, charts, tables and other graphic presentations. The maps and data are analyzed together in order to determine the accessibility of settlements and functions for people living in various parts of the region. The analyses are then used to identify functional "gaps" in various services, facilities, infrastructure and productive activities, and to delineate the service areas of existing settlements. In some cases, regional planners are interested in identifying marginal or peripheral areas that do not have sufficient numbers of central places to serve their residents, where access to functions is weak or nonexistent, and where linkages among settlements are poorly developed. Combined with more detailed economic and technical studies, sectoral analyses, or "demand analyses," the information about the settlement system can be used to help develop regional investment strategies and to identify specific projects for particular settlements or areas.

The spatial information is mapped and interpreted to help regional planners deal with the following types of issues or questions:

1. Which settlements in the region are central places with "adequate" functions and service areas, and need only investments that maintain and strengthen their current comparative advantages?

2. Which settlements are functionally "deficient," or could serve a greater hinterland with strategic investments in services and

177

facilities that are currently absent but could be supported in the settlement, or by strengthening their linkages with higher or lower order settlements?

3. Which settlements lack important services and facilities or infrastructure but show little or no potential for economic growth and diversification and therefore should have low priority for investment?

4. Which centers have the potential for economic growth and diversification and could be "upgraded" to a higher level in the settlement hierarchy with a "package of projects" designed to add to their functional diversity?

5. Which settlements that do not now serve as central places might be upgraded with investments in new services and facilities?

6. How can existing non-central places that do not seem to have potential for growth and diversification be linked more strongly to existing or potential central place settlements?

7. How can the access of people now living in marginal or peripheral areas be increased so that they can be served by facilities, infrastructure or social and commercial activities that must be located in towns or cities?

8. How can the existing settlement system be used more effectively to distribute services, facilities and infrastructure more widely and to serve larger numbers of people?

9. How can the settlement system be changed to make it more articulated and integrated and to allow it to provide a physical base for more widespread economic development?

10. How can linkages among settlements be strengthened to promote development in strategic places spontaneously?

These are only some of the issues about which spatial analysis can provide information. It should be stressed again, however, that the analyses do not provide answers to these questions. The answers require careful judgment based on an intimate knowledge of the region and its people's needs and desires. The analyses provide information that allow planners and policy-makers to make better and more informed judgments. Moreover, the spatial analyses provide only some of the data needed to make informed judgments. They must be combined with other analyses, with information about potential needs and demands, with assessments of economic and political feasibility, and with appraisals of institutional capability to carry out programs and projects.

This chapter describes phases four through six of the UFRD approach: analytical mapping, accessibility analyses, and identification of functional and settlement service areas. From these studies functional "gaps" and unserved or marginal areas of the region can be identified. These analyses are used in turn to help planners add a locational dimension to the formulation of investment strategies and projects, phases of UFRD that will be described in more detail in Chapter 7.

ANALYTICAL MAPPING

Experiences with UFRD projects in the Philippines and Bolivia suggest that one of the most important tasks of regional planners is to present information and analyses in ways that are easy to understand and to visualize. This is especially important when they are dealing with policy-makers who may not be familiar with spatial analysis techniques, and with government officials and local leaders who may not be highly trained in statistical analysis and, indeed, may not even have a high level of formal education. Unless those who must make decisions can "see" the implications, it is highly unlikely that they will make use of spatial analyses. Moreover, if the studies are too complicated or the presentation of results too abstract, they may generate hostility among decision-makers rather than convince them of the importance of locational and spatial factors in regional planning and policy.

Roy and Patil,[1] in their manual on area development planning in India, suggest that two types of maps are essential:

1. Topographic maps that record physical features of a region--such as rivers, forests, roads, and terrain; and

2. Thematic maps that concentrate on a set of activities, characteristics or socio-economic features of the region such as population distribution, location of infrastructure, movements of goods and services, economic characteristics of settlements or other important factors that can be drawn or symbolized.

In addition to these, the UFRD approach makes use of other forms of graphic presentation, including tables, charts, graphs and diagrams. Obviously, the process of mapping and organizing information goes on throughout a UFRD project and is not all done at a single point in the process. In this sense, calling this activity a "stage" or "phase" of the UFRD approach is somewhat misleading. A number of graphic presentations are prepared in earlier phases of analysis--the regional profile tables, settlement system scalograms, and linkage analysis all require some sort of graphic,

statistical or diagrammatic presentation. Moreover,
maps, charts, tables and graphs are prepared in subse-
quent stages of analysis as well--in accessibility
analysis, delineation of service areas and formulation
of investment strategies and programs. However, it is
usually after the regional profile, settlement system
and linkage analyses are completed that information can
be analyzed in new ways and summarized most effectively
on maps in order to prepare for its further analysis,
interpretation and application.

There are a wide variety of graphic and statistical presentation methods that can be used to in
regional planning. Dickinson, perhaps, most concisely
summarizes and describes the range of techniques that
can be used in the UFRD approach.[2] He notes that:

1. _Statistical diagrams_ can be used to show the
relationship between quantities when the presentation
of spatial distribution is not important. Among the
most effective statistical diagrams are:

    a. Line graphs
    b. Bar graphs
    c. Circular graphs
    d. Scatter graphs or scatter diagrams

Statistical diagrams can also be used to show the division of characteristics into components--usually in
percentages or absolute numbers. Among the most effective statistical diagrams for showing parts or components of a whole are:

    a. Compound line charts
    b. Bar graphs
    c. Divided circle or "pie" charts
    d. Divided rectangles
    e. Triangular graphs

2. _Statistical maps_ can be used to show the
spatial distribution of social or economic characteristics, population, activities, resources or other features that exist at different levels or in different
quantities in various parts of a region. When differences in degree or level are to be shown in a non-
quantitative manner, various symbols, letters or levels
of shading can be used at different locations on the
map.

When it is important to show on the map quantities
distributed among places, the following devices can be
used:

    a. For showing the quantities distributed at
       specific _points_:
       1) Repeated unit symbols--such as a small
          drawing of a cow at each location repre-
          senting 100 head of cattle raised in that
          place
       2) Proportional bars--representing different
          levels or amounts at each place

        3) Squares, circles, spheres or cubes--with
           each symbol representing different amounts
           or proportions
        4) Graduated range of symbols--such as circles
           of different sizes representing larger
           amounts or percentages
        5) Repeated statistical diagrams
    b. For showing the quantities distributed in an
       area:
       1) Dots--with the density of dots representing
           the amount within the area
       2) Shading--the darker the shading, the
           greater the amount or percentage
       3) Proportional shading
       4) Isolines--connecting areas with equal
           amounts or levels and forming areas within
           an area
    c. For showing quantities distributed along a
       line--such as a road, river, or railroad--
       bands with proportional widths or graduated
       size indicating the level or amount.

The most effective type of map, table or chart to
use depends on the types of data to be presented, the
emphasis or focus that is desired, and the ability of
the audience to comprehend the information. There are
graphics that are more or less appropriate to different
types of data: for example, population or commodity
flow data along roads are most appropriately highlighted by proportional width bands along the line of
flow. But other means might be used to highlight other
data. Part of the planners' responsibility is to
select those graphic techniques that are most likely to
highlight the relevant implications of the data and
that are most likely to be understood by those who must
make decisions about the information presented.

In the Bicol River Basin, most of the forms of
presentation listed earlier were used at one stage or
another of the UFRD project. Information about the
levels of development and accessibility of settlements
was mapped together with information about the distribution of functions and the network of linkages. The
maps were used to determine the "areas of influence" of
various settlements, the service areas of selected
functions, and the location of marginal or peripheral
areas within the region where the population was poorly
served by central places.

Moreover, the data were used to delineate sub-
systems of settlements and major economic areas within
the Basin and to compare those to existing planning
units. Transport and physical accessibility maps
showed areas of the Basin that could be reached by
roads, water transport and railway. The volumes of
goods flowing through major markets were mapped to show

the "reach" of each market center and the sources and destination of commodities traded. The maps delineated the secondary and periodic markets in rural areas that participated in trade relationships with larger markets. Travel volume and origin and destination data were derived from the modal transport study and were mapped along with the service areas of selected institutions and public facilities.

The project staff made a number of transparent overlays that could be used with a base map to show the distribution of services and facilities among settlements and that could be employed for comparison and evaluation after development plans were implemented. They also produced the first comprehensive map of barangay settlements in the Bicol River Basin that would be important in future development planning.[3]

In both the Bicol River Basin and the Department of Potosi in Bolivia, the base and analytical maps were important tools for organizing and interpreting the regional profile, settlement system and linkage analyses and in determining the accessibility of settlements and functions for rural residents.

ACCESSIBILITY AND SERVICE AREA ANALYSIS

A crucial feature of the UFRD approach is that is is designed to collect and analyze spatial and functional data to help planners make investment decisions that will promote economic growth with a high degree of social and geographic equity. That is, the UFRD approach is based on the premise that new investments in services, facilities, infrastructure and productive activities should be located in such a way as to promote equitable growth by increasing the access of the population living in rural hinterlands to the functions that are located in central-place settlements. Before such locational decisions can be made, however, it is necessary to know how accessible existing settlements and functions are to the population living within the settlement and to those living in immediately surrounding areas.

One dimension of accessibility is physical--the amount of time and the distance people must travel from the places where they live to the places where functions are located. In rural regions, especially, physical accessibility is a major factor determining which groups can participate in the activities located in towns and cities.

Obviously, however, it is not the only factor. Perhaps equally important are the disposable income and purchasing power of potential clients or customers, people's knowledge about the existence of facilities, their level of education, their skill in making use of the facilities and services, and other social and political factors. But physical distance does play an important role in accessibility. It determines to a large degree the differential cost of a service or facility for people living at different distances from its site. People's knowledge of the existence or use of a service or facility is also determined in part by their physical access to it. And to some extent the effective demand for a service or facility is determined by the probability that people can have physical access to it. Living near a school, for example, makes people more aware of the existence of educational services. It lowers their cost of travel and increases the probability that they will be able to attend or to send their children.

Moreover, all things being equal, the closer people live to a service or facility, the greater their chances of being able to make use of it during the hours of the day when it is provided or made available, and the more likely that they will be able to get convenient transportation to it. Thus, although physical distance between the location of a function and its potential clients or customers does not in itself determine accessibility (e.g., a family may live next to a general hospital but not have an income high enough to pay for its services), the physical location of services and facilities does play an important role in determining the number of people who are likely to have access to them. Moreover, the comparison of locations of population and functions can provide a surrogate for, or an effective initial indicator of, accessibility that can be refined with information about income, knowledge, and effective demand. As with all other techniques of analysis employed in the UFRD approach, accessibility studies are most effectively used in conjunction with other methods to cross-check and refine them.

Several methods have been used to determine the service areas of functions, and in combination, that of settlements. Usually the service areas of settlements are composite indicators of the accessibility of major functions located within them. These methods include functional service area indexes, market area and commodity flow networks, service area cluster maps, and accessibility models.

Functional Service Area Index

Southall suggested the use of a functional service area index in the UFRD project in Upper Volta. The index determines accessibility of functions for people living in settlements or villages,[4] and in a sense, complements and extends the scalogram. It helps show the relationship among functions in a settlement and the average access of the population to them. Southall suggests the following procedures:

1. Record the distance of each settlement to surrounding towns or villages and to other areas where there is a significant distribution of population;

2. Assume that on average the distance of the total population of one settlement from a service or function located in another settlement is the distance from each settlement's physical center. For very large cities, this assumption could be redefined.

3. On the basis of 1 and 2, calculate the distance of each settlement from each function and calculate the total population at each interval of distance from each function.

4. If all services are ranked and weighted, then the overall score of Service Access adequacy or inadequacy can be calculated for any settlement or any group or network of settlements.

For example, the accessibility of functions in a district or province for people living in Town A could be determined by measuring the distance of Town A to functions located in the district or province. Assume that people living in Town A were the following distances from these functions:

Town Hall	0 kms (one located in Town A)
Primary School	5 kms
Health Clinic	10 kms
Hospital	20 kms
Secondary School	20 kms

If it was very difficult for people to travel more than 15 kilometers from Town A because of poor roads or rough terrain, one could consider the population living in the town to be within the service areas of the town hall, primary school and health clinic functions, but not within the effective service areas of the hospital and secondary school functions.

Similarly the functional service areas for a region could be determined by calculating the proportion of population in the region at each distance interval from various functions:

	0 kms.	1-5 kms.	6-10 kms.	11-20 kms.	more than 20kms.
Town Hall	60%	30%	10%		
Primary School	30%	40%	30%		
Dispensary	20%	30%	30%	20%	
Hospital	10%	15%	20%	25%	30%
Secondary School	10%	15%	20%	25%	30%

The Service Access Index method can also be modified to use time required to reach a function rather than simply distance. Depending on the terrain and the availability of transportation, time interval measurements may be far more accurate indicators of accessibility than distance measures.

In any case, the adequacy of accessibility can be judged only be establishing desirable criteria for time or distance required to reach a function. If, for example, it is considered important that at least 50 percent of the population of an area should be within 5 kms. of a secondary school, then the accessibility of secondary schools for population living in the district or province described above would be considered inadequate. The implication would be that the feasibility of locating a secondary school in or nearer to settlements that were more accessible should be explored. If it is assumed that at least 50 percent of the population should be within 10 kms. of a town hall, the accessibility of that function in the previous example would be more than adequate.

Market Area and Commodity Flow Networks

In those settlements that are market centers, the settlement's area of influence can often best be determined by tracing the flow of commodities into and out of the market and by mapping the distance from which buyers and sellers come to trade in the market place. The information gathered from the scalogram, market center and transport linkage studies can be used to trace the commodity flow networks of a settlement. Market area maps constructed from the combination of commodity flow networks can determine marginal or peripheral areas that have little or no access to organized market systems.

In the Bicol River Basin, for example, commodity flow networks were derived from major goods traded in regular and periodic markets through data gathered in the market center and from transportation linkage analyses. The flows were traced for each major commodity traded in each market. The distance from which goods came and were sold, the time and cost of transporting them and the type of transportation route were recorded during the market center studies. Flows were traced through intermediate as well as final markets.

For example, Figure 6-1 shows the origin and destination of salt water fish, through Payatan, one of the six periodic markets surveyed in the Bicol River Basin during the UFRD project. Since Payatan was a mountainous barangay located near the foot of Mt. Isarog, it had no direct access to the sea, and depended for its salt water fish supplies primarily on

186

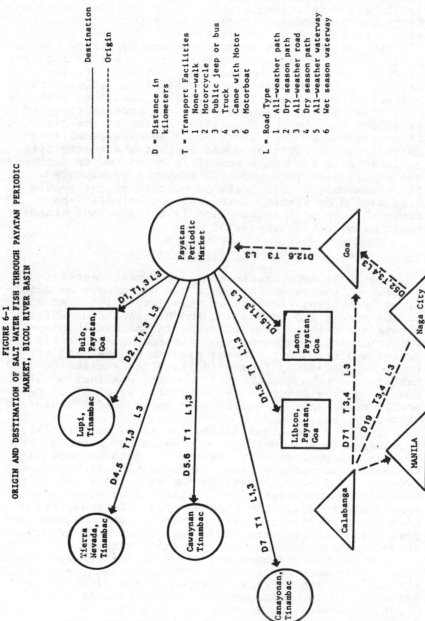

FIGURE 6-1

ORIGIN AND DESTINATION OF SALT WATER FISH THROUGH PAYATAN PERIODIC
MARKET, BICOL RIVER BASIN

D = Distance in kilometers

T = Transport Facilities
1 None--walk
2 Motorcycle
3 Public jeep or bus
4 Truck
5 Canoe with Motor
6 Motorboat

L = Road Type
1 All-weather path
2 Dry season path
3 All-weather road
4 Dry season path
5 All-weather waterway
6 Wet season waterway

———— Destination

- - - - Origin

markets in Calabanga. Fish were supplied through
markets in Naga City and Goa. Some came directly to Goa
from Calabanga, others from middle-men or wholesalers in
Naga City.

Studies also found that Payatan served about 18
barangays in a 10 kilometer radius. Payatan was primarily a palay (unmilled rice) and rice trading point,
obtaining its supplies from the barangays of Lupi,
Tierra Nevada, Tinambac, Quinale, Cawaynan, Canayonan,
Libtong and Laon, as well as Bulo, Maysalay, Tabgon and
Balaynan. Palay and rice were sold primarily in the
larger, regular markets in Goa, Tigaon and Naga. In
addition, the market at Payatan traded in clothing,
nearly all of it made in Manila and shipped in through
Naga City and Goa; school supplies from the same
sources; sugar from Pili and Goa, which was sold to
traders in smaller barangays; canned and prepared foods
from Manila, Naga and Goa; and dried fish. Moreover,
the periodic market at Payatan served as a collection
point for coconut, livestock and vegetables which were
sent to the Goa market for further distribution.

Through the commodity flow networks, planners were
able to show the market area of Payatan and the network
of linkages through which traders distributed goods from
the rural hinterlands, the networks through which processed and manufactured goods came into the area, and
the barangays that had access to the market. They also
identified the rural areas that were outside of the
market area and in which people had little or no access
to places where they could sell their goods or obtain
the items traded in organized markets.[5]

Service Area Clusters

Another technique of determining the service area
of a settlement is by clustering the service areas of
major functions located within it. The approach,
described in more detail by R.S. Dick, requires a map of
the service ranges of individual functions measured in
any direction from a central place.[6] To construct the
service area cluster (see Figure 6-2) for the settlement, the following steps are followed:

1. Measure the service range of the function outward from the center along sixteen radials
   corresponding to the sixteen principal compass
   directions (N, NNE, NE, ENE, etc.).
2. Index the separate radial directions clockwise
   from 1 to 16--labelling N as 1, NNE as 2, NE as
   3, and so on.
3. Along the given radial i (i=1,2, ... 16) the
   actual ranges r_{ji}(j= 1,2, ..., n) are measured
   and the mean service range r_i

FIGURE 6-2

GRAPHIC ILLUSTRATION OF SETTLEMENT SERVICE AREA AS COMPOSITE
OF FUNCTIONAL SERVICE AREAS

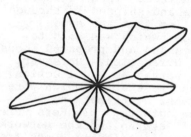

Function 1 Service Area

Function 2 Service Area

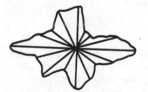

Function 3 Service Area

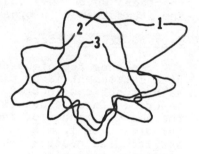

Settlement Service Area

$$\overline{r}_i = \frac{1}{n} \sum_{j=1}^{n} r_{ji}$$

is determined.

4. Deviations from the mean range are recorded, ignoring sign, and the mean deviation is calculated:

$$\overline{d}_i = \frac{1}{n} \sum_{j=1}^{n} \left| r_{ji} - \overline{r}_i \right|$$

5. The degree of correspondence of service area boundaries around a settlement is determined by a measure of relative variability of service range, defined by the following ratio expressed in percent:

$$V = \frac{(100D)}{R}$$

where:

D = average of the mean deviations ($\overline{d}_i$) r recorded for each of the 16 radials drawn, i.e.,

$$D = \frac{(\sum \overline{d}_i)}{16}$$

R = overall mean service range obtained as the mean of 16 separate r_i

Possible values for V range from zero percent--which indicates complete coincidence of all service boundaries--to higher values indicating varying degrees of discordance. Generally, the higher the value of V, the higher the degree of variability and the lower the degree of correspondence among the service areas of functions located within the settlement.

Dick notes that in many regions, the high degree of variation found in service areas for some functions is due to erratic government investment criteria or to the fact that service areas for some public facilities or infrastructure are mandated by law. In any case, when information is available about the service areas of functions, analyses of their correspondence can provide a good indication of the service area of settlements. As Smailes has pointed out, "the service areas of a variety of functions correspond sufficiently closely to

allow broad recognition of general or composite urban
fields at a series of functional levels which accord
with the more clearly defined ranks of the urban hierarchy."[7] Thus, this method can be used to cross check
and refine the functional hierarchy defined by the
scalogram analysis.

Through the use of a combination of time-distance
analyses, linkage analyses, analytical mapping and
service area clustering, planners in the Bicol River
Basin were able to outline broadly not only the service
areas of various functions, and of the major settlements, but also of functional subsystems of settlements
within the region. Indeed, the analytical maps, linkage studies and accessibility and service area analyses
confirmed earlier indications that the Bicol River
Basin was not an integrated economic or physical
region. Independent functional subsystems of settlements, instead, tended to cluster around the two urban
centers of Naga and Legaspi, each primarily serving a
small network of towns and villages in its immediately
surrounding area and within its own province. Transport routes to the rest of each province converged at
these two cities, which were also the largest markets
in the Basin. Smaller market centers were usually
linked to one or the other of these central markets.
Most of the higher order services and facilities were
concentrated in Naga and Legaspi.

However, the accessibility and service area
studies showed that relatively little interaction
occurred between the two provincial cities. The level
of market trade between Naga and Legaspi was neglig-
ible. Travel volume was less than 230 person-trips per
day, a low and insignificant volume for a region with
700,000 hectares of land and 1.7 million people. The
service areas of major functions located within each
center deteriorated rapidly with distance.

Iriga City, in the center of the Basin acted as
another node for a smaller number of settlements and
had a few linkages with Naga City but relatively little
physical, economic or social interaction with Legaspi.

In Camarines Sur province, some local services
were available to rural people living in the areas
immediately surrounding Calabanga, Goa, Pili and Bato.
In Albay Province the towns of Lagao, Polangui, Guinobatan and Tobaco provided services to nearby barangays.
But accessibility to town-based services and facilities
for much of the rest of the Basin was found to be weak.
Large portions of the region were relatively inaccessible and had few central places of any significance.

The Manila South Road provided the most important
physical linkage and means of access to services and
facilities for people living outside of the major
towns. People living only a few kilometers off of the

main road often had to travel long periods of time to get to towns and market centers. The cost of transporting goods to market for farmers who lived off the main roads was nearly six times that of farmers living along the Manila South Road or a connecting provincial road. The clustering of settlements by functional service areas and linkages in Bicol is depicted in Figure 6-3.[8] The white or blank areas on the map are places that generally have little or no access to towns and the functions located in them; these marginal and peripheral areas had the highest levels of poverty.

Accessibility Models

In the UFRD project in Potosi, Bolivia, an attempt was made to delineate more precisely the service areas of settlements and the accessibility of people living in various parts of the region to town-based services and facilities. A model was designed by John Dickey and Hugh Evans to measure the level of access of the population in different zones of the region to specific functions.[9] The model was later used to evaluate alternative investment strategies for improving physical access either by upgrading transportation to towns where functions already were located or by locating them in new places. The model was constructed in the following way (see Figure 6-4):

1. <u>Identify zones and zone centroids</u>: zones can be delineated on the basis of existing political boundaries, economic criteria, physical features or other standards, depending on the factors that are most important for planning in the region. A centroid is chosen for each zone. It should approximate the population center of that zone. To simplify the analysis, it is assumed that all trips to the zone are made to and from this centroid.

2. <u>Identify transport links among centroids</u>: information can be obtained from an appropriate government agency, from reliable maps or from the UFRD linkage analysis, on the transport network in each zone. Each major link is assigned a number. Those centroids not connected to the primary network are assigned links following the best path (a tertiary road or commonly used footpath or river) to that link. Also a "pseudo link" is created for each centroid to simulate the network for travel <u>within</u> the zone. A table is constructed to show the numbers and travel time of each link.

3. <u>Compute interzonal travel times</u>: a map can be used to compute zone-to-zone travel times. A table is then constructed to list the inter- and intra-zonal travel times. The total time for each link is added to find the zone-to-zone travel time.

192

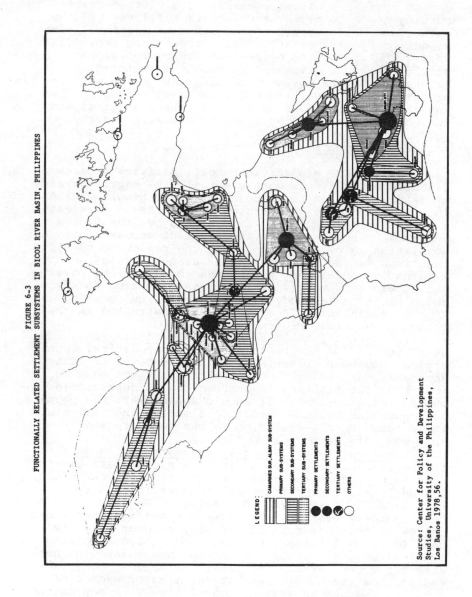

FIGURE 6-3

FUNCTIONALLY RELATED SETTLEMENT SUBSYSTEMS IN BICOL RIVER BASIN, PHILIPPINES

LEGEND:

CAMARINES SUR, ALBAY SUB-SYSTEM

PRIMARY SUB-SYSTEMS

SECONDARY SUB-SYSTEMS

TERTIARY SUB-SYSTEMS

PRIMARY SETTLEMENTS

SECONDARY SETTLEMENTS

TERTIARY SETTLEMENTS

OTHERS

Source: Center for Policy and Development
Studies, University of the Philippines,
Los Banos 1978,56.

FIGURE 6-4

GRAPHIC ILLUSTRATION OF ACCESSIBILITY MODEL

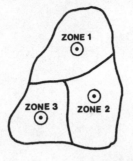

a.   Zone map with centroids

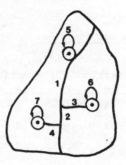

b.   Transport links connecting centroids

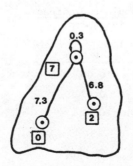

c.   Function travel convenience

(continued)

194

Figure 6-4 (Continued)

d. Zone to Zone Travel Times

From Zone	To Zone		
	1	2	3
1	0.3	6.8	7.3
2	7.0	0.5	4.0
3	7.4	3.9	0.4

e. Zonal Characteristics and Functions

Zone	Population	No. of Function A	No. of Function B
1	10,000	7	3
2	6,000	2	0
3	4,000	0	0

f. Function Travel Convenience Indices
(Numbers of Function/hours)

Zone	Function	
	A	B
1	23.63	10.00
2	5.00	0.43
3	1.46	0.41

Figure 6-4 (Continued)

g. <u>Zonal and Function Accessibility Indices</u>
   <u>Base Case</u> (x 1000)

| Zone | Functions | | Total |
	A	B	
1	7561	1500	9061
2	960	39	999
3	187	24	211
Total	8708	1563	10,271

h. <u>Weighted Accessibility Indices Base Case</u>
   (x 1000)

| Zone | Functions | | Total |
	A	B	
1	2520	500	3020
2	960	39	999
3	94	12	116
Total	3574	551	4125

4. <u>Develop indices of function travel conveni-</u><u>ence</u>: the number of establishments or occurrences of functions in each zone is divided by the travel time to that zone. The resulting fractions for all zones are added. The formula for the calculation is as follows:

$$A_{ij} = \sum_{k=1}^{n} (N_{kj}/T_{ik})$$

where N_{kj} = the number of establishments of function j in zone k

T_{ik} = the travel time from zone i to zone k

5. <u>Weight the functions by level of importance</u>: it is assumed that all functions found in a zone are not of equal importance. Some play a more crucial role in the daily lives of residents or are more crucial than others in the development of the locality. One empirical indicator of the importance of a function is its annual average number of visit-hours (number of visits x hours of travel per visit). It is assumed that if people are willing to spend more time for more visits to a particular function it must be proportion-ately more valuable to them. A table is made to list the visit-hours weight of each function.

6. <u>Develop population weights</u>: assuming that the location of a function or linkage that reaches more people is better than one that reaches fewer, the accessibility index should reflect the population of the zone. A total individual access index, A_i, for each zone for all functions is:

$$A_i = \sum_{j=1}^{m} (A_{ij} \times W_j)$$

where W_j = weight assigned to function j

$= N_j \times T_j \times P_j$

and N_j = average number of visits by a household in time t, to the function j;

T_j = average travel time to function j;
P_j = proportion of the population that uses function j.

7. <u>Calculate accessibility indices</u>: finally, an accessibility index, $A(P)_i$, for each zone and each function can be calculated using the following formula:

$$A(P)_i = A_i \times P_i = \sum_{j=1}^{m} A_{ij} \times W_j \times P_i$$

Obviously, the statistical methods used in Potosi require a great deal more information than the graphic methods used in the Bicol River Basin. To use the accessibility model effectively, information must be collected on the population of each settlement and rural area of each zone; average speed along, and distances of all road links; and the number of establishments or occurences of each function in each zone. Such information could be collected at the same time that a scalogram survey is done, or independently at a later stage in the UFRD analysis.

In Potosi, information on frequency of visits and travel times to functions was gathered through a survey of randomly selected households in 96 zones (see 6-5). Data were collected for 24 functions including health and education facilities, shops and stores, government offices and services for mining and agriculture.

The calculation of the average number of visits for different functions was handled in different ways. For schools and health facilities, for example, where the visit was made by only one individual, averages were based on observations for appropriate individual members of the household. For other functions, such as farm supply stores, processing plants, pharmacies, gas stations, post offices, or government offices, where the visit usually benefits the whole family, averages were based on the total number of visits made by all members of the household. For such functions as markets, clothing or grocery stores, where counts for all members of the household might exaggerate the number of trips, averages were based on the total number of visits made by all household members divided by the number of people in the family who made the trips.

Evans points out in his analysis of the results of the survey that schools were the most frequently visited function. The average travel time was about 15 minutes for primary and high schools and was slightly greater for middle schools.[10] The average travel time, however, masked the fact that children in some parts of the region had to travel up to two hours between home and school. The next most frequently visited function was grocery stores. In most zones these small family shops selling basic consumer goods were visited once or twice a week by people who had to travel an average of one-half hour. Families visited markets about three times a month and took an average of two hours to get to them. Stores selling cooking and heating fuel were visited about twice a month and it took an average

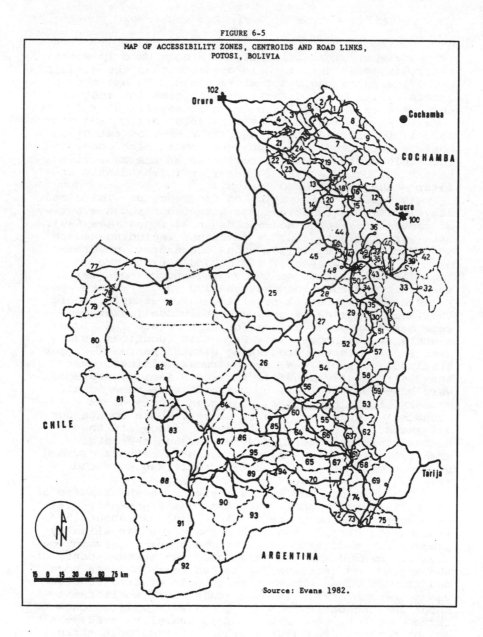

FIGURE 6-5
MAP OF ACCESSIBILITY ZONES, CENTROIDS AND ROAD LINKS,
POTOSI, BOLIVIA

Source: Evans 1982.

of nearly two and a half hours to reach them. People
in the region seldom had access to doctors or hospitals, both because they could not afford to visit them
and because both functions were highly concentrated in
only a few centers in the region. Farm-related services and facilities were among the least accessible
functions primarily because they were located in so few
places in the department. They were visited only once
or twice a year and they required a four to five hour
journey.[11] (See Table 6-1)

Evans further notes that using the methods of
accessibility analysis applied in Potosi, the most
important and accessible function turned out to be the
market, followed by the grocery store, fuel store,
pharmacy, primary and middle schools, and post offices.
The indices show that health facilities and agricultural supply stores were among the least accessible
functions in Potosi. But Evans emphasizes that the
indices are based on current usage, and given the scarcity of functions in most settlements in the region
they do not give an accurate estimate of the inherent
worth of these functions, or provide good information
on the potential demand for the functions if they were
more accessible.[12]

The same data were used to examine the distance-
decay relationships for each function--that is, the
decline in the number of visits that people made to a
function as the length of the journey increased. A
slow decline in the relationship indicates that the
function is not highly sensitive to distance; people
are willing to travel long distances in order to obtain
the good or service it offers. The observations are
plotted on a graph with the number of visits and the
length of journey as the two axes. Table 6-2 summarizes the cumulative percentages of visits over time for
the ten most frequently used functions. As the table
indicates, the distance-decay relationship declined
most rapidly for grocery stores; 83 percent of the
visits were to places within 15 minutes travel time.
Seventy percent of the trips to high schools were
within the same travel-time interval. Over seventy
percent of the trips to post offices and doctors'
clinics were less than one-half hour. The decline was
slower for fuel stores, pharmacies, hospitals and
markets. They reached their seventieth percentile
after two hours. The slowest decline was for farm supplies, which reached that level only after five hours.

The analysis confirmed the preliminary conclusions
of the linkage analyses. Evans points out that instead
of visitng a doctor's office nearby, people often
travelled to a hospital farther away to obtain better
care. The farmers' persistence in visiting distant
farm supply stores suggested that there could be

Table 6-1

WEIGHTED ACCESSIBILITY INDEXES FOR FUNCTIONS IN POTOSI, BOLIVIA

Function	Number of Observations	N_j	T_j	P_j	Weight
Market	179	32	2.15	1.00	68.8
Grocery store	100	73	0.54	1.00	39.4
Cooking and heating fuel store	151	24	1.39	1.00	33.4
Radiocommunication and t'phones	17	25	1.33	1.00	(20.0)
Pharmacy	141	5	2.03	1.00	10.1
Junior school	159	200	0.27	0.16	8.6
Banks	11	12	1.34	0.49	(7.9)
Junior-high school	82	196	0.29	0.13	7.4
Post and telegraph office	94	10	0.73	1.00	7.3
Mineral processing plant	6	44	1.22	0.13	(7.0)
Shoe and clothing store	180	2	3.04	1.00	6.1
Silo or farm produce storage	3	2	4.40	0.60	(5.3)
Mining Bank depository	8	12	3.24	0.13	(5.1)
High school	43	200	0.25	0.10	5.0
Training Center	6	200	0.30	0.08	(4.8)
Hospital or health center	224	3	1.56	1.00	4.7
Domestic appliance store	203	1	3.80	1.00	3.8
Farm produce processing plant	48	3	1.95	.060	3.5
Hardware store	65	1	3.32	1.00	3.3
Farm tools and equipment store	60	1	4.85	0.60	2.9
Seeds and fertilizer store	51	1	4.61	0.60	2.8
Prefect/mayor/civil registrar	133	2	1.03	1.00	2.1
Doctor's clinic or nurse's post	146	2	0.92	1.00	1.8
Police station or magistrate	84	4	0.35	1.00	1.4

N_j = average number of visits per year to function j

T_j = average time in hours of journeys to function j

P_j = proportion of the population that normally uses the function j

Weighting factor $W_j = N_j \times T_j \times P_j$

Figures in (parentheses) should be interpreted cautiously due to the limited number of observations.

Source: CORDEPO, Funciones Urbanas en el Desarrollo Rural: Resultados del Estudio en Potosi, Vol. 2, CORDEPO, Potosi, 1981; and Hugh Evans, Urban Functions in Rural Development: The Case of the Potosi Region in Bolivia, Washington: USAID, 1982.

Table 6-2

CUMULATIVE PERCENTAGES OF VISITS TO SELECTED FUNCTIONS BY TRAVEL TIME, POTOSI, BOLIVIA

Travel Time		High School	Post Office	Doctor's Clinic	Farm Supplies	Grocery Store	Pharmacy	Cooking Fuel	Market	Hospital	Farm Equipment
Hours	Minutes										
0	15	70.0	52.5	62.7		83.0	35.0	48.0	35.3	56.0	5.0
0	30	97.5	72.5	71.1	25.0	84.4	43.0	59.3	46.3	63.8	10.0
0	45		75.5						47.8		
1	00		78.5	73.1	30.5	88.4	55.0	63.3	55.7	65.8	13.0
1	30	100.0	82.8	76.5	35.5	92.4	65.0	70.1	64.5	69.8	20.0
2	00		92.8	81.5	43.5	94.0	74.0	83.1	74.2	74.8	41.0
3	00		98.1	94.9	58.5	96.8	85.0	90.1	83.8	86.4	60.0
4	00		98.3	98.9	65.5	98.0	89.3	95.1	89.7	89.4	66.0
5	00		98.7		67.0	98.6	91.6	95.4	90.4	93.4	69.0
6	00										75.0
7	00				80.5		94.3				83.0
8	00				85.0		96.3	97.3	94.6	97.8	88.0
9	00		100.0	100.0	90.0				96.6		
10	00										
12	00						97.5	99.1			
14	00										
16	00				100.0						
18	00							100.0			
20	00					100.0	100.0				
22	00								100.0	100.0	
24	00										
48	00										100.0

Source: CORDEPO, Funciones Urbanas en el Desarrollo Rural: Resultados del Estudio en Potosi, Vol. 1, CORDEPO, Potosi, 1981; and Hugh Evans, Urban Functions in Rural Development: The Case of the Potosi Region in Bolivia, Washington: USAID, 1982.

large potential demand for such functions if they were located in more accessible places throughout the region.[13]

The results of the accessbility study were used together with those of the scalogram and linkage analyses to delineate the service areas of functions and settlements and to refine the functional hierarchy of settlements derived from the scalogram. Although the accessibility model could have been used to determine the market areas of settlements in each level of the hierarchy, it was actually used only to delineate the rural areas of the region. These rural areas were to form what later would become the basic planning units for regional development.[14]

The rural areas were intitially delineated by preparing maps of the effective service areas of rural centers for each function normally found at the third tier of settlements in the scalogram. Weekly markets, health centers, and fuel and drug stores were representative functions. These maps were then superimposed on each other, in much the same way as is done in preparing service area cluster maps. In this way the service areas of different functions of a settlement could be compared. While the degree of variability was high, the effective market or functional economic areas of rural centers could be delineated in terms of those zones having effective service to the majority of functions. Where residents of a zone had access to functions in more than one center, the zone was assigned to the market area of that town providing the greatest accessibility.

The definition of an "effective service area" is always the subject of some debate. But in Potosi it was considered to be those areas having zones with a level of access at least 50 percent of the maximum observed in settlements located outside of the city of Potosi. Travel pattern data gathered from survey of households showed not only that the number of visits to a function tended to fall off with increasing journey time and distance, but also that the proportion of families making journeys also declined. Evans points out that it might be, for example, "that in the case of pharmacies, 90% of the families use such a facility when the travel time is less than half an hour, 75% when the journey is less than one hour, and 50% when it is less than three hours. If 'effective' service is defined in terms of observed use, say where at least 50% of families made use of the facility, then the effective area would include only those zones where the journey time is less than three hours,"[15] (See Table 6-3).

The region of Potosi was nearly always identified with the political-administrative boundaries of the Department, although the UFRD studies found that many

Table 6-3

SUB-REGIONAL CENTERS IN THE DEPARTMENT OF POTOSI, BOLIVIA

Sub-region	Rural Area	T_{max} (hrs)	km^2	Local area
NORTH Center: Llallagua/	Llallagua/Uncia	5.54	3,300	Llallagua/Uncia Chayanta Entre Rios
	Colquechaca	2.28	2,700	Colquechaca Macha Pocoata
	None Corresponding			Ocuri Sacaca S.P.de Buena Vista
CENTRAL Center: City of	City of Potosi	3.11	3,200	City of Potosi Caiza "D"
	Betanzos	1.99	1,600	Betanzos Colavi
	Puna	0.72	600	Puna
	None Corresponding			Punutuma Otavi Vitichi
SOUTH Center: Tupiza	Tupiza	3.58	4,300	Tupiza
	Villazon	4.06	2,500	Villazon
	Atocha (part of)	5.27	5,300	Atocha Rosario Tanza
	Cotagaita	1.41	2,400	Costagaita
	None Corresponding			S.P.de Lipez
WEST Center: Uyuni	Uyuni	3.24	8,000	Uyuni Pulcayo
	Llica	2.50	4,100	Llica Huanaque
	Atocha (part of)	5.27	5,300	Atocha
	None Corresponding			Colcha "K" S.P.de Quemez Rio Mulatos

T_{max} = estimated maximum travel time from any zone in the rural area to the rural center.

Source: Hugh Evans, Urban Functions in Rural Development: The Case of the Potosi Region in Bolivia, Washington: USAID, 1982.

areas on the periphery of the department were more closely tied economically to nearby regions and capitals of other departments. The city of Potosi did serve as a regional center for a number of functions, including higher education through the university and other technical training institutes; the communications media through newspapers and television, and as a unit of government administration. Most of the institutions representing region-wide functions were concentrated in the city of Potosi and did serve a good portion of the department.

The accessibility studies also allowed planners to discern quite clearly four subregional centers-- Llallagua-Uncia-Siglo XX, the city of Potosi, Uyuni and Tupiza. Such functions as banks, savings and loan associations, legal services, wholesaling and import-export activities, and retail outlets for furniture and domestic appliances were concentrated in them and they served a wide surrounding area. These subcenters also contained some government offices and daily markets. Some had farm supply stores and hospitals. The maximum travel time from the periphery of the areas in which these sub-regional centers were located to the center itself was nearly the same in all four areas--about 10 hours--except for the western region where the terrain was much flatter and the roads in better condition, where it was about 4 hours.

The accessibility study also identified rural service centers providing basic, frequently-used household goods and services, and sometimes a gas station, vocational school or farm supply store. Some settlements, such as the City of Potosi, which are clearly regional or subregional centers, also functioned as rural service centers because they contained many of the establishments that provided goods or services primarily to rural households. This can be expected in areas of a region where service areas are hierarchical and "nested."

Finally, local centers were also identified as places that provided only the most basic goods and services and those that were most frequently used. The service areas of these centers were quite small and accessibility to them was very poor.[16]

IMPLICATIONS OF THE SPATIAL ANALYSES

In both the Department of Potosi and the Bicol River Basin, planners were able to describe and analyze the settlement structure, distribution of functions, service areas of settlements and accessibility of important functions and centers to rural populations more effectively after mapping and interpreting spatial information from the UFRD studies.

In Potosi, the studies made clear that the urbanization process in that part of Bolivia was only in its incipient stages. The settlement system through which development would have to proceed in the region was still unarticulated and unintegrated. Evans and his associates found that "the regional capital, the sub-regional centers and a number of lower level service centers have established themselves, although some of these, particularly the smaller settlements serving the farming communities are weak and in some cases show signs of decline."[17] In large parts of the region, especially in the north, there were few central places with adequate facilities and infrastructure to function as service centers for their rural areas, and from which rural people could obtain the inputs needed to increase agricultural production or their incomes.

The accessibility and service area studies confirmed that interaction among settlements in Potosi were only strong along the main roads from Potosi to Sucre and Villazon, and between Llallagua-Uncia and cities outside of the region. In much of the Department, physical access to even subregional centers was weak. Roads were in such bad condition that whatever services and facilities were located in rural and local centers were barely accessible to people living outside the settlements. "In sum, it is fair to say that by far the greater part of the region remains poorly integrated into the main urban-rural system," Evans concluded, "particularly the provinces of Ibanez, Bilbao and Charcas in the north, the periphery of Linares and Saavedra, even many communities in Frias and Quijarro in the middle and almost the whole of the west."[18]

From the analytical maps and accessibility studies planners delineated 18 functionally related areas that could be used for coherent sub-regional planning and for developing regional investment strategies and programs. (See Figure 6-6) The region was then divided into five major sub-regions encompassing these 18 planning units. Each had a settlement as the subregional center except the Southwest, where there was no town large and functionally diversified enough to perform that function. Each subregion encompassed from two to four provinces, each having a rural service center. Table 6-4 lists the subregions, the 18 planning units and the rural service centers in each unit.

The analytical maps and functional-settlement service area analyses also allowed planners in the Bicol River Basin to draw more definite conclusions about characteristics of the the spatial system. They found, for example, that the major services, facilities, infrastructure and productive activities in the region were heavily concentrated in Naga and Legaspi and that the lack of an articulated and integrated

206

FIGURE 6-6

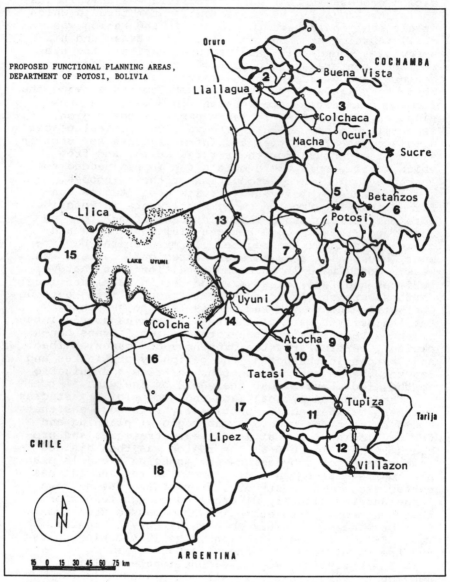

PROPOSED FUNCTIONAL PLANNING AREAS,
DEPARTMENT OF POTOSI, BOLIVIA

Table 6-4

PROPOSED SUBREGIONAL PLANNING AREAS AND CENTERS
POTOSI, BOLIVIA

Sub-region	Sub-regional Center	Rural Area	Rural Center
North	Llallagua/Uncia		
		1. North of Potosi	Acasio
		2. Bustillos	Llalagua/Uncia
		3. Chayanta	Colquechaca
Central	City of Potosi	5. *Potosi	City of Potosi
		6. Betanzos	Betanzos
		7. Quijarro East	Punutuma
		8. Vitichi	Vitichi
South	Tupiza	9. Cotagaita	Cotagaita
		10. Atocha	Atocha
		11. Tupiza	Tupiza
		12. Villazon	Villazon
North-west	Uyuni	13. Rio Mulatos	Rio Mulatos
		14. Uyuni	Uyuni
		15. D. Campos	Llica
		16. Nor Lipez	Colcha "K"
South-west	None	17. S.P. de Lipez	S.P. de Lipez
		18. Sud Lipez	(to be determined)

*Rural are #4 was subsequently absorbed into rural area #5, Potosi.

Source: H. Evans, Urban Functions in Rural Development: The Case of the Potosi Region in Bolivia, Washington: USAID, 1982.

system of settlements within the region prevented a
large percentage of the population living on the periphery and away from the Manila South Road from having
access to the functions concentrated in the cities.
They noted that "people in the Basin, therefore, have
little choice but to go directly to these two cities
even for basic services that should have been available
in nearer places." They pointed out that "the domin-
ance of existing urban centers has stunted the growth
of other sub-regions of the Basin and has slowed down
the growth of intermediate-and smaller-sized cities."

Moreover, as noted earlier, they were able to
determine that the majority of the rural population
was scattered in small barangays or villages with less
than 300 households: "too small to support services
or facilities of any developmental significance.
Against this pattern of scattered, small communities,
is the absence of enough central places, sufficiently
dispersed to provide farmers with access to needed
farm inputs and to markets where their produce can be
sold at fair prices."[19]

The analytical maps and service area studies also
confirmed earlier indications that linkages among
rural settlements and between them and the larger
central places in the region were extremely weak. The
weaknesses were due to the fact that

1. Transport connections are poor between rural
   areas and periodic markets and regular
   markets; and between market towns and the two
   provincial capitals of Naga and Legaspi;
2. There is a lack of specialization and division of labor among settlements along with
   dependence upon Metro Manila for manufactured
   commodities; and,
3. Public service delivery linkages from town
   centers to rural barangays are intermittent,
   weak, unorganized and discouraged by poor
   access.[20]

They found that the few functions located within most
smaller settlements of the Basin usually served only
the populations of those settlements and rarely provided access to people living in surrounding areas.

Examining the plans of the Bicol River Basin
Development Program (BRBDP), the UFRD staff concluded
from the spatial analysis that adjustments would be
needed in investment strategy in the future.

First, they suggested that BRBDP plans that were
based on the assumption that the Basin was a cohesive
economy be re-examined and that fundamental changes be
made in planning strategy to integrate the Basin economically and spatially. They found that at least five
subarea economies operated almost independently of each
other. As the scalogram had indicated, Naga and

Legaspi cities and their immediate rural hinterlands formed two largely autonomous economic areas and a cluster of villages surrounding the smaller city of Iriga formed another. Smaller, primarily subsistence, agricultural trade areas were scattered in rural municipalities of the Basin operating at relatively low levels, in virtual isolation. They were centered on small regular or periodic markets. Finally, relatively isolated rural areas with subsistence agricultural and fishing economies and with access only to small periodic markets, or to none at all, were found in coastal and peripheral areas of the Basin.

Second, the BRBDP's IAD boundaries, which were drawn on the basis of water resource and physical criteria, would be less useful for economic development planning later, since they took virtually no cognizance of economic and spatial subsystems in the Basin. In fact, they divided what seemed to be economically related clusters of communities. The staff suggested that more attention be given to how IAD development will integrate rural production areas with urban-centered marketing towns, and promote market center growth, spatial specialization and division of labor and exchange among settlements. The UFRD's settlement system analysis, analytical maps and linkage studies could be used to redraw IAD boundaries. (See Figure 6-7).

Third, it was suggested that the BRBDP and other national ministries operating in the Basin give immediate attention to providing increased transportation access to a larger number of rural areas. The planners noted the improbability of BRBDP attaining its goals of increased agricultural production, economic diversification and more equitable distribution of services and facilities without first extending transportation access. A network of all-weather and farm-to-market roads was found to be an essential precondition for extending services to rural people, locating agro-processing facilities in rural areas and providing access to the services, facilities and productive activities that were located in the larger towns, or for decentralizing those functions to smaller communities.

Fourth, they noted that the paucity of markets and market towns within the Basin required the immediate attention of the BRBDP. Future investments in services, facilities and infrastructure would have to be located strategically in existing or incipient rural service centers to stimulate the growth of markets. Without a well-dispersed, integrated and easily accessible network of market centers in rural areas it would be unlikely that farmers could increase

210

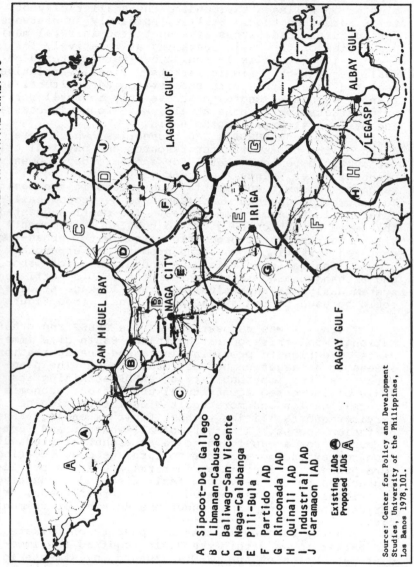

FIGURE 6-7

PROPOSED CHANGES IN SUBREGIONAL PLANNING UNITS BASED ON SPATIAL ANALYSIS

A Sipocot-Del Gallego
B Libmanan-Cabusao
C Baliwag-San Vicente
D Naga-Calabanga
E Pili-Bula
F Partido IAD
G Rinconada IAD
H Quinali IAD
J Industrial IAD
J Caramaon IAD

Existing IADs
Proposed IADs

Source: Center for Policy and Development
Studies, University of the Philippines,
Los Banos 1978,101.

production to the levels projected by the BRBDP. The BRBDP had, to this point, concentrated on planning for the provision of agricultural inputs to stimulate production, but had given little attention to marketing and distribution. Experience in the Philippines and other developing nations clearly showed that both must be done simultaneously. The UFRD study pinpointed the location of existing or incipient market centers and the analysis, supplemented by more intensive marketing studies, could be used to plan the location of investments that would stimulate rural market-center growth.

Finally, the UFRD study provided a descriptive profile of all settlements and of the distribution of services and facilities in the Basin that could be used to develop more detailed locational criteria for projects. Plans then had to be made for increasing the access of the rural poor to town-based services and facilities, building and integrating settlements of sufficient size to support a diversity of productive and social functions, and coordinating agricultural with industrial development projects.[21]

In sum, these spatial analyses can help planners understand locational implications in formulating investment strategy and in designing "packages of investments" and specific projects for individual settlements or particular areas of the region. It is to these issues that attention turns in the final four phases of the UFRD approach.

212

NOTES

1. Prodipto Roy and B.R. Patil, Manual for Block Level Planning, Delhi: The Macmillan Company of India, 1977.

2. G.C. Dickinson, Statistical Mapping and the Presentation of Statistics, 2nd Ed., London: Edward Arnold, 1973, especially Chapter 2.

3. Bicol River Basin Development Program, Urban Functions in Rural Development: A Research Project in Spatial Analysis and Planning, Pili, The Philippines: BRBDP, 1978.

4. Aiden Southall, "Urban Functions in Rural Development: Report on a Visit to Upper Volta," unpublished report, (Washington: U.S. Agency for International Development, 1978).

5. Center for Policy and Development Studies, University of the Philippines, Los Banos, Urban Functions in Rural Development, Bicol River Basin Development Program, Vol. III-B: Case Study of Six Periodic Markets in the Bicol River Basin, College, Laguna, CPDS, 1977.

6. Ross S. Dick, "Central Place Service Areas and Urban Fields: New Measures of Spatial Character," Queensland Geographical Journal, Vol. 5 (1979), pp. 65-78.

7. A.E. Smailes, The Geography of Towns, (London: Hutchinson, 1966), p. 145.

8. Center for Policy and Development Studies, op. cit.

9. Hugh Evans and John Dickey, "A Technique to Help Evaluate Function and Linkage Packages," unpublished paper, Potosi, Bolivia: Urban Functions in Rural Development Project, 1980.

10. Hugh Evans, Urban Functions in Rural Development: The Case of the Region in Bolivia, Vol. 1 (Washington: USAID, 1982), pp. 66-68.

11. Ibid. p. 68.

12. Idem.

13. Idem.

14. Ibid., p. 80.

15. Idem.

16. Ibid., pp. 81-86.

17. Ibid., p. 88.

18. Idem.

19. Bicol River Basin Development Program, op. cit. p. 99.

20. Idem.

21. See Dennis A. Rondinelli, "Spatial Analysis for Regional Development: A Case Study in the Bicol River Basin of the Philippines," Resource Systems Theory and Methodology Series, No. 2 (Tokyo: United Nations University, 1980), pp. 37-38.

7
Integrating Spatial Analysis
in Regional Planning

The final phases of UFRD focus on integrating spatial analysis with sectoral, economic and technical
planning. They are concerned with promoting the use of
locational information and standards in the on-going
processes of planning and decision-making that most
directly affect the region's development. Phases seven
through ten of UFRD include: formulating a broad spatial strategy for regional development; identifying
possible programs and projects for various areas and
settlements within the region; establishing monitoring
and evaluation procedures to assure that programs and
projects are implemented on schedule and to assess
their impact on the regional settlement system; and
integrating spatial analysis methods into institutionalized processes of regional planning and policy-making.
As explained in Chapter Two, the aim of doing spatial analyses is not necessarily to produce a comprehensive physical plan for the region, but rather to
identify the spatial and locational factors that should
be taken into account in future development decisions.
Initially, the UFRD approach yields a detailed report
on the settlement system and conclusions and recommendations for promoting integrated regional development.
This is less a plan, however, than a set of policy
recommendations. In later iterations, it is often more
desirable to integrate the methods of spatial analysis
described here into the general process of regional
planning rather than to carry them out as separate
activities. To the extent that they can be integrated
with other forms of planning it will be more likely
that physical and spatial factors will be considered
seriously in program and project design. But in its
intitial application the UFRD approach can make an
important contribution to planning and policy-making by
providing planners with the information needed to
suggest a broad strategy for spatial development.

FRAMEWORK FOR STRATEGIC PLANNING

In its initial application, the UFRD approach can yield detailed information about the physical and spatial characteristics of the region and can be used to formulate a broad strategy for spatial development. That information can also help policy-makers to locate services, facilities, infrastructure and productive activities in places that provide greater access to larger numbers of people and that will allow greater spread effects to surrounding areas.

There are relatively few ways in which planners and policy-makers can intervene to create a more articulated and integrated settlement system in a region. They include:

1. Strengthening the capacity of existing settlements to perform a wider range of functions by investing in higher order services and facilities or new types of functions in strategically located central places;

2. Strengthening existing linkages between central places where functions already exist in currently unserved or peripheral areas of the region;

3. Creating new settlements in unserved areas to act as central places for a specified range of functions;

4. Creating new linkages to reduce the travel time and cost of reaching places with appropriate functions from peripheral or unserved areas; and,

5. Enacting or changing regulations or policies affecting the operation of functions or linkages in ways that will increase the nonphysical access of people in various income groups to those functions.

These activities can be carried out on a region-wide basis or in various areas within the region in the currently existing settlements, that is, a regional urban center, intermediate-sized cities and towns, area-wide service centers, market towns, rural service centers or villages. Spatial development planning attempts to match activities that are best suited to the appropriate settlement in the appropriate areas. (See Figure 7-1.)

These strategies require a thorough understanding of the settlement system of a region as well as the historical and political reasons for its emergence in its current form, and the comparative strengths or weaknesses of areas within the region for future development. Effective regional planning and development also require an understanding of how alternative forms of economic, social, and political intervention affect, and are affected by, physical and spatial development. Just as there are relatively few alternatives for shaping physical and spatial development,

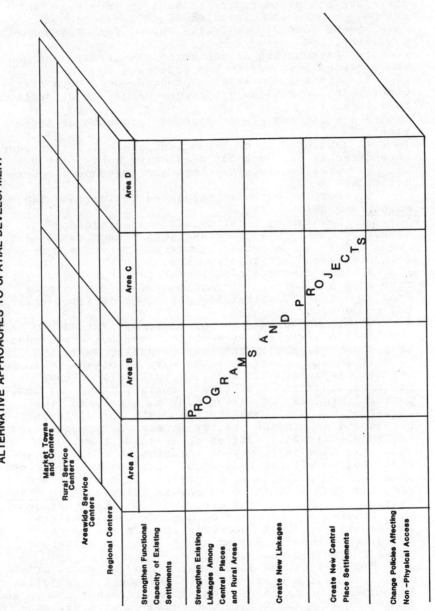

FIGURE 7-1

ALTERNATIVE APPROACHES TO SPATIAL DEVELOPMENT

there are a limited number of ways to intervene to
change the pace and direction of regional economic
development (See Figure 7-2). These, John Friedmann
has identified as:[1]

1. Discovering or capturing new markets for goods
and services produced in the region;

2. Finding new ways to produce goods more efficiently and economically through changes in production
functions;

3. Producing new or improved products or services;

4. Building up or extending physical infrastructure directly relevant for productive activities;

5. Creating local savings and investment opportunities;

6. Developing human resources to increase labor
supply and skills;

7. Developing local natural resources and
improving the locational advantages of the region and
areas within it to produce goods and services more
effectively and efficiently; and,

8. Building the capacity of institutions to provide more and better information and to disseminate
knowledge that is useful for planning, decision-making
and production.

Within any given region, these activities can be
promoted in a variety of sectors: agriculture, industry, commerce, social services or public works.

It is also clear that the pursuit of any of these
sectoral strategies in a region is likely to have
different impacts on different social, income or occupational groups. Any investment is likely to create
different kinds of benefits and costs for different
groups and to provide greater access to opportunities
for people living in different areas of the region.
Although there is no way of ensuring that any investment program will provide equal benefits to all groups
in a region, packages or portfolios of projects and
programs can be designed to ensure relatively equitable
development by providing a combination of investments
that benefit a wide range of groups--town dwellers,
landowners, landless laborers, small scale entrepreneurs, farm tenants and others--living in different
parts of the region.

Regional planners are most often concerned primarily, if not exclusively, with sectoral strategies.
The impacts of those strategies on different groups and
geographical areas within the region are rarely considered. Spatial analysis, along with social-impact
studies, can add a physical and locational dimension
that helps planners and policy-makers to calculate the
potential impact of investment programs on beneficiaries while at the same time forging a coherent

FIGURE 7-2

SECTORAL STRATEGIES FOR ACHIEVING REGIONAL ECONOMIC GROWTH

Means [1]	Sectors	Agriculture	Industry	Social Services	Infrastructure	Energy and Utilities	Health	Education	Commercial Enterprise	
Create new markets for existing goods										
Identify new ways to produce old products										
Produce new or improved goods and services		P	R	O	J	E	C	T	S	
Create new organizations for production										
Build-up or extend physical infra-structure				A	N	D				
Create local savings and investment opportunities										
Develop human resources		P	R	O	G	R	A	M	S	
Develop local natural resources										
Provide better information and knowledge										

[1]Adopted from John Friedmann, <u>Urbanization, Planning and National Development</u>, Beverly Hills: Sage Publications, 1973.

development policy for the entire region. (See Figure 7-3.)

All of this must usually be done, however, in an environment in which the capacity to formulate and implement detailed comprehensive development plans is extremely limited. Participants in regional planning and decision-making usually pursue their own interests. Action must be taken incrementally and with limited resources. Political factors often outweigh all others in resolving conflicts and disputes over proper courses of action. In most developing countries institutional dynamics make coordination and cooperation among the participants highly unlikely. Thus, planners must realize that however comprehensive and integrated their proposals may be, they are unlikely to be understood in their full complexity, agreed to entirely by other groups or implemented totally.[2]

Because of the difficulty of formulating and carrying out regional development plans comprehensively, investment plans and programs must be designed strategically and disaggregated by area so that projects can be made incrementally and sequentially. It is to this task that spatial analysis can make an important contribution.

FORMULATING SPATIAL INVESTMENT STRATEGIES

The findings of the Urban Functions in Rural Development studies were used in both the Bicol River Basin and the Department of Potosi to help formulate broad regional development strategies.

Spatial Strategy for Potosi

In Potosi, before the UFRD project began, the Departmental Development Corporation (CORDEPO) had already begun preparing a medium-term plan for the regional economy with investment programs for agriculture, mining, industry, transportation, tourism, infrastructure and other important sectors. The spatial and locational implications, however, had not been taken into consideration. The UFRD studies introduced a spatial dimension to regional planning and for the first time planners in CORDEPO began not only to identify sectoral investments but also to consider the most effective location for projects. As Evans points out: "This required a complex procedure for rationalizing and coordinating the projects proposed by each of the teams involved in global, sectoral and spatial planning. Prior to that, however, it was necessary to ensure that objectives and strategies, particularly those related to the global and spatial components of the plan, were consistent with one another."[3]

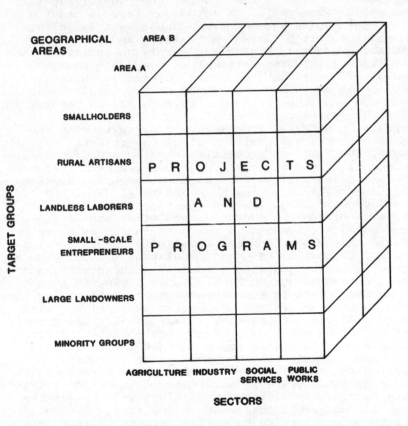

FIGURE 7-3

INTEGRATING SPATIAL, SECTORAL AND TARGET GROUP PLANNING

For the region, the plan sought to maximize the growth of the local economy in order to reduce the growing gap in income and wealth between Potosi and other regions of the country and to increase productivity and income within the Department to reduce the even wider gap in living conditions between urban and rural areas.

The economic and spatial analyses pointed to a number of common conclusions, which made the process of integrating the two much easier. First, both showed that despite the high level of mining activities in the region, the Department of Potosi was the most economically backward area of the country and was falling further behind each year. As noted earlier, it had the lowest per capita income of any department in Bolivia, the highest rate of infant mortality, and the slowest population growth. Mining was merely an enclave activity, valuable to the national economy as a source of foreign exchange, but of little benefit in increasing the incomes or living conditions of the local population. On the other hand, agriculture was the sector in which the majority of Potosi's population earned its living. It suffered from severe underinvestment and neglect by both national and local governments. As a result, the value of production was low and declining. Therefore, it was clear to CORDEPO's planners that more widespread and equitable development required substantial investment in agriculture and rural development.

Moreover, these analyses indicated that the distribution of health, education and other social services among settlements in the Department was closely related to the settlements' level of economic development and proportion of urban population. Incomes were higher in urban occupations such as manufacturing and commerce than in agriculture. Those living in towns had better access to a wider array of services, facilities, infrastructure and productive activities. With severe resource constraints, it was equally clear that such functions could be provided efficiently and economically only to towns, implying that a second component of development strategy had to be to locate services and facilities in such a way as to encourage people to concentrate in small and medium-sized settlements rather than disperse themselves widely over the rural landscape. Infrastructure and facilities would have to be provided to encourage farmers to live in clustered settlements.

In addition, the analyses revealed that with few exceptions the mining towns had been gaining while farming towns had been losing population. The scalogram analyses, however, showed that seven of the eleven third-tier settlements in the hierarchy (rural centers) and almost half of the fourth-tier (local centers) were

mining towns, although they represented a smaller proportion of the total number of towns and villages. The
relatively higher level of infrastructure and social
services found in mining towns was due to the fact that
investment in farming towns had been largely ignored.
Planners therefore saw the need to reduce this imbal-
ance by increasing investment in social services and
infrastructure in selected rural service centers that
were accessible to the farming population.

Furthermore, as Evans pointed out, "it was evident
from an examination of the distribution of other urban
functions that there was a widespread lack of the
infrastructure and services required for agricultural
production, such as irrigation, storage facilities,
farm supply stores for seeds, fertilizers, tools and
equipment, as well as mills and other plants for processing farm produce. This once again reflected the
low priority previously given to agriculture in the
region."[4] It also reflected the weak demand for such
facilities due to the low level of rural household
income. Future development policy therefore would have
to pay more attention to the provision of such infrastructure.

The studies of linkages and accessibility under-
lined the importance of rural roads in connecting small
communities to towns and urban centers and in providing
access for the rural population to the functions provided in them. Moreover, the studies found rural roads
to be major factors in giving farmers access to markets
for their surplus goods and in providing them with the
incentives to increase output. High priority, therefore, had to be given in future investment plans to
extending transportation access to rural areas and
integrating outlying and poorly served rural communities.

Finally, both the economic and spatial analyses
pointed out that if agriculture was to become the
cornerstone of development in Potosi, investments
would have to be made in related service and processing
industries and in diversifying the economies of rural
communities to provide employment and stimulate the
demand for local farm produce. Analyses indicated that
there would be strong potential demand for storage and
packaging facilities, mills, slaughterhouses and other
small labor-intensive food processing operations if
agricultural development strategy was successful.
Agricultural production would not be able to increase,
however, without substantial investment in farm-related
infrastructure and services such as irrigation works,
production and marketing cooperatives, and agricultural
credit. "The promotion of new industries related to
agriculture in small and middle-sized settlements also
served other goals of the plan," Evans noted. "The

prospect of better jobs, coupled with the policy of
upgrading the provision of infrastructure and services
in selected towns and villages, is designed to provide
the incentives necessary to encourage the rural population to resettle in urban centers. The increased
urbanization of the population is expected in turn to
facilitate the diffusion of developmental impulses and
to act as a catalyst in exposing farmers to more modern
methods of production."5

The spatial implications of the strategy were
clear. Action would have to be taken to strengthen the
hierarchy of central places in the region, particularly
the small-and intermediate-sized settlements that had
few functions, and to improve the linkages between them
and their surrounding communities in order to integrate
isolated or peripheral areas into the regional economic
system. Investments had to be made initially in
facilities to support agricultural production and to
meet the basic needs of the rural population. Planners
began to choose the towns and villages that would act
as rural and local service centers by three criteria:
1) the economic potential of the locality and its long-
term prospects for continued growth and diversification; 2) the strength of the settlement's linkages with
other towns and with the surrounding rural areas; and
3) the existing range of functions found in the settlement. Particular attention was given to the possi-
bility of revitalizing traditional farming towns that
had recently lost population.

Linkages would be improved by upgrading main roads
between the larger towns in the region and building
feeder roads to connect service centers to surrounding
rural areas. This would both increase the access of
the rural population to functions located in urban
service centers and expand the potential market for
manufacturing and commercial establishments located in
them.

Strengthening the urban hierarchy also meant
investing in new functions in settlements where they
were missing and rationalizing the distribution of
existing facilities to increase the access of rural
population to them.

The strategy recognized the need to build on the
productive potential and comparative advantages of each
area within the region. The design of the "package of
projects" for each area would thus begin by identifying
the main economic activities of the area, and determining the infrastructure and services--such as credit,
irrigation, technical assistance, storage and market
facilities--needed to support those activities. Investments would also be made in education, health care and
other social services to meet basic needs. Evans noted
that "in Potosi, the concept of designing packages of

projects for specific areas, as opposed to the more conventional approach of individual projects in each
sector, introduced a new perspective on the allocation
of investments." In previous years, he pointed out,
"the discussion had always been in terms of sectoral
needs and priorities, now for the first time the distribution of resources in different parts of the Department
was taken into account explicitly: planners and
decision-makers were able to consider instead the
options of giving priority to specific provinces or
areas of the region."[6]

Spatial Strategy in the Bicol River Basin

As in Potosi, the Bicol River Basin Development
Program had already formulated a number of regional
development plans, all of which were sectoral or technical and none of which explicitly included spatial or
locational factors. Although Integrated Area Development (IAD) units were created to identify projects for
particular places in the region, these units were based
on natural resources and not on the functional and economic characteristics of settlements. Indeed, some of
the IAD boundaries had broken up functionally-related
settlement sub-systems into two or three different planning units.

The BRBDP's comprehensive plan for the region
sought to achieve six major goals:
1. To accelerate growth in the agricultural
   sector;
2. To stimulate investment in manufacturing and a
   tertiary industries;
3. To expand employment opportunities;
4. To distribute equitably income and wealth;
5. To improve social services; and,
6. To promote maximum popular participation in
   planning and implementation.[7]
Projects were classified sectorally under four major
development categories: physical development, including
water resources and transport; agricultural development;
agribusiness and rural manufacturing; and health, nutri-
tion and social services development.

The general problems of development were well known
through extensive sectoral and technical studies prior
to the formulation of the comprehensive plan. These
problems included the region's physical isolation from
Manila and other centers of national economic activity;
a hostile physical environment with extensive flooding
and salinity intrusion; inefficient agricultural production and marketing technology; capital scarcity for
investment in appropriate physical infrastructure and
services; rapid population growth and outmigration; high
levels of ill-health in rural households, malnutrition

and poor environmental sanitation; inequitable land tenure arrangements; and ineffective delivery of government services.[8]

All of these problems were addressed to one degree or another in the BRBDP's development plans (See Figure 7-4). However, the plans did not have a strong locational or spatial dimension. Little attention was given to where projects would be located. But the UFRD study was done after the comprehensive plan had largely been formulated and was not completed until after the plan had been published. Thus, the UFRD study was seen primarily as a pilot project to test methods and techniques of spatial analyses and as a background study to provide information that would be used in future development plans and programs.

The planners who carried out the UFRD study in Bicol, nonetheless, derived from it the outlines for a spatial development strategy. As noted earlier, the UFRD studies indicated quite clearly that:

1. Services, facilities and infrastructure were heavily concentrated in a few of the largest settlements in the Basin and in those towns and villages along the Manila South Road.

2. Only a few settlements in the Bicol River Basin served as central places for other communities and rural areas. Naga City, Legaspi, Iriga and a few others were the only settlements that acted as area-wide service centers. The large majority of settlements--over 95 percent--were noncentral places. Their average population was about 300 households and most contained only very basic functions such as a small grocery stall or a few small shops.

3. Linkages of all kinds among places in the Basin were extremely weak. Little social, physical or economic interaction took place between the two provinces of the Basin or among municipalities that were not connected by the Manila South Road. The functions located in the towns, therefore, served only the residents of the town and few nearby communities; access for rural people who lived off of the main highway was limited.

4. Large disparities in income and living conditions existed between the more urbanized centers of the Basin and the rural peripheral areas. Large gaps also existed in the services, facilities, infrastructure and productive activities between the few urban centers in the region and the large number of small villages and towns.

5. The settlement system of the Basin was neither well-articulated nor well-integrated. Rather, clusters of economically and functionally autonomous settlements existed around some of the larger towns in the Basin, which were neither integrated with each other nor with the rural areas surrounding them. Services and facilities could not be arranged in a hierarchical fashion to

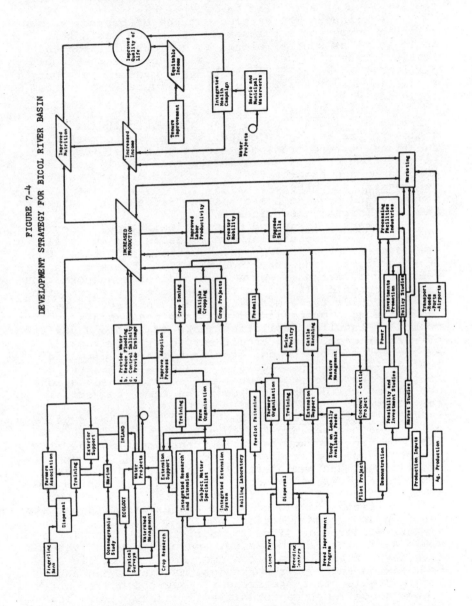

FIGURE 7-4

DEVELOPMENT STRATEGY FOR BICOL RIVER BASIN

serve differing needs in the Basin, and those communities located off of the all-weather roads received very few services on a regular basis.[9]

The planners who carried out the UFRD studies identified a number of settlements within the Basin that could serve as central places at various hierarchical levels. They also delineated the functions they could perform if adequate investments were made in services, facilities and infrastructure (see Figure 7-5). These included:[10]

1. Rural Service Centers, which would contain services and facilities to assemble agricultural commodities for marketing, provide local periodic marketing functions, extend transport access to market towns and larger urban centers, accommodate small-scale agro-processing and handicrafts, distribute credit, market information and other technical inputs, mobilize savings, and provide basic health, recreation, education and administrative services;

2. Market Towns and Centers, which would provide an areawide exchange point for trade in agricultural commodities, processed goods, household and common consumer products, and farm inputs; offer access to an all-weather road network; serve as a node of transportation and distribution linked to regional centers within the Basin, provide the preconditions and infrastructure to stimulate agro-processing plants and small-scale bulk commodity handling facilities; make available a variety of rural financial and credit services; meet rural energy and utility needs; provide higher-level administrative services that could be found in rural service centers; and offer vocational and secondary education, health and child care services, and rural commercial services; and

3. Regional Centers that would be linked physically to each other and to urban centers outside the Basin by frequent and reliable transportation and all-weather roads; offer diversified commercial, financial, professional and administrative services; accommodate regional offices of national government ministries and branch offices of provincial government agencies; provide facilities for large-scale and diversified markets; function as a communications node for a broad rural hinterland; provide sites for agri-business and large-scale agricultural processing, and offer incentives for a variety of small-scale consumer goods industries, tool-making and repair workshops, machine shops and light durable goods industries. They could also offer higher educational opportunities and more specialized vocational training, and provide diversified and multi-purpose hospitals and health clinics.

The planners who conducted the spatial studies also argued that more equitable development in the Basin

FIGURE 7-5

SERVICES, FACILITIES AND INFRASTRUCTURE PROPOSED FOR EACH SETTLEMENT LEVEL,
BICOL RIVER BASIN

General Functions	Rural Service Centers	Market Towns and Centers	Regional Urban Centers
Transport and Communications	-Surfaced, All-Weather Roads -Farm Access Roads -Bus Stop -Regular Bus or Jeepney Service to Rural Collection Points -Gas Station -Telegraph Service -Postal Service	-Asphalted, All-Weather Roads -Bus Terminal -Trucking or Bulk-Distributing Services -Regular Bus or Jeepney Service to Rural Service and Regional Urban Centers -Gas and Service Station -Auto Spare Parts Retail Store -Telegraph-Radiogram Service -Telephone Station -Postal Services	-Concrete Highway to Major Urban Centers -Bus Terminal with Major Repair Facilities -Auto & Machine Repair Shops -Vehicle and Machine Spare Part Shops -Regional and interregional Trucking and Bus Services -Gas and Service Stations -Railroad, Port and Air Terminals -Telegraph, Telegram, Telex Services and Facilities -Telephone Exchanges linked to Major Urban Centers and Market Towns -Postal Distribution Centers
Marketing, Trade and Shopping	-Periodic Market Facilities -Farm Implements and Agricultural Supply Shop -Marketing Cooperative Outlet -Storage Facilities -General Store or Sari-Sari Stores -Milling Facilities	-Daily Market Facilities -Retail Outlets for Farm Supplies -Wholesale Outlets for Farm Implements -Cold Storage and Warehouse Facilities -Grocery Shops -Household Goods Retail Shops -Grading and Bulk Assembly Facilities	-Diversified Daily Market -Distribution Outlets and Sales Offices for Farm Machines -Farm Supply Wholesalers -Cold Storage and Warehousing -Agricultural Commodity Brokers and Distributers Outlets -Diversified Commercial Retail and Wholesale Establishments -Retail Outlets for Consumer Goods, Household Goods -Consumer Specialty Shops

(continued)

General Functions	Rural Service Centers	Market Towns and Centers	Regional Urban Centers
Industrial and Manufacturing	-Cottage Industry -Small Scale Craft Shops -Small Machine Repair Shops and Metal Shops	-Bulk Commodity Processing Facilities -Agricultural Processing Plants -Small Scale Consumer Goods Manufacturing Facilities -Small Machine, Implement and Metal Shops	-Agro-Industry and Agribusiness Facilities -Commodity Processing and Packaging -Rural Goods Production and Distribution Facilities -Small Tool and Implement Production Facilities
Finance	-Rural Bank -Credit Cooperative	-Commercial and Savings Bank Facilities -Rural Bank with Nonagricultural Loan Programs -Credit Cooperatives -Moneylenders and Pawnshops	-Development and Commercial Bank Branch -Savings and Loan Associations -Insurance and Financial Establishments -Urban and Rural Credit Coops -Brokerage Firms -Chambers of Commerce -Small Industry and Business Incentive Programs
Public Utilities	-Piped Water Supply Points -Small Water Filtration Facilities -Residential Electricity	-Electrical Energy Station -Residential Piped Water Supply -Residential and Commercial Area Drainage Systems	-Electric Supply Grid -Piped Water System -Sewerage and Drainage System -Waste Disposal System
Administration	-Municipal Service Office -Barangay Government Office -Police or PC Sub-station -Municipal Court Branch -Agricultural Extension Station	-Municipal or Barangay Govt. Office -IAD Team Headquarters Office -Police or PC Station -District Office of Agricultural Extension -Judicial Facilities -National Ministry Program District Offices	-Provincial Government Offices -Municipal Hall and Administrative Offices -Regional Planning and Development Agency Offices -Municipal and Provincial Court -Branch Offices of National Ministries -Regional Office Headquarters

General Functions	Rural Service Centers	Market Towns and Centers	Regional Urban Centers
Administration	-Municipal Service Office -Barangay Government Office -Police or PC Sub-station -Municipal Court Branch -Agricultural Extension Station	-Municipal or Barangay Govt. Office -IAD Team Headquarters Office -Police or PC Station -District Offices of Agricultural Extension -Judicial Facilities -National Ministry Program District Offices	-Provincial Government Offices -Municipal Hall and Administrative Offices -Regional Planning and Development Agency Offices -Municipal and Provincial Court -Branch Offices of National Ministries -Regional Office Headquarters
Recreation and Social	-Paved Basketball Court -Multi-purpose Community Center	-Paved Basketball Court -Small Gymnasium/Auditorium -Restaurants and Coffee Shops -Cinema -Playground with Facilities	-Paved Basketball courts -Parks and Plazas -Cinema with Daily Run -Hotel with Nightclubs -Restaurants -Gymnasium/Auditorium -Multipurpose Community Center -Diversified Social Activities
Education	-Primary Schools -Vocation Education Facilities	-Primary Schools -High Schools -Vocational Schools -Extension and Home Economics Classes -Agricultural Demonstration Facilities	-Primary and Secondary Schools -Small Colleges and Technical Schools -Specialized Vocational Training Programs -Regional Agricultural Research Station
Health	-Dispensary-Clinic -Maternal/Child Care Service	-Multi-Purpose Clinic -Area Health Office -Physicians, Dentists -Drugstores	-General Hospital -Public Health Offices -Physicians, Dentists, Surgeons -Retail Pharmaceutical Outlets

would require better physical linkages between rural areas and towns. Among the most important linkages were farm-to-market roads and all-weather arterials between market centers and larger cities. It was inconceivable, they contended, that the BRBDP would be able to attain its goals of increased agricultural production, economic diversification and equitable distribution of income and wealth without first improving transportation. Substantial portions of the northern and northwestern areas of the Basin and the peripheral areas of the southwestern coast were completely inaccessible by road.[11] In both the Bicol River Basin and the Department of Potosi, the spatial analyses allowed planners for the first time to assess the settlement system in the region and to derive from that assessment spatial and locational implications for regional development. The suggestions for broad strategies of spatial development, however, had to be integrated with sectoral and technical proposals for specific projects and programs.

FORMULATING INVESTMENT PROGRAMS AND PROJECTS

The UFRD analyses can be used not only to outline a broad spatial development strategy, but also to identify specific projects and programs needed to provide essential functions and to strengthen the settlement system's capacity to promote development.

As in strategy formulation, the spatial analyses must be used together with economic, sectoral, social and technical analyses to help planners and policy-makers form better judgments about the types of projects and programs that are needed and where they might be located. Often, the most important contribution that the UFRD analyses can make to the process is to raise further questions and lead planners to think in different ways about the allocation of investments and the design of projects. There are specific methods and techniques that can be used at this phase of the UFRD approach to help planners cope with spatial and locational issues, but again these must be used in conjunction with other forms of analysis and planning in order to be most useful. They include demand analysis, relative partitioning methods to find the most efficient location for new settlements, project "package" identification methods, distance-access-equity assessment methods and locational sensitivity analyses.

Demand Analyses--Household and Social Surveys

Much of the methodology used in the UFRD approach is "supply" oriented. It assesses the degree of articulation and integration in the settlement system by the distribution of functions within a region and assumes

that the continued survival of those functions is an
indication of demand. A more direct method of ascer-
taining demand, of course, is by asking those people who
live in the region and in various settlements throughout
the region what types of functions they need and want.

In both Potosi and the Bicol River Basin household
sample surveys were used to determine the location of
functions and to obtain some indication of what types of
services and facilities people desired. In Potosi,
questions were included in the household surveys used to
gather information for the scalogram, linkage and
accessibility analyses about services and facilities
that were needed in communities. The questions could be
asked quickly and inexpensively during the functional
inventory.

In the Bicol River Basin an extensive and systematic set of social surveys were carried out under the
auspices of the Social Survey Research Unit (SSRU) of a
local university--the Ataneo de Naga. The surveys
included both large sample studies of households
throughout the Basin and stratified and occupation group
studies of households in specific municipalities.
Studies were done of the problems and needs of rice
farmers, fishpond owners, cooperative members, credit
association members, those living on land consolidation
projects, people living in areas where proposed projects
were to be located, irrigation users, people living in
flooded areas, the unemployed, local elite groups, and
those suffering from particular types of health and
nutritional problems.

Moreover, the SSRU surveys included large-scale
household studies of people's needs and desires and
baseline studies of living conditions. A sample of over
1,000 Basin farmers was questioned in the mid-1970s, for
example, about the most significant problems with which
they had to cope. The survey was one means of identifying projects that might be undertaken to deal with
development problems. In decreasing order of frequency,
people identified the following as their most important
problems: threats to peace and order, flooding, lack of
roads, unemployment, poor drinking water, ineffective
community organizations, lack of transportation, lack of
access to electricity, dirty and unsanitary surround-
ings, and high prices.[12] A sample of 3,240 household
heads yielded a great deal of information about what
factors people in Bicol thought were related to an
improved quality of life. They indicated that the following were most important: to have a respectable job
and an adequate income; to have a sturdy home, to have
adequate food and drink and sufficient furnishings; to
enjoy esteem and status in their community, and to participate in small group activities and community
affairs.[13]

The surveys further indicated that people in Bicol region "have a market orientation and accept the idea that modern practices and increased production and income lead to a higher quality of life." The surveyors found that for Bicolanos, quality of life "tends first to revolve around the concept of job and income, second around the concept of adequate housing and food, and third around the concept of formal and informal group affiliation."[14]

The projects included in the Bicol River Basin Development Program's plans coincided with eight of the ten major concerns of the people revealed by the household surveys. Peace and order and social acceptance were considered goals that had to be pursued through community and national efforts and that might only indirectly result from economic development and social progress in the region.

In both Potosi and Bicol, household and social surveys were used to cross-check "supply-oriented" methods of analysis and to identify projects and programs that were needed and wanted by people living in those regions. In Bicol a substantial effort was made to include a wide range of group leaders in IAD planning units and in the BRBDP's planning and policy-making activities. Both the demand analyses and the continuing participation of a variety of occupational, geographic and economic interest groups allowed planners to attach priorities to project proposals and to assess the need and desire for functions in various locations within the region.

Partitioning Methods for the Location of New Centers

A relatively simple method of choosing preliminary sites for the location of a new settlement or for selecting settlements to be upgraded to higher order central places is available through relative partitioning. It involves the following procedures:[15]

1. Identify the largest and most functionally complex settlement in the area.
2. Search in all directions for other settlements inside or outside of the area (but not farther outside than the approximate diameter of the area).
3. Draw lines from the most important place to settlements of approximately equal importance identified in step 2, using transport routes if places are connected by reasonably direct links or, otherwise, straight lines.
4. Bisect each of these lines and construct perpendicular lines at these points of bisection.

5. The innermost area formed by the intersection
    of these perpendicular bisectors delineates the
    area that will be served from the most import-
    ant centers with functions not offered by sub-
    sidiary centers, and other areas will be served
    from other central places.
6. Identify settlements of local importance per-
    forming some functions found in higher level
    centers within the area of this boundary.
7. Select subsidiary centers to become lower order
    service centers from among these places, so
    that they are distributed approximately uni-
    formly over the boundary area.

The selection of subsidiary centers can follow one
of three models (See Figure 7-6): choose settlements at
the edges of the boundaries between major centers,
choose settlements at the corners of the boundaries
between major centers or choose settlements on either
side of the boundaries between major centers.[16] Partitioning methods should be used, however, only to obtain
preliminary indications, based on physical distance, of
where central places might be strengthened. Much more
detailed studies must then be made of the settlements
chosen through partitioning techniques to take into consideration topography, population distribution, transportation access and social interaction patterns as well
as economic growth potential, and comparative advantage.
Relative partitioning techniques, tested in area development planning in India, were introduced in the Potosi
and Bicol projects, but were not used because in neither
case had the planning agencies yet turned their attention to the creation of new settlements or the deliberate upgrading of existing settlements.

Use of Service Standards for Equitable Distribution of Functions

National ministries use service standards as a
means of allocating investments in nearly all developing
countries. Usually the criteria are based on the number
of people each function should serve--for example, one
health clinic or primary school for every three thousand
people in an area. But there are a variety of standards
that can be used to improve the distributional equity of
functions when spatial factors are taken into consideration. Morrill and Symons define efficient location of a
function as "one in which some societally predetermined
level or volume of service is met at minimum total system cost of operation and travel. Alternatively, but
similarly, an efficient pattern could be that which max-
imizes the volume of service within a predetermined budget constraint."[17] They point out that the concept of
distributional equity could take three different forms:

FIGURE 7-6

SELECTION OF SUBSIDIARY SERVICE CENTERS USING RELATIVE PARTITIONING TECHNIQUES

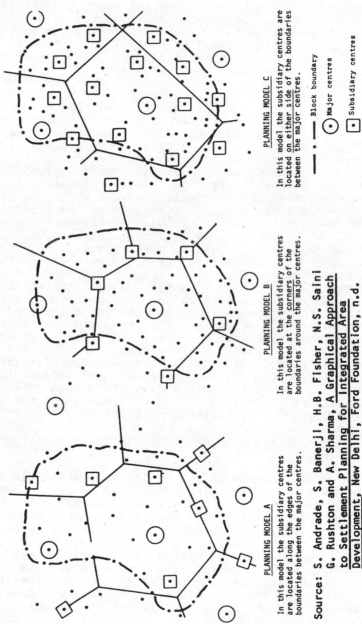

PLANNING MODEL A

In this model the subsidiary centres are located along the edges of the boundaries between the major centres.

PLANNING MODEL B

In this model the subsidiary centres are located at the corners of the boundaries around the major centres.

PLANNING MODEL C

In this model the subsidiary centres are located on either side of the boundaries between the major centres.

—— Block boundary

⊙ Major centres

☐ Subsidiary centres

Source: S. Andrade, S. Banerji, H.B. Fisher, N.S. Saini G. Rushton and A. Sharma, A Graphical Approach to Settlement Planning for Integrated Area Development, New Delhi, Ford Foundation, n.d.

1. System equity--in which average travel times to
    facilities should be no more than a prescribed
    number of minutes or kilometers of distance.
    The average travel time criterion provides some
    degree of uniformity in choosing the location
    of functions, but does not address the issue of
    disparities within the range of travel times
    that constitute the average. Usually, level of
    access to a set of functions can be raised
    using this standard by providing a larger
    number of smaller facilities distributed more
    widely throughout an area. Although average
    travel time would be reduced, in some cases
    efficiency might decline and average costs
    could increase.

2. Minimum standard--in which no more than a
    socially acceptable small percentage of people
    are more than some critical distance from a
    good or service; for example, no more than 10
    percent of the school age population will be
    more than 3 kilometers from an elementary
    school. Often, the only way that minimum
    standards can be reached effectively is to
    shift investment in services and facilities
    from more densely to less densely populated
    areas. Again, this may increase the access of
    more people who had previously been farther
    away than the minimum acceptable distance, but
    at an increased cost for those living in more
    densely populated areas and perhaps with a
    reduction in efficiency of operation. Where
    income is higher in more densely populated
    areas, however, the increased costs to richer
    people of providing greater access to poorer
    families may be a socially acceptable trade-
    off.

3. Range of Variability--in which the frequency
    distribution of time or distance required to
    travel to a set of functions is used as the
    basis for making location decisions and in
    which reduction of variability about the mean
    indicates a more equitable location pattern.
    The range of variability could be reduced for
    many functions simply by locating them in a
    regular system of central places, in a lattice-
    like pattern, over an area. If population den-
    sity and income vary greatly throughout the
    area, the reduction in the range of variability
    might come at increased cost and reduced effi-
    ciency of operation.

Some combination of standards could be used, or
different standards could be applied for different functions. Also, substitution of complementary services--

such as clinics with paramedic staff and referral
services for physician-staffed health stations or
hospitals--could increase access without shifting the
locations of higher order services.[18]
     Oberg has summarized concisely the strategies
available to planners for locating services and facilities to attain different combinations of equity and
efficiency goals:
     1.   If the major goal is urban system efficiency
and the purpose is to provide access to as many people
as possible, then functions should be located in as many
of the largest central places as possible.
     2.   If regional equity is the main objective with
the aim of giving people in as many different parts of
the region as possible access to functions, then they
should be located in a pattern of spatial dispersion,
with priority given to central places away from existing
supply points.
     3.   If sectoral efficiency is a major objective in
order to increase competition among providers of
services, then priority would be given to those lcations
already having the functions;
     4.   If settlement system equity is the goal, that
is, to increase the access of people who currently have
little or no access to services and facilities, then the
functions should be located in centers that have few or
none of them.
     5.   If temporal efficiency in the settlement system
is considered important, functions would be located in
centers with growing populations in order to provide
access to services in anticipation of actual need.[19]
     Again, depending on local goals and objectives some
combination of these standards, or different standards
for different functions, can be used in identifying and
formulating projects and programs for regional development.

Identification and Design of Project Portfolios

     A process for identifying and selecting projects
aimed at promoting development through a well-
articulated and integrated settlement system emerged in
the UFRD project in Potosi, Bolivia. Based on information obtained in the regional profile, settlement
system, linkage and accessibility analyses, planners in
Potosi--working through an iterative and lengthy process
in interdisciplinary teams--were able to integrate
spatial and sectoral criteria in preparing "packages" or
"portfolios" of projects for various areas of the
region. The process involved the following steps:[20]
     1.   The comparative economic advantages or poten-
tially productive activities in each area of the region
were identified. Information was derived from previous

economic and sectoral studies and from UFRD surveys of
towns and market centers.

2. Using this information, and personal knowledge
of the areas, planners proposed two or three key agricultural production or rural development projects, and
estimated the potential outputs or impact of them.

3. Preliminary proposals were made for essential
supporting activities, services or facilities, such as
mills, agro-processing enterprises, or packing plants.
These could be identified through a quick sketching of
forward and backward linkages of the key projects.

4. Preliminary estimates of required inputs--such
as irrigation facilities, extension agents, credit, or
agricultural supplies--were made, based on knowledge of
the area and information about existing facilities from
the scalogram analysis.

5. The need for infrastructure directly related to
the key projects--such as electricity, water, market
facilities, or roads--was identified using the scalogram
and linkage analyses.

6. Proposed locations for the key projects and
supporting facilities and services were identified--
again using the scalogram, linkage and accessibility
studies as well as information from economic and technical studies.

7. A timetable, year-by-year, sequence of activities and schedule of related investments were made for
each area. Each timetable started with "year 1" rather
than any specific date, since it was not known when the
project would be approved, funds could be obtained and
the plans would be implemented.

8. The timetables were used to estimate the costs
of the project portfolio or package over the first five
years. The estimates included sources of funding,
amounts required from each source, and investments
needed from the private sector. Annual cost estimates
were summed for each project by sector and each area.

An initial portfolio for the area "Norte de Potosi"
is illustrated in Table 7-1. This somewhat physically
isolated area, with great potential for agricultural
development, had few roads to connect farm areas with
markets or existing settlements with larger urban centers. Therefore, improving the road linking the area
with markets in Llallagua, Siglo XX, and the Department
of Cochabamba received high priority in the investment
program, and the construction of feeder roads to connect
Acasio--the settlement chosen to be the rural service
center--to nearby communities was also proposed in the
investment plan. Work would begin on building irrigation systems in the second year, along with construction
of a potato packing plant. During the third year, it
would be possible to provide farm supplies, technical
assistance, credit and other inputs needed to increase

TABLE 7-1

PROPOSED PROJECT PORTFOLIO FOR NORTE DE POTOSI AREA
OF POTOSI, BOLIVIA

Project	Location	Organization	1	2	3	4	5
Agriculture							
Irrigation	various	CORDEPO		----	----		
Extension service	various	IBTA			----	----	----
Credit	RC	BAB			----	----	----
Construction	various	CORDEPO		----	----		
Farm Supplies	RC	MACA/CORDEPO			----	----	----
Wheat	Arampampa	MACA/CORDEPO			----	----	----
Corn	Acasio/Aram	MACA/CORDEPO			----	----	----
Potatoes	Acasio/Aram	MACA/CORDEPO			----	----	----
Sheep raising	Sacaca	INFOL/MACA/CORD				----	----
Mining							
Machinery hire	various	CORDEPO/BAMIN			----	----	----
Industry							
Mill	RC	MinInd/CORDEPO			----		
Animal feed plant	RC	MinInd/CORDEPO			----		
Dried oca plant	RC	MinInd/CORDEPO			----	----	
Tourism							
Resource survey	various	IBT/CORDEPO			----		
Craft Workshop	San Pedro	IBT/CORDEPO			----	----	----
Transport & Comms.							
Highways	Uncia-Anzaldo	SENAC/CORDEPO	----	----			
Feeder roads	RC to LCs	ALDE/CORDEPO	----	----			
Telephones	RC	ENTEL	----				
Post Office	RC	MinTC	----	----			
Energy							
Grid extension	various	ENDE	----				
Local generators	RC & LCs	CORDEPO	----	----			
Education							
High schools	RC & LCs	MinEd/CORD			----	----	----
Training center	RC	MinEd			----	----	----
Literacy Program	various	MinEd			----	----	
Health							
Health center	RC	UnSan/CORD			----	----	----
Clinics	LCs	UnSan/CORD				----	----
Infrastructure							
Drinking water	RC & LCs	CORDEPO		----	----		
Sewerage	RC	CORDEPO		----			
Market	RC	CORDEPO	----	----			
Institutions							
Producers coop	various	IPTK/MACA			----	----	----
Marketing coop	RC	IPTK/MACA			----	----	----
Field office	RC	CORDEPO	----	----	----	----	----

RC = Rural center = Acasio;
LC = Local center = Arampampa, Sacaca, Toro Toro and S.P. de Buena Vista.

production of wheat, corn and potatoes, the major crops
grown in the area. A plant was also needed to dehydrate
oca, a local vegetable.

Because Acasio was only a small village, the project portfolio had to include investments in a wide
range of functions that would allow it to act as a rural
service and marketing center. These included a post and
telegraph office; a high school; a health center staffed
by doctors equipped with jeeps so that they could visit
neighboring communities; a gas station and repair shop;
and a market, agricultural supply store and warehousing
facilities. Four nearby local centers were to receive
drinking water systems, high schools, post offices, and
small health clinics.[21]

In the Bicol River Basin a combination of partitioning techniques, physical distance analyses and
information from the scalogram and linkage studies were
used, along with the analytical maps, to delineate eight
settlements that could serve as market centers. With
appropriate facilities, these places could incorporate
large unserved or marginal areas into the regional
marketing system. Bicol planners chose the following
places to be considered as sites for a market development investment package: 1) Sipocot in the western part
of the Basin, 2) Naga City in the Center of Camarines
Sur province, 3) Tinambac north of Naga; 4) Iriga City
in the center of the Basin; 5) Goa in the eastern portion of the Caramoan peninsula; 6) Ligao in the upper
part of the Basin; 7) Legaspi covering the northern,
southern and western part of the Albay Gulf; and 8)
Tabaco north of Legaspi. It was around these market
centers that the planners proposed re-drawing IAD planning boundaries so that projects and programs would be
oriented toward economic rather than flood-plain development. The market areas for each center would be the
proposed IADs depicted in Figure 7 in Chapter Six.

The scalogram analysis served as a guide in formulating an investment package for the market centers,
indicating which important functions were lacking and
which might be improved or upgraded. As noted earlier
the investment portfolios for market centers would consist of projects to construct or improve all-weather
asphalt roads to connect them to rural service centers,
telephone lines connecting the market centers to the
larger urban centers within the Basin, permanent market
facilities, warehousing and cold storage facilities,
utilities, finance and credit services, and agricultural
extension services.

In some of the market centers, general services
would also be improved, including health clinics or
small hospitals, vocational schools, and essential
social services. These market centers would also be
high-priority locations for the development of agro-

processing industries and related small-scale manufacturing.[22]

Incentives for private investment in these centers
would be offered, based on the following criteria: 1)
that it reinforce the central marketing and trading
functions of the town; 2) that it contribute to agro-
processing activities; 3) that it strengthen transport
access from within its agricultural supply areas; 4)
that it widen its non-agricultural commercial or service
capacities, especially in finance, distribution and
social services; or 5) that it contribute to increasing
the administrative capacity of organizations located
there to serve people living in the rural hinterlands.[23]

The accessibility model described in Chapter Six
can also be used to do sensitivity analyses of proposed
project packages. The procedure consists of assessing
various combinations of functions that might be located
in a zone to see how they affect time-distance relationships.

It should be noted, however, that final decisions
about the package of projects proposed for an area must
depend on a variety of analyses and the judgments of
planners, decision-makers and representatives of local
groups. No statistical technique will provide answers
or even objectively "optimal" choices. They will merely
provide information that can be used in the decision
making process.

MONITORING, EVALUATION AND INSTITUTIONALIZATION
OF SPATIAL ANALYSIS METHODS

The final stages of UFRD are concerned with creating an evaluation system for monitoring the implementation of projects and for determining the impact of
development activities on spatial development. They are
also concerned with finding the best ways of integrating
spatial analysis into the overall process of regional
planning and policy-making.

Monitoring and Evaluation

As noted earlier, the intent of the UFRD approach
to spatial analysis is not to create a "one-shot" comprehensive plan for the region, but to test and apply
methods of analysis that allow planners and policy-
makers to assess the spatial and locational dimensions
of regional development on a continuing basis.

One important task is to determine the degree of
frequency with which various methods of analysis should
be applied. The regional profile analysis, for example,
should be up-dated periodically when new data become
available from secondary sources. The ten-year interval

between national censuses is probably too long in most
regions, and ways should be found of obtaining up-dated
population, social and economic data on the region every
four or five years.

Information systems can be established to allow
planners to up-date the scalogram analysis annually or
bi-annually. In some countries municipal officials are
required to report annually on changes in the types of
services and facilities located in their jurisdictions,
and this information can be collected and used to revise
the scalogram. Check-lists of functions for each major
settlement could be distributed annually to key informants, such as the town clerk or high-school prinicpal,
to fill-in information about the presence or absence of
functions in order to update the scalogram.

Linkage and accessibility studies, which require
far more elaborate surveys, might be done every five
years or after major linkage investments--such as new
highways or markets--are made in the region. If the
region is divided into planning areas, as was done in
Bicol and Potosi, a full-scale UFRD study might be done
for some of the zones each year on a three-to-five-year
rotating basis.

One means of monitoring and evaluating project
portfolios for various areas within the region is to
formulate and design them using what the U.S. Agency for
International Development calls the "Logical Framework."[24] This framework organizes information about the
project package into four major categories:

1. Project Goals--stated in the form of single,
    coherent objectives toward which progress can
    be verified in terms of time, quantity or
    quality. They provide the reason for the pro-
    jects and identify the ends toward which they
    are directed.
2. Project Purpose--stated in a way that defines
    the terminal conditions of success. It
    expresses in quantitative or qualitative terms
    what will be created, accomplished or changed
    through the project in order to solve develop-
    ment problems.
3. Project Outputs--stated functionally by kind
    and magnitude so that progress toward them can
    be verified. They are the specific results
    that can be expected from the effective manage-
    ment of the inputs provided through the pro-
    jects.
4. Project Inputs--stated as activities that will
    produce outputs. They are the goods, services,
    and other resources provided from various
    sources in order to produce the specific out-
    puts identified earlier. (See Figure 7-7.)

FIGURE 7-7
PROJECT DESIGN SUMMARY
LOGICAL FRAMEWORK

Life of Project:
From FY _____ to FY _____
Total Funding: _____
Date Prepared: _____

Project Title & Number:

NARRATIVE SUMMARY	OBJECTIVELY VERIFIABLE INDICATORS	MEANS OF VERIFICATION	IMPORTANT ASSUMPTIONS
Program or Sector Goal: The broader objective to which this project contributes: (A-1)	Measures of Goal Achievement: (A-2)	(A-3)	Assumptions for achieving goal targets: (A-4)
Project Purpose: (B-1)	Conditions that will indicate purpose has been achieved: End-of-Project status. (B-2)	(B-3)	Assumptions for achieving purpose: (B-4)
Project Outputs: (C-1)	Magnitude of Outputs: (C-2)	(C-3)	Achieving outputs: (C-4)
Project Inputs: (D-1)	Implementation Target (Type and Quantity) (D-2)	(D-3)	Assumptions for providing inputs: (D-4)

For each of these categories, information is provided on objectively verifiably indicators, means of
verification and important assumptions for achieving the
goals, purposes, and outputs, and for providing the
inputs.

The "Logical Framework" not only can help planners
to design investment portfolios more carefully and systematically, but also to monitor the actual progress
toward goals and purposes by measuring the inputs and
outputs over time.

Institutionalizing Spatial Analysis in Regional Development Planning and Policy-Making

The final stage of the UFRD approach is to integrate spatial analysis into the on-going planning and
decision-making processes of organizations involved in
regional development. This must be done differently in
every region, since the organizational structure,
authority of regional planning agencies, scope of participation, institutional relationships and political
structure usually differ substantially even among
regions within the same country.

To some degree the methods are institutionalized
through building the skills of planners during the initial UFRD project, and by making national, regional and
local technical and economic planners, government officials and local group leaders familiar with the uses of
spatial analyses in regional planning and investment
programming.

As with the introduction of any innovation or
change in established organizations and procedures, the
integration of spatial analysis often requires a con-
certed initial effort and a long period of gestation.

It is important for spatial analysts to emphasize
at the outset that the intent of this process is not to
supplant, but to supplement, existing planning procedures. It is equally important to underline the fact
that the UFRD approach is not intended to produce a comprehensive plan for the region, but only to add the
spatial and locational dimensions to economic, technical
and sectoral planning.

Indeed, the underlying assumptions of the UFRD
approach are that in most regions the most effective
form of planning is strategic and incremental. In few
places are there the resources, skills and administrative capacity to formulate and implement long-range com-
pehensive plans. The UFRD approach is designed to provide basic information quickly, to be adjunctive and
indicative, and to raise critical questions about the
settlement system and locational implications of development decisions which require more detailed studies to

answer effectively. It seeks to provide quickly marginally better information about the spatial dimensions of regional development so that locational factors can be considered in decisions that must be made rapidly and that cannot await time-consuming systematic research. The UFRD approach is most useful where planners seek to transform conditions gradually. Indeed, the approach is designed to promote a transformational approach to development.

Rondinelli and Ruddle have defined <u>transformational development</u> as a process that "seeks to increase incrementally the productivity of indigenous institutions and practices, reinforcing and building on those appropriate to local conditions and needs and adaptive to changing circumstances, gradually displacing those that are not."[25] The characteristics of transformational development include:

1. Building on existing culturally embedded resources, institutions and practices;
2. Involving local people, who will be affected by transformation and change, in the processes of development planning and implementation;
3. Adapting modern technologies, services and facilities to local conditions;
4. Promoting specialization in production and exchange activities based on existing spatial comparative advantages;
5. Using appropriate, low-cost, culturally acceptable methods of change to generate "demonstration effects" that lead to widespread adoption of those methods that prove successful;
6. Planning for displacement of unproductive and unadaptable traditional institutions and practices as change occurs;
7. Establishing, through planning based on "strategic intervention," the preconditions for transformation and change in social, technical, political, economic and administrative structures and processes, and in elements of the spatial structure; and
8. Creating a planning process that is flexible, incremental, adaptive and that provides for experimentation and adjustment as transformation takes place.

Development planning rarely begins with a clean slate. In every region existing problems and circumstances, which often evolved over centuries, establish the environment for change. Although it is almost a cliche to argue that development plans should be based on a thorough understanding of existing conditions and emerging needs, this basic principle is often lost in the urgency to formulate and implement projects and programs.

One of the recurrent lessons of development experience, however, is that the most pervasive changes can be attained by transforming existing resources. Local social and economic systems survive because they perform useful or necessary functions. They are usually adaptive mechanisms suited to cultural peculiarities that meet the needs of those who maintain them. Understanding their operations is crucial to designing effective plans and programs for promoting change. The use of existing resources and culturally embedded traditions, moreover, can be more effective and less costly than attempting wholesale substitution of "modern" but alien institutions and practices.

Building on existing resources, institutions and practices requires involving local people who will be affected by transformation and change in development planning and implementation. The information, experience and insights of local residents are essential in identifying local needs, the most effective channels of change, and the types of change that they will support. Only by involving local people in the process of planning and implementation can decisions be tailored to their needs and can their latent talents and skills be developed.

Transformational development also implies building on the comparative advantages of organizations and settlements and strengthening those functions they can perform most effectively and efficiently compared with other organizations and places. This requires assessing the advantages and deficiencies of existing settlements to determine their potential roles, the extent and nature of their linkages to other settlements and their complementarities.

A fundamental obstacle to investment in many rural regions is the lack of information on local conditions, which makes evaluation of location decisions difficult, uncertain, and risky. The ability of public and private decision-makers to act to meet the needs of a region depends on their ability to perceive correctly current problems and opportunities. Most regions lack organizations that collect, aggregate and analyze data on regional social, economic, and technological trends. In some cases a regional development agency can compile information already collected by other agencies and firms as the basis for analysis, or it can generate new data. Ultimately, however, successful planning for regional development must be tailored to the needs and constraints of individual communities.

A fundamental weakness of centralized national planning is its insensitivity to uniquely local problems and opportunities. Regions in developing nations often differ drastically in their resource bases, comparative advantages, levels of development and potential for

future growth, as do communities within regions. Not
all regions or communities suffer the same deficiencies
or require the same services and facilities to promote
productive investment. The requirements for building
intermediate cities differ from those for market towns
and village service centers. Decisions concerning allocation of investment and location of urban services and
facilities should be based on the types of analyses of
rural hinterlands and of existing central places that
are offered by UFRD.

Much of the transformation needed to increase the
productivity of settlements in developing nations can be
achieved through methods that are low in cost, adaptable
to local conditions, and that generate "demonstration
effects" that encourage communities to experiment with
successful technologies, services and facilities. As
spatial structure, traditional institutions and indigenous practices change, the least productive and adaptive are eventually displaced. Their roles and functions must be assumed by more appropriate successors.
Examples of transformational displacement in developing
nations are numerous and commonplace--day laborers and
bullock ploughmen are replaced by mechanized tractors
and tillers, ferrymen operating small barges at river
crossings are rendered jobless by the construction of a
bridge, charcoal makers are ousted from their livelihood
by rural electrification, periodic markets disappear as
new transport linkages between rural areas and larger
towns increase access to more diversified daily markets,
the economic base of whole cities deteriorates as new
industrial technologies or competitive markets for their
goods or services emerge.

Since displacement is inevitable as development
occurs planners must attempt to mitigate its adverse
impacts. But the lessons of history document the frus-
trations of attempting to preserve artificially unadap-
tive institutions. The fundamental role of development
planning is to facilitate and promote processes of productive change, while attempting to anticipate and mitigate the adversities and traumas of transformation.

Yet governments can never be omnipotent in planning
for development. Rarely, if ever, is it possible to
anticipate accurately or to control comprehensively the
consequences of change. Indeed, there are only limited
actions that governments can take to promote economic
growth, and these are confined to those identified at
the beginning of this chapter. But few governments in
developing nations have the resources even to undertake
all of these activities. At best, government intervention can usually only establish the essential preconditions for change and attempt to manipulate strategic
factors that obstruct development or set in motion
chains of activities that are likely to accelerate

transformation. Among the most important preconditions that can be established by government agencies are: providing social overhead capital and physical infrastructure required for productive investment by public and private organizations, ensuring that at least minimum levels of health, education and other social services are available to a majority of the population, removing obstacles to increased productivity and exchange in economically lagging regions and among disadvantaged groups, and ensuring equitable and wide opportunities for individual advancement.

Beyond providing these preconditions governments can plan their own resource allocations and investments to encourage the growth of strategic points in the spatial hierarchy--rural service centers, market towns, intermediate cities and metropolitan areas--and to strengthen the linkages among them. Regional development agencies using the UFRD approach can assist provincial, district and local governments and private firms to locate services and facilities in ways that build the productive capacity of central places and strengthen linkages among them, by:

1. Helping to identify specific sites for establishing new plants or expanding existing enterprises to take maximum advantage of economies of agglomeration, scale, and proximity to supplementary and complementary economic and social activities;

2. Analyzing social overhead expenditures, public services and facilities needed to sustain proposed development projects and new private ventures and to adapt technological innovations to regional and local conditions;

3. Identifying and analyzing backward, forward and lateral linkages of existing economic activities and delineating opportunities for new investment in the production of goods currently imported to the region;

4. Monitoring the investment activities of local, provincial and national government agencies that construct infrastructure and develop utility, transportation and service facilities in the region;

5. Analyzing the impact of that infrastructure on regional and local comparative advantages and on production, marketing and transport costs for important sectors of the regional economy; and

6. Identifying major public and private capital investments that would yield high, immediate multiplier effects for the region's major economic activities and settlements, and recommending their inclusion in national and regional investment plans.[26]

Social, economic and technological changes play an important role in promoting regional development. Changes in transportation, technology, service delivery and economic linkages, it was noted earlier, vitally affect the locational advantages of villages, market centers, and small and intermediate cities. Changes in agricultural, mining, and manufacturing production techniques have been significant in creating comparative advantages of some communities and destroying those of others. The ability of regional decision-makers to perceive opportunities and adopt technological innovation is critical to regional development.

Regional planning agencies can play an important role in helping to establish an environment for innovation, transformation and entrepreneurship by acting as an intermediary and channel of communication between organizations within rural regions and those outside—national ministries, private firms, financial institutions, universities, research groups and individual entrepreneurs—with resources that could be invested in regional activities. As an intermediary and promoter of innovation and entrepreneurship, a regional development agency can:

1. Transfer information concerning innovations in production technology, marketing, transportation, organization and processing techniques to public and private organizations within the region;

2. Identify public and private sources of capital for new ventures—by monitoring new national development programs, changes in interest rates, new sources of government grants and loans to industry, and by actively participating in the creation of cooperatives;

3. Promote regional agricultural goods and manufactured products locally and in markets outside the region—by assisting local entrepreneurs to pool resources for promotion, advertising, and marketing in intermediate cities and metropolitan areas;

4. Development agencies can also help improve the skills of regional entrepreneurs and public administrators by contracting for and conducting training, by conducting workshops and seminars through which successful entrepreneurs disseminate their experience to others, and by mobilizing teams of experts and practitioners within the region to evaluate potential projects and existing business and government operations.

Because the very purpose of development planning is to trigger a set of interrelated actions, which through multiplier and spread effects generate productive change, the planning process itself must be change-oriented. It has to remain flexible, incremental and adaptive. It must foster experimentation and adjust policies and programs to the consequences of previous investments.[27]

CONCLUSIONS

In summary, the applied methods of spatial analysis and planning described here are designed to help planners to:

1. Understand the comparative advantages and weaknesses of a region's economic, human and physical resources in the national space-economy;

2. Identify areas within the region that have greater and lesser developed resources and capacities to promote economic growth;

3. Determine the pattern of human settlement, the distribution of important services, facilities, infrastructure and productive organizations among settlements, and the degree to which settlements in the region serve people living in the rural areas surrounding them;

4. Identify the types and strengths of linkages among settlements, the degree of access they provide for rural residents to town-based functions, and the degree of interaction that takes place among them;

5. Determine those functions that are not well distributed within the region, those that are available only to people living in some areas of the region and the pattern of association among functions within particular areas of the region;

6. Identify areas in which people are not well served by central place settlements or which are weakly linked to towns and cities that contain the functions needed for economic development and social progress;

7. Determine, on the basis of the existing distribution of functions, how to locate new investments to fill crucial gaps, provide complementary services and facilities, or build potential comparative locational advantages; and,

8. Identify means of locating new investments in ways that increase the capacity of settlements to support and promote "spontaneous" economic growth without further government intervention or investment.

The spatial and locational dimensions of regional planning can be ignored, but only if governments are willing to accept the high costs of locating expensive services and facilities in places where they may not generate the intended benefits or where they will not produce the maximum spread effects. The methods of analysis suggested here can help regional planners to gather information rapidly to minimize those risks. They can help investors to locate services and facilities in places where they are more likely not only reach intended beneficiaries but also to increase the capacity of those places to serve a larger population. In so doing, they may not only be able to promote economic growth more rapidly but also to distribute the benefits more equitably.

250

NOTES

    1.   John Friedmann, Urbanization, Planning and National Development, (Beverly Hills: Sage Publications, 1973), pp. 115-116.

    2.   The argument is made in more detail in Dennis A. Rondinelli, Development Projects as Policy Experiments: An Adaptive Approach to Development Administration, London: Methuen, 1983.

    3.   Hugh Evans, Urban Functions in Rural Development: The Case of the Potosi Region in Bolivia, Part I (Washington: USAID, 1982), p. 90.

    4.   Ibid., p. 92.

    5.   Ibid., p. 95.

    6.   Ibid., p. 97.

    7.   Bicol River Basin Development Program, Ten-Year Develop- ment Plan, 1978-1987, Baras, Canaman, Philippines: BRBDP, 1977.

    8.   U.S. Agency for International Development, Philippines: Bicol Integrated Rural Development Project, 1977-1981, Project Paper, Manila: USAID, 1976, 1976.

    9.   Center for Policy and Development Studies, University of the Philippines--Los Banos, Urban Functions in Rural Development: A Research Project in Spatial Analysis and Planning, College, Laguna, Philippines; CPDs, 1978), pp. 99-102.

    10.   See Dennis A. Rondinelli, "Spatial Analysis for Regional Development: A Case Study in the Bicol River Basin of the Philippines," Resource Systems Theory and Methodology Series, No. 2 Tokyo: United Nations University, 1980.

    11.   Center for Policy and Development Studies, op. cit., pp. 102-104.

    12.   Frank Lynch, S.J., "Let My People Lead: Rationale and Outline of a People-Centered Assistance Program for the Bicol River Basin," Manila: Institute of Philippine Culture, 1976.

    13.   Robert C. Salazar and Frank Lynch, S.J., "The Perceived Quality of Bicol Life in the Early 1970s," Naga City: Social Science Research Unit, Ateneo de Naga University, 1974.

    14.   Frank Lynch, S.J., "Social Soundness Analysis of Bicol Integrated Rural Development Project," (Manila: U.S. Agency for International Development, 1976), p. 5.

    15.   C. Andrade, S. Banerji, H.B. Fisher, G. Rushton, N.S. Saini, and A. Sharma, A Geographical Approach to Settlement Planning for Intergrated Area Development, (New Delhi: Ford Foundation, no date), pp. 43-48.

    16.   See Prodipto Roy and B.R. Patil, Manual for Block Level Planning (New Delhi: The Macmillan company of India, 1977); pp. 28-29.

17. Richard L. Morrill and John Symons, "Efficiency and Equity Aspects of Optimum Location," _Geographical Analysis_, Vol. IX ((July 1977) pp. 215-225; quote at p. 26.

18. _Ibid._, pp. 223-224.

19. Sture Oberg, _Methods of Describing Physical Access to Supply Points_, Lund Series in Geography, No. 43 (Stockholm: Royal University of Lund, 1976).

20. The process is described in more detail in Evans, _op. cit._, pp. 98-106.

21. See Evans, _op. cit._, Part II, pp. 77-86.

22. Center for Policy and Development Studies, _op. cit._, pp. 104-105.

23. _Ibid._, p. 105.

24. U.S. Agency for International Development, _Design and Evaluation of AID-Assisted Projects_, Washington: USAID, 1980.

25. Dennis A. Rondinelli and Kenneth Ruddle, _Urbanization and Rural Development: A Spatial Analysis for Equitable Growth_, (New York: Praeger, 1978), p. 181.

26. See Dennis A. Rondinelli and Barclay G. Jones, "Decision-Making, Managerial Capacity and Development: An Entrepreneurial Approach to Planning," _African Administrative Studies_, No. 13 (1975), pp. 105-118.

27. See Rondinelli, _Development Projects as Policy Experiments op. cit._, Chapter 5.

Bibliography

Anrade, C., et al. A Geographic Approach to Settlement
     Planning for Integrated Area Development. New
     Delhi: Ford Foundation, no date.
Beals, Ralph L. The Peasants' Marketing System in
     Oaxaca. Berkeley: University of California Press,
     1975.
Bendavid-Val, Avrom. Regional and Local Economic Ana-
     lysis for Practitioners. New York, Praeger, 1983.
Berry, Brian J. L. Geography of Market Centers and
     Retail Distribution. Englewood Cliffs, N.J.:
     Prentice-Hall, 1967.
Berry, Brian J. L. "Policy Implications of an Urban
     Location Model for Kanpur Region." P. B. Desai et
     al. (eds.). Regional Perspective of Industrial and
     Urban Growth: The Case of Kanpur. Bombay:
     Macmillan, 1969.
Berry, Brian J. L. and Garrison, William. "Recent
     Development in Central Place Theory." Papers and
     Proceedings of the Regional Science Association.
     Vol. IV, 1958.
Berry, Brian J. L. and Horton, Frank E. Geographic
     Perspectives on Urban Systems. Englewood Cliffs,
     N.J.: Prentice-Hall, 1970.
Bicol River Basin Development Program. Ten Year Devel-
     opment Plan, 1978-87. Baras, Canaman, Philippines:
     BRBDP, 1977.
Bicol River Basin Development Program. Urban Functions
     in Rural Development: A Research Project in
     Spatial Analysis and Planning. Pili, Philippines:
     BRBDP, 1978.
Bromley, R. Periodic and Daily Markets in Highland
     Ecuador. Ann Arbor, Michigan: University Micro-
     films, 1975.
_____. "Market Center Analysis in the Urban Func-
     tions in Rural Development Approach." Paper pre-
     sented at International Symposium on Small Towns
     in National Development. Bangkok: Asian Institute
     of Technology, 1982.

253

_____. "Market Centers in the Urban Functions in
   Rural Development Approach." Working Paper.
   Worcester, MA: Clark University Settlement and
   Resource Systems Analysis and Management Project,
   1983.
Center for Policy and Development Studies, University of
   the Philippines, Los Banos. Urban Functions in
   Rural Development: A Research in Spatial Analysis
   and Planning. College, Laguna, Philippines: 1978.
Conroy, Michael E. "Rejection of Growth Center Strategy
   in Latin American Regional Development Planning."
   Land Economics. Vol. XLIX, No. 4, 1973.
Corwin, Lauren Anita. "The Rural Town: Minimal Urban
   Center." Urban Anthropology. Vol. 6, No. 1,
   1977.
Croxton, F. E., Cowden, D. and Klein, S. Applied
   General Statistics. Englewood Cliffs, N.J.:
   Prentice-Hall, 1967.
Dannhaeuser, Norbert. "Commercial Relations Between
   Center and Periphery in Northern Luzon: Detri-
   mental Dependence or Generative Interdependence?"
   Philippine Studies. Vol. 29, 1981.
Darwent, D. F. "Growth Poles and Growth Centers in
   Regional Planning--A Review." Environment and
   Planning. Vol. 1, 1969.
Davis, Diane E. "Migration, Rank-Size Distribution and
   Economic Development: The Case of Mexico."
   Studies in Comparative International Development.
   Vol. XI, No. 1, 1971.
Dick, Ross S. "Central Place Service Areas and Urban
   Fields: New Measures of Spatial Character." Geo-
   graphical Journal. Vol. 5, 1979.
Dickinson, G. C. Statistical Mapping and the Presenta-
   tion of Statistics. 2nd ed. London: Edward
   Arnold, 1973.
Doherty, P. A. and Ball, J. M. "Central Functions of
   Small Mexican Towns." Southeastern Geographer.
   Vol. XI, No. 1, 1971.
Evans, H. Urban Functions in Rural Development: The
   Case of Potosi Region in Bolivia. Parts I and II.
   Washington: U.S. Agency for International Develop-
   ment, 1982.
Evans, Hugh and Dicky, John. "A Technique to Help Eval-
   uate Functions and Linkage Packages." Unpublished
   Paper. Potosi, Bolivia: Urban Functions in Rural
   Development Project, 1980.
Fass, S. "Urban Functions in Upper Volta: Final
   Report." Washington: USAID, 1981.
Fisher, H. Benjamin. "Methods of Identification of
   Agro-Urban Centers at the Kabupatin and Provincial
   Levels." Jakarta: Ford Foundation, 1975.
Fisher, H. B. and Rushton, G. "Rural Growth Centers:
   Experiences in the Pilot Research Project 1969-

1974." Paper presented at the Annual Meeting of the Association for Asian Studies. San Francisco, 1975.

Friedmann, John. Regional Development Policy: A Case Study of Venezuela. Cambridge, MA: MIT Press, 1966.

Friedmann, John. Urbanization, Planning and National Development. Beverly Hills: Sage Publications, 1973.

Friedmann, John and Douglass, Mike. "Agropolitan Development: Towards a New Strategy for Regional Planning in Asia." Paper presented at the Seminar on Industrialization Strategies and the Growth Pole Approach to Regional Planning and Development. Nagoya, Japan: United Nations Center for Regional Planning, 1975.

Fuller, Theodore D. "Migrant Evaluation of the Quality of Urban Life in Northeast Thailand." Journal of Developing Areas, Vol. 16, No. 1, October 1981.

Gilbert, Alan. "A Note on the Incidence of Development in the Vicinity of a Growth Center." Regional Studies, Vol. 9, 1975.

Government of the Kingdom of Thailand, National Economic and Social Development Board. South Thailand Regional Planning Study, Vol. 2. Bangkok: Hunting Technical Service, Ltd., N.D., 1979(?).

Grove, D. and Huszar, L. The Towns of Ghana. Accra: University of Ghana Press, 1964.

Haggett, P., Cliff, A. D. and Frey, A. Location Analysis in Human Geography. New York: Wiley, 1977.

Hansen, Niles. "The Role of Small and Intermediate Sized Cities in National Development Processes and Strategies." Paper delivered at Expert Group Meeting on the Role of Small and Intermediate Cities in National Development. Nagoya, Japan: United Nations Center for Regional Development, 1982.

Hirst, M. A. "A Functional Analysis of Towns in Tanzania." Tidschrift Voor Econ. en Soc. Geographie. Vol. 64, No. 1, 1973.

Ho, Sam P. S. Small-Scale Enterprises in Korea and Taiwan. World Bank Staff Working Paper No. 384. Washington: World Bank, 1980.

International Labour Office. Poverty and Landlessness in Rural Asia. Geneva: ILO, 1977.

Isard, W. Methods of Regional Analysis. New York: John Wiley, 1961.

Johnson, E.A.J. "Scale Economies in Small Agro-Urban Communities." F. Helleiner and W. Stohr (eds.). Proceedings of the Commission on Regional Aspects of Development of the International Geographical Union. Vol. II. Toronto: International Geographical Union, 1974.

Johnson, E.A.J. The Organization of Space in Developing Countries. Cambridge, MA: Harvard University Press, 1970.

Knapp, Ronald G. "Marketing and Social Patterns in Rural Taiwan." Annals of the Association of American Geographers. Vol. 11, No. 1. March 1971.

Leonard, David K. "International Linkages for Decentralized Rural Development: Overcoming Administrative Weaknesses." G. S. Cheema and Dennis A. Rondinelli (eds.). Decentralization and Development: Policy Implementation in Developing Countries. Beverly Hills: Sage Publications, 1983.

Leeds, Anthony. "Towns and Villages in Society: Hierarchies of Order and Cause." in T. W. Collins (ed.). Cities in a Larger Context. Athens, Georgia: University of Georgia Press, 1980.

Lindblom, Charles E. and Cohen, David K. Usable Knowledge: Social Science and Social Problem Solving. New Haven: Yale University Press, 1979.

Lombardo, Jr., Joseph F. "Introduction to the Human Settlement System in Honduras." Unpublished Report. Tegucigalpa, Honduras: U.S. Agency of International Development, 1982.

Lynch, Frank. "Social Soundness Analysis of Bicol Integrated Rural Development Project." Manila: U.S. Agency for International Development, 1976.

Lynch, Frank. "Let My People Lead: Rationale and Outline of a People-Centered Assistance Program for the Bicol River Basin." Manila: Institute of Philippine Culture, 1976.

Marshall, John U. The Location of Service Towns. Toronto: University of Toronto Press, 1969.

McNulty, Michael and Conroy, Michael E. "An Evaluation Report on Potential Sites in Bolivia and Paraguay for the Urban Functions in Rural Development Project." Washington: U.S. Agency for International Development, 1977.

Misra, R. P. and Sundaram, K. V. "Growth Foci as Instruments of Modernization in India." A. Kuklinski (ed.). Regional Policies in Nigeria, India, and Brazil. The Hague: Mouton, 1978.

Morrill, Michael L. and Symons, John. "Efficiency and Equity Aspects of Optimum Location." Geographical Analysis. Vol. IX, July 1977.

Obudho, R. A. Urbanization in Kenya: A Bottom Up Approach to Development Planning. Landam, MD: University Press of America, 1983.

Oberg, Sture. Methods of Describing Physical Access to Supply Points. Lund Series in Geography No. 43. Stockholm: Royal University of Lund, 1976.

Onyemelukwe, J.O.C. "Settlement Structures as Sociocultural Constraint on Nigerian Rural Development." Ekistics. Vol. 7, No. 284, 1980.

Parent, Jean. "The Problem of Transferring Technology from Branch to Branch and the Multiplier."

Organization for Economic Cooperation and Development, Choice and Adaptation of Technology in Developing Countries. Paris: OECD, 1974.

Parr, John B. "Growth Poles, Regional Development and Central Place Theory." Papers of the Regional Science Association. Vol. 31, 1973.

Preston, David A. Farmers and Towns: Rural-Urban Relations in Highland Bolivia. Norwich: University of East Anglia - Geo Abstracts, 1978.

Ragragio, Junio M. "The Design for Identification of the Hierarchy, Centrality and Threshold of the Central Place System in the Bicol River Basin." Project Discussion Paper. College, Laguna: Center for Policy and Development Studies, University of the Philippines--Los Banos, 1977.

Republic of Malawi. Development of District Centers Feasibility Study: Final Report. Vol. I. Dusseldorf, Germany: GEITEC Consult GMBH, 1980.

Republic of Philippines. Census of Population and Housing. Manila: National Census and Statistics Office, 1974.

Rice, E. B. and Glaeser, E. "Agriculture Sector Studies: An Evaluation of AID's Recent Experiences." AID Evaluation Paper No. 5. Washington: U.S. Agency for International Development, 1972.

Richardson, Harry W. and Richardson, Margaret. "The Relevance of Growth Center Strategies to Latin America." Economic Geography. Vol. 51, No. 2, April 1975.

Richardson, Harry W. "Policies for Strengthening Small Cities in Developing Countries." Paper prepared for Expert Group Meeting of the Role of Small and Intermediate Cities in National Development. Nagoya, Japan: United Nations Centre for Regional Development, 1982.

Riley, H. M. and Harrison, K. M. "Vertical Coordination of Food Systems Servicing Large Urban Centres in Latin America." Paper prepared for United Nations Food and Agriculture Organization. Conference on the Development of Food Marketing Systems for Large Urban Areas in Latin America. Rome: FAO, 1973.

Rondinelli, Dennis A. "Adjunctive Planning and Urban Development Policy." Urban Affairs Quarterly. Vol. 7, No. 1, 1977.

_____. "Applied Policy Analysis for Integrated Regional Development Planning in the Philippines." Third World Planning Review. Vol. 1, No. 2, Autumn 1979.

_____. Development Projects as Policy Experiments: An Adaptive Approach to Development Administration. London: Methuen, 1983.

_____. "Regional Disparities and Investment Allocation Policies in the Philippines: Spatial Dimensions of Poverty in a Developing Country." Canadian Journal of Development Studies, Vol. 1, No. 2, Fall 1980.

_____. Secondary Cities in Developing Countries: Policies for Diffusing Urbanization. Beverly Hills: Sage Publications,1983.

_____. "Spatial Analysis for Regional Development: A Case Study in the Bicol River Basin of the Philippines." Resource Systems Theory and Methodology Series. No. 2, Tokyo: United Nations University, 1980.

_____. Urban and Regional Development Planning: Policy and Administration. Ithaca: Cornell University Press, 1975.

Rondinelli, Dennis A. and Evans, Hugh. "Integrated Regional Development Planning: Linking Urban Centers and Rural Areas in Bolivia." World Development. Vol. 11, No. 1, January 1983.

Rondinelli, Dennis A. and Jones, Barclay G. "Decision Making, Managerial Capacity and Development: An Entrepreneurial Approach to Planning." African Administrative Studies. No. 13, 1975.

Rondinelli, Dennis A. and Ruddle, Kenneth. "Appropriate Institutions for Rural Development: Organizing Services and Technology in Developing Countries." Philippine Journal of Public Administration. Vol. XXI, No. 1, 1977.

_____. "Coping with Poverty in International Development Policy." World Development. Vol. 6, No. 4, 1978.

_____. "Integrating Spatial Development." Ekistics. Vol. 43, No. 257, April 1977.

_____. "Local Organization for Integrated Rural Development: Implementing Equity Policy in Developing Countries." International Review of Administrative Sciences. Vol. XLIII, No. 1, January 1977.

_____. "Political Commitment and Administrative Support: Preconditions for Growth with Equity Policy." Journal of Administration Overseas. Vol. XVII, No. 1, 1976.

_____. Urbanization and Rural Development: A Spatial Policy for Equitable Growth. New York: Praeger, 1978.

Roy, Prodipto and Patil, B. R. Manual for Block Level Planning. Delhi: The Macmillan Company of India, 1977.

Ruddle, Kenneth and Rondinelli, Dennis. Transforming Natural Resources for Human Development: A Resource Systems Approach to Development Policy. Tokyo: United Nations University Press, 1983.

Salazar, Robert C. and Lynch, Frank. "The Perceived Quality of Bicol Life in the Early 1970s." Naga City: Social Survey Research Unit, Ateneo de Naga University, 1974.

Santos, Milton. "Underdevelopment, Growth Poles and Social Justice." Civilisations. Vol. 25, Nos. 1 and 2, 1975.

Schatzberg, Michael. "Islands of Privilege: Small Cities in Africa and the Dynamics of Class Formation." Urban Anthropology. Vol. 8, No. 2, 1979.

Schwimmer, Brian. "Periodic Markets and Urban Development in Southern Ghana" in Carol A. Smith (ed.) Regional Analysis, NY: Academic Press, 1976, 123-146.

Shah, S. M. "Growth Centers as a Strategy for Rural Development: India Experience." Economic Development and Cultural Change. Vol. 22, No. 2, January 1974.

Skinner, G. W. "Marketing and Social Structure in Rural China." Part 1. Journal of Asian Studies. Vol. 24, No. 1, November 1964.

Smailes, A. E. The Geography of Towns. London: Hutchinson, 1966.

Smith, Carol Ann (ed.). Regional Analysis. Vols. I and II. New York: Academic Press, 1976.

Southall, Aidan. "Urban Functions in Rural Development: Report on Visit to Upper Volta." Unpublished Report. Washington: U.S. Agency for International Development, 1978.

Southall, Aidan. "What Causes Overconcentration on Decentralization in the Urbanization Process?" Urbanism Past and Present. Vol. 7, No. 13, Winter-Spring 1982.

Stohr, Walter and Todtling, Franz. "Spatial Equity-- Some Anti-Thesis to Current Regional Development Doctrine." Papers of the Regional Science Association. Vol. 38, 1977.

Swetnam, John J. "Interaction Between Urban and Rural Residents in a Guatemalan Market Place." Urban Anthropology. Vol. 7, No. 2, 1978.

Symanski, R. and Bromley, R. "Market Development and the Ecological Complex." Professional Geographer. Vol. 26, No. 4, 1974.

Taylor, D.R.F. "The Role of the Smaller Place in Development: The Case of Kenya." S. El Shakhs and R. Obudho (eds.). Urbanization, National Development and Regional Planning in Africa. New York: Praeger, 1974.

Tria, III, Agapito M. SSRU Municipal Inventory. Naga, the Philippines: Social Survey Research Unit, Bicol River Basin Development Program, 1974.

Thomas, M. D. "Growth Pole Theory: An Examination of Some of Its Basic Concepts." N. Hansen (ed.). Growth Centers in Regional Economic Development. New York: Free Press, 1972.

United Nations Economic and Social Commission for Asia and the Pacific. Guidelines for Rural Centre Planning. New York: United Nations, 1979.

260

United States Agency for International Development,
      Office of Urban Development. Urban Functions in
      Rural Development Project Paper. Mimeographed.
      Washington: USAID, 1976.
United States Agency for International Development.
      Design and Evaluation of AID Assisted Projects.
      Washington: USAID, 1980.
United States Agency for International Development.
      Philippines: Bicol Integrated Rural Development
      Project, 1977-1987. Project Paper. Manila:
      USAID, 1976.
United States Bureau of the Census. Planning for
      Internal Migration: A Review of Issues and Poli-
      cies in Developing Countries. ISP-RD-4. Washing-
      ton: U.S. Government Printing Office, 1977.
Uphoff, Norman T. and Esman, Milton J. Local Organiza-
      tion for Rural Development: Analysis of the Asian
      Experience. Ithaca: Cornell University Center for
      International Studies, 1974.
Voelkner, H. E. Shortcut Methods to Assess Poverty and
      Basic Needs for Rural Regional Planning. Part II.
      Geneva: United Nations Research Institute for
      Social Development, 1978.
Voelkner, H. E. "The Structural Complexity Growth Model
      and Scalogram Analysis of Development and Human
      Ecosystems." Unpublished paper. Washington: World
      Bank, 1974.
Ward, R. G. and Ward, M. G. "The Rural-Urban Connection--
      A Missing Link in Melanesia." Malaysian Journal
      of Tropical Geography. Vol. 1, September 1980.
World Bank. Rural Development Sector Policy Paper.
      Washington: World Bank, 1975.
      . Rural Enterprises and Nonfarm Employment.
      Washington: World Bank, 1978.
      . World Development Report, 1978. Washington:
      World Bank, 1978.
      . World Development Report, 1980. Washington:
      World Bank, 1980.
      . Village Water Supply. Washington: World
      Bank, 1976.
Wunsch, J. "Political Development and Planning in
      Ghana: A Comparative Study of Two Medium Cities."
      R. A. Obudho and S. El Shakhs (eds.). Development
      of Urban Systems in Africa. New York: Praeger,
      1979.

Index

262

Douglass, M., 9, 17, 23, 25

Ecuador, 2
Educational services, 30,93, 110, 197, 199, 220
Employment, 70-78, 82
Entrepreneurship, 248
Equity, 216, 233-236
Evaluation, 37, 240-243
Evans, H., 22, 25, 79, 94, 138, 139, 171, 175, 176, 191, 197, 202, 212, 218, 221, 250, 251

Factor analysis, 45
Fass, S., 22, 39, 48
Fisher, H.B., 6, 22, 23, 117, 250
Frey, A., 138
Friedmann, J.R., 9, 23, 53, 63, 97, 216, 250
Fuller, T.D., 24
Functions. See Urban functions

Ghana, 15
Gilbert, A., 20, 26
Glasser, E., 48
Grove, D., 22
Growth centers, 4, 8-9
Growth poles, 3-4, 20
Guatemala, 10, 14, 15
Guttman scale, 106-114, 121, 125

Haggett, P., 138
Hansen, N., 22, 23
Harrison, K.M., 174
Health services, 18, 30, 110, 166, 169, 220, 226
Hirst, M.A., 25
Ho, S., 24
Honduras, 14, 15, 16, 17
Household surveys, 230-232
Huszar, L. 22

India, 2,6,7,13,33, 115
Indonesia, 2,6, 115
Industry, 13, 20, 75-77, 83, 221

Innovations, 248
    agricultural, 8-9
    dissemination of, 9, 10
Institutional development, 5, 243-248
International Labor Organization (ILO), 27
"Investment packages," 37, 222, 230-240
Ivory Coast, 16

Johnson, E.A.J., 5, 13, 23, 24, 47, 174
Jones, B.G., 54, 97, 251

Kenya, 2
Knapp, R.G., 174
Korea, Republic of, 13

Leeds, A., 9, 24
Lindblom, C.E., 44, 48
Linkages
    administrative, 147-148, 169-173
    analysis of, 32, 141-173, 239, 241
    economic, 144, 185-187
    physical, 9, 10, 11, 18, 19, 30, 33, 142, 160-164, 222, 224
    political, 147-148, 169-173
    social, 145-146, 164-169
    technological, 145
Location, 58, 59
Location quotients, 84-87
"Logical Framework," 241-243
Lombardo, J.F., Jr., 25
Lynch, F., 250

Malawi, 2
Mali, 16
Maps, analytical, 179-182, 202, 205, 208
Market areas. See Service areas
Market centers, 8, 10, 14-15, 148-160, 209
Market movement surveys, 152-154, 185-187